MW00719750

STAND BY FAITH...
OR NOT AT ALL

Orville K. Andvik

WinePress Publishing  *Mukilteo, WA 98275*

STAND BY FAITH ... OR NOT AT ALL
Copyright © 1994 by Orville K. Andvik

Published by WinePress Publishing
PO Box 1406
Mukilteo, WA 98275

Cover by **DENHAM**DESIGN, Everett, WA

ISBN 1-883893-65-8

I dedicate this book to my wife, Helen. The writing of it was undertaken as a consequence of her encouragement, (one of her strongest gifts), and her continued support throughout.
Thank you for your love!!!
Also—
to Brad Boardman, a wonderful brother in the Lord,
for his excellent help in editing.

CONTENTS

FOREWORD

There are many New Testament scripture passages whose precise meaning is of critical importance to us who live in these last days. We are living in a time of increasing uncertainty, violence and immorality. There does not appear to be any light at the end of the tunnel for this world short of the triumphant return of the Lord Jesus Christ. We who believe in Jesus Christ need to be diligent, considering these days we are living in, to assure that our spiritual standing is firm and is rooted in a correct understanding of the Word of God. When the day of Jesus' return arrives, I do not want to find too late that I have built my spiritual life on sand. Jesus said at the conclusion of His Sermon on the Mount:

> *24"Therefore everyone who hears these words of mine and puts them into practice is like a wise man who built his house on the rock. 25The rain came down, the streams rose, and the winds blew and beat against that house; yet it did not fall, because it had its foundation on the rock. 26But everyone who hears these words of mine and does not put them into practice is like a foolish man who built his house on sand. 27The rain came down, the streams rose, and the winds blew and beat against that house, and it fell with a great crash"* (Matt. 7:24-27).

The Bible clearly states that we must be diligent and alert in these days so that His coming does not catch us unawares. Jesus said about His return:

32"No one knows about that day or hour, not even the angels in heaven, nor the Son, but only the Father. 33Be on guard! Be alert[a]! You do not know when that time will come. 34It's like a man going away: He leaves his house and puts his servants in charge, each with his assigned task, and tells the one at the door to keep watch.
35Therefore keep watch because you do not know when the owner of the house will come back—whether in the evening or at midnight, or when the rooster crows, or at dawn. 36If he comes suddenly, do not let him find you sleeping. What I say to you, I say to everyone: 'Watch!'"[b]
(Mark 13:32-37).

If some would think that these words do not apply to believers, it should be noted that they were spoken by Jesus to four of His twelve disciples: Peter, James, John and Andrew (Mark 13:3-5). What He said to them, He says to everyone: *"Watch!"*
Again, in the book of Revelation it is stated:

15"Behold, I come like a thief! Blessed is he who stays awake and keeps his clothes with him[c], so that he may not go naked and be shamefully exposed" (Rev. 16:15).

We must take care that we are not asleep, spiritually speaking, as we approach these last days. We need to understand what the Lord expects of us, and there are some vital things that we must know. These truths are revealed in His Word. We will examine some of these critical truths, taking a look at them in the light of both the Old and New Testaments.

Old Testament books of the Bible are much more important to the understanding of the New Testament than many people realize. I believe that we may be subject to an improper or incomplete understanding of some New Testament passages if we have not viewed them in context with Old Testament scriptures.

---

[a]Some manuscripts say *alert and pray.*
[b]Emphasis added
[c]Emphasis added

This study will make extensive use of the Old Testament to amplify and clarify what has also been said in the New Testament.

One of the great values of the Old Testament is that it helps us to know and understand God better. We are able to learn much about His character, His faithfulness, His love, His patience and kindness, and other attributes by and through His dealings with the people of that day. We see through their experiences, what pleased Him and what did not, what He expected of His people, and how He upheld them and worked in their behalf when they trusted Him, obeyed Him and believed His promises. This knowledge serves to enrich our own faith and encourages us to be diligent in our walk with Him. We are also able to see clearly the awesomeness of our God. He did not treat sin lightly. While He was patient and forgiving, His patience grew thin over continued rebellion. When we see how God dealt with those who continually disobeyed Him and rejected all of His warnings, we are encouraged not to take God lightly, but to give Him the respect and the honor which is His due. Psalm 111:10 says;

"The fear of the LORD is the beginning of wisdom; all who follow his precepts have good understanding..."

Also in Proverbs 1:7:

"The fear of the LORD is the beginning of knowledge, but fools despise wisdom and discipline."

To sit down and write such a book is a little scary. I mean, what qualifies me to write a book of this kind? I don't want to be presumptuous. I have to realize that I am not writing about any old subject, but one that deals with the Word of God. If I will be saying things in this book which take issue with the way some people interpret scripture, then I have to be very careful and prayerful that I do not go beyond the Word of God. This could be enough of a concern to keep me from writing anything at all.

Also, I consider myself to be a rather average fellow, and I am sure that friends and relatives consider me the same way. "Is this average guy writing a book?", they might ask. I know there have been a few times when I have become so excited about the word of God and certain truths that I see, that I have spilled over in ways that border on being a little overbearing. This book might be viewed as just another outburst from a sometimes strange person whom they may like but perhaps don't understand too well.

Several years ago, and occurring over a period of a year or so, the Lord opened a series of scriptures to me which drastically changed my life. During these last ten years, my belief in the importance of these scriptures has not changed. Neither has my belief that they need to be shared with others. I don't believe I am being presumptuous when I say that an understanding of these scriptures is vital for all who believe in Jesus.

So, in spite of my misgivings, I have set out to share these things in writing. I hope that those who read the book will not be inclined to accept or reject what is said based upon their view of me, but rather that they will receive it and measure it solely by the light of scripture itself. I shall do my best to avoid saying anything which is not supported by clear scriptural evidence.

Let me ask one thing of you, the reader. Some conclusions may be drawn in this book which are contrary to beliefs you currently hold. Be willing to change your views, no matter how popular they may be, if you see that there is scriptural support for doing so, and let the LORD bring about the changes that He desires.

With that final word, I commit this book into the Lord's hands.

AUTHOR'S PREFACE

The primary focus of this book begins with the Biblical account of the Israelites sojourn in Egypt as documented in the book of Exodus. However, for the reader who desires to place all of this in proper context, it may be beneficial to review the history leading up to their internment in Egypt including their origins as a people and as a nation as it began with the man Abram (Abraham). This history is summarized in the addendum **"God's Beginnings–The Nation of Israel"**.

CHAPTER 1

Players and Places— A Likeness to Today

The slavery of the Israelite people in Egypt, their exodus from Egypt, the wilderness journey to the promised land and the events in between are actual history that outline God's dealings with the nation of Israel. But, by God's marvelous design, they are also a type or representation of truths and teachings found in the New Testament that are fundamental to the Christian experience today. The events that took place were a shadow of things to come, that have found their fulfillment in Jesus Christ (1 Cor. 10:1-11; Heb. 8:6-13). If this were not the case, the sacrifices and ceremonial requirements placed upon the Israelites in their worship of God would not make sense. In fact, they would appear as so much superstitious mumbo-jumbo. However, they do make sense now because of the subsequent appearing of Jesus Christ and the things which He has accomplished by His life, death and resurrection. This is one of the many wonderful things which testify to the Divine inspiration of the Bible.

What are some of the types or representations that we can see in this history?

PHARAOH

This man held absolute power over Egypt and over the Israelite people who were his slaves. The Israelites had no hope of escaping, through their own strength, from his power and dominance over them.

Pharaoh is a type or representation of Satan (the devil, the "evil one"), whom the New Testament says has taken mankind captive to do his will (2 Tim. 2:26). He holds a power over people that they cannot break in their own strength and by their own good works, but which can only be broken through faith in Jesus Christ and the deliverance He has made available (Col. 1:13-14; Eph. 2:8-9). Satan resists those who want to be free, just as Pharaoh did, and tries to keep them from hearing and heeding the truth that will set them free (Luke 8:12). He has no love for those who are his slaves, but only takes from them, and his end purpose is to steal, kill and destroy (John 10:10).

Pharaoh was a visible ruler. Satan is not. There may be many who would think that Satan doesn't really exist, or that he certainly doesn't rule over them. Yet, the Bible says that everyone who is born into this world, except for Jesus Christ, is under the power of this evil one (Acts 26:16-18; 1 John 5:19; Rom. 3:9-12-23) and is in need of deliverance from him.

EGYPT

Pharaoh's evil control and influence effected every aspect of Egyptian life, including politics, commerce and religion. Similarly, we find that in this world Satan's influence pervades every aspect of our daily lives.

Egypt is, therefore, a representation of this present evil world, a world that is under control of the "evil one" (1 John 5:19) who is also identified as the prince of this world (John 12:31). Everything in the world—the cravings of sinful man, the lust of his eyes and the boasting of what he has and

14

does—comes not from the Father but from the world (1 John 2:15-17). The wisdom of this world is foolishness in God's sight (1 Cor. 3:19). God has set a day when He will judge the world with justice by the man He has appointed, that is, Jesus Christ (Acts 17:31).

Yes, this world is under the control of the "evil one." How can we think otherwise when we see that evil seems to always rise up in spite of mans' best efforts to stop it. Any thinking person must be led to wonder just what, or who it is that continually motivates evil in our society. We don't have to train people to do wrong. No special classes are required for people to learn how to lie, cheat, steal, commit child abuse, murder, and every kind of evil. The Bible says the reason for it is that every inclination of man's heart is evil from childhood (Gen. 8:21).

We all understand that we have to be diligent to train and correct our children as they grow up, because it is so easy for them to go the wrong way. As a society, we try to counsel, train, correct and even imprison people that they might learn to obey the law and do what is right, and yet we are unable to keep up with the tide of wrongdoing that sweeps our land. It has to be obvious, when we take time to think about it, that there is some power at work in this world which motivates us to go in the wrong direction. A power that pits people against people, nation against nation. A power that puts people in bondage to alcohol and drugs and every kind of evil. The Bible says that the source of that evil is Satan, who comes as a thief to steal and kill and destroy (John 10:10).

It must also be noted that Egypt worshipped many gods and the starry hosts of heaven. So today, many gods are worshipped around the world. There is a myriad of religious beliefs, "new-age" philosophies and evolutionary doctrines which Satan has initiated to confuse the minds of men. He does so, that he might prevent them from knowing the TRUTH that can set them free.

15

THE ISRAELITES BROUGHT OUT OF EGYPT

The Israelites heard the message that Moses brought, that God wanted to deliver them from slavery and Pharaoh's dominion over them. They made a decision to believe and accept God's offer of deliverance, and God miraculously set them free to serve him.

This is a representation of individuals who, by an act of their own will, choose to be delivered from the dominion of darkness and to be brought into the kingdom of the Son of God in whom they have redemption and the forgiveness of sins (Col. 1:13-14). By this act they join the ranks of those who are identified as "believers" or "Christians" (Acts 11:26)—individuals who were at one time the slaves of sin and Satan (Rom. 6:16-18; Gal. 3:22; Eph. 2:1-3), without hope, and without God in the world (Eph. 2:12), who then heard and acted upon God's promise of deliverance, a promise given to all who would acknowledge their fallen state and would be willing to repent and forsake the ways of the world (Acts 26:20). Through faith, they are provided salvation (deliverance) by the power of God through Jesus Christ, and are supernaturally turned from darkness to light, from the power of Satan to God (Acts 26:17-18) in order to be rescued from this present evil age (Gal. 1:4). This way of deliverance has been made available through Jesus Christ to all who will hear, believe and enter in (2 Peter 3:9).

Someone might say, "Well, I don't need that, because I have lived a good life and been a pretty good person all of my life." However, according to the Bible, all individuals have sinned and come short of the glory of God (Rom. 3:23). All have been tainted by sin and cannot measure up to God's standards for holiness. So, all individuals, whether they want to recognize it or not, are separated from God and as has been said previously, are under the power of a cruel taskmaster.

However, God has provided a way to be delivered from the power of Satan. It comes when we realize that our lives do

16

not measure up to God's standard of holiness and we make a wholehearted decision to repent of our sins, come to Jesus Christ by faith, to receive Him as our Savior and to obtain forgiveness and cleansing from our sins. As it says in Rom. 10:8-13:

> [8] "...'The word is near you; it is in your mouth and in your heart,' that is, the word of faith we are proclaiming: [9]That if you confess with your mouth, 'Jesus is Lord,' and believe in your heart that God raised him from the dead, you will be saved. [10]For it is with your heart that you believe and are justified, and it is with your mouth that you confess and are saved. [11]As the Scripture says, 'Anyone who trusts in him will never be put to shame.' [12]For there is no difference between Jew and Gentile—the same Lord is Lord of all and richly blesses all who call on him, [13]for, 'Everyone who calls on the name of the Lord will be saved.'"

It is in this life (now, at this present time) that we must make the choice that can cause us to become heirs to an inheritance which God holds in store for those who will come to Him (2 Cor. 6:1-2; Heb. 9:27-28). Jesus has come to deliver us from Satan's power and to bring us out of the bondages of sin in this world (Acts 26:17-18). When we hear this message of deliverance and of the inheritance which is promised to us, we must make a decision (John 3:16-18). We can remain in unbelief or rebellion and thereby reject that deliverance that He so graciously offers us; or we can believe it, receive it and act on it by submitting ourselves to Him in faith and obedience. When we make this choice and act on it out of sincere hearts, we are born again spiritually by the power of God (John 3:1-8). We become children of God (John 1:12-13) and heirs to all the treasures of the Kingdom of God (Rom. 8:15-17; James 2:5).

When we receive Jesus by faith, our lives are supernaturally transformed. We become new creatures in Christ where old desires have passed away, and all things become new

(2 Cor 5:17). We receive a new nature that wants to follow Jesus wholeheartedly. Then, we are no longer to be conformed to the practices of this world (Rom. 12:2). Friendship with the world and it's ways is hatred toward God and anyone who chooses to become a friend of the world becomes an enemy of God (James 4:4-5). We are no longer to love the world or anything in it. If we love the world, the love of the Father is not in us. For everything in the world—the cravings of sinful man, the lust of his eyes and the boasting of what he has and does—comes not from the Father but from the world (1 John 2:15-17). God has said: *"I will live with them and walk among them, and I will be their God, and they will be my people."* Therefore, we are not to be yoked together with unbelievers, with wickedness, with darkness, but we are to come out from among these things and be separate, and touch not the unclean thing that the Lord may receive us unto himself (2 Cor. 6:14-18).

THE WILDERNESS

The wilderness was the place where the Israelites went when they left Egypt. It was not intended to be a place for the Israelites to stay, but only to pass through on their way to the promised land. It was to be a place of transition or transformation; of change from the old to the new. A place where they would either learn to know the ways of God or would rebel against him.

The wilderness was barren. It was a dangerous place. It was a thirsty and waterless land that was full of snakes and scorpions. Food was very scarce there. It was a place of difficulties which would come to sorely test and try the hearts of the Israelites. Would they learn how to trust and obey God? Would they be able to make it through this barren land, or would they become discouraged, lose heart and want to turn back? If they weren't obedient, they could die there, and never make it to the land that had been promised to them. If they did not learn the lessons of the wilderness, of trust and obedience to God, it would be impossible for them to drive out the inhabitants dwelling in that land of promise in their own strength. They would fail to enter into their inheritance.

The journey in the wilderness could not be circumvented. It had to be faced and conquered.

The wilderness represents a place of transformation for us also. A place where we really come to know God in an intimate way. A place where we are taught, with regard to the former way of life, to put off our old self, which is being corrupted by its deceitful desires; to be made new in the attitude of our minds; and to put on the new self, created to be like God in true righteousness and holiness (Eph. 4:22-24). A place where we learn to offer our bodies a living sacrifice unto God and to no longer conform to the patterns of the world. It is where we can be transformed by the renewing of our mind. It is here also that we are able to test and approve what God's will is—his good, pleasing and perfect will (Rom. 12:1-2).

We are called to face tests and trials in our wilderness journey also. We know that these trials come so that our faith—of greater worth than gold, which perishes even though refined by fire—may be proved genuine and may result in praise, glory and honor when Jesus Christ is revealed (1 Peter 1:6-7). We should consider it pure joy when we face such trials recognizing that the testing of our faith develops perseverance. Perseverance must finish its work so that we may be mature and complete, not lacking anything. The persons who persevere under trial are blessed, because when they have stood the test, they will receive the crown of life that is promised to those who love God (James 1:2-4, 12).

If we are to enter into our inheritance, we must first learn these lessons of the wilderness. The wilderness is a dangerous place for us, just as it was for the Israelites. It is full of difficulties which can cause us to lose heart, to doubt and to turn aside from that which we have been promised and from that which we seek (2 Peter 2:20-22; Heb. 10:35-39; 12:1-13). However, if we do not learn the lessons of the wilderness, that is, of trust, obedience and submission to the Lord, we may not finally enter in at all. As it says in Revelation, *"To him who overcomes and does my will to the end,[a] I will give authority over the nations—He will rule them with an iron scepter; he will dash them to pieces like pottery'—just as I have received authority from my Father"* (Rev. 2:26-27).

We who trust in Jesus must go through the wilderness with him, that we might enter into our promised inheritance.

THE PROMISED LAND

The "promised land" was the object the Israelites were seeking—the inheritance promised by God to Abraham, Isaac, Jacob and their offspring. The one who ultimately led them into that land was Joshua. Earlier in his life, Joshua was called simply Hoshea, meaning "salvation." Later, Moses changed Hoshea's name to Joshua (Num. 13:8,16), meaning "The LORD saves" (or "The LORD gives victory"). The Greek form of this name is Jesus. Joshua led them to battle, to conquer that land of Canaan, and to bring them to victory. Today it is Jesus Christ who leads us to salvation and victory.

There is a tremendous inheritance promised to all who will follow Jesus Christ (Eph. 1:18-19; 1 Cor. 2:9; 1 Pet. 1:3-5). However, there is a spiritual warfare to be waged before we can enter into our full inheritance (Eph.6:12; 2 Cor. 10:3-5). We do not have the strength to gain that battle's victory in and of ourselves. We can only be victorious with Christ (our Joshua) as we submit ourselves to Him in true faith and obedience and put on the armor that He provides (Eph. 6:10-18).

This conquest and our access to this promised inheritance began at Calvary where Jesus laid the foundation for total victory (Col. 2:15; Heb. 2:14-15). It continues today in

---

[a]Emphasis added

20

efforts to reach out to those in this world who are entrapped in Satan's power and who are subject to the wrath of God unless they turn to Jesus Christ (John 3:36). It will continue until all things in the heavens and the earth are brought under one head, even Jesus Christ, at His triumphant return (2 Thes. 2:8; Rev. 19:11-21; 20:1-3; Eph. 1:9-10). This conquest is not to be accomplished so that evil might again have an opportunity to reign, as is so often the case with the wars of this world, but rather that a rule of peace, justice and righteousness might be established. As it says in scripture, the government will be on His (Jesus Christ's) shoulders. He will be called Wonderful, Counselor, Mighty God, Everlasting Father, Prince of Peace. Of the increase of His government and peace there will be no end. He will reign on David's throne and over his kingdom, establishing and upholding it with justice and righteousness from that time on and forever. The zeal of the Lord Almighty will accomplish this (Is. 9:6-7).

The inheritance promised to the saints does not stop with the subjugation of Satan, this earth, and the evils that exist here, but extends to the coming of a new heaven and a new earth (Rev. 21:1-7), and to the fulfillment of all the promises that God has given to those who believe, both now and for eternity (John 3:16; James 2:5; 2 Pet. 1:3-4; 3:13). When the land of Canaan was conquered, it became the land of Israel, the place where David's throne and kingdom were established. Jesus is the ultimate and final heir to the throne of David. He will reign forever and His kingdom will never end (Luke 1:32-33).

MOSES

A likeness to Christ, who comes with a message of hope to lead us out of our slavery to Satan and sin. (see following chart, MOSES AS A LIKENESS TO CHRIST)

MOSES...AS A LIKENESS TO...CHRIST

1. Of priestly ancestry (Exod. 2:1)

Of holy ancestry

• Of the tribe of Levi, a priestly tribe

• Father - God

2. Raised in royalty (Exod 2:10)

Of Supremely Royal lineage.

• Son of Pharoah's daughter
• Born of a Hebrew woman but adopted by Pharoah's daughter

• Son of God
• Born of a virgin but conceived by the Holy Ghost.

3. Hidden as a child from Pharaoh to avoid being killed. Then later fled to Midian at age 40, when Pharaoh again sought to kill him. (Exod. 2:1-2, 15)

Taken as a baby to Egypt by Joseph and Mary to avoid death at the hands of Herod. (Matt. 2:13-16) Satan finally succeeded in killing Jesus on the cross.

4. Saw his brethren suffering in Egypt under Pharaoh (Exod. 2:11; 3:7, 9)

Saw mankind suffering in bondage under sin and Satan.

5. Chose to identify with the people of God and suffer affliction with them. He regarded disgrace for the sake of Christ as of greater value than the treasures of Egypt (Heb. 11:25-26)

Chose to identify with those He created (his brothers) and to enter into their sufferings. (Heb. 2:10-12, 17-18). He shared in our humanity so that by His death He might destroy him who holds the power of death—that is, the devil—and free those who all their lives were held in slavery by their fear of death (Heb. 2:14-15)

6. Left his place in Pharaoh's household (Exod. 2:15; Heb. 11:24) and became a sheep herder.

Left His throne in glory. He was in very nature God, but made himself nothing, taking the very nature of a servant, being made in human likeness. (Phil. 2:6-8; Heb. 2:14-17)

MOSES...AS A LIKENESS TO...CHRIST

7. Was identified as ruler and judge. (Exod. 2:14; Acts 7:27,35)

The Ruler who will reign for ever and ever (Rev:11:15) and the ultimate Judge before whom all will stand (Acts 10:42).

8. Not recognized as deliverer by those he came to deliver. (Exod. 2:14; Acts 7:25)

"He came to that which was his own, but his own did not receive him." (John 1:11)

9. Was a stranger in Egypt along with the other Israelites. (Gen. 15:13)

Christ, a temporary resident on earth, came from, and returned to the Father in heaven (John 16:28)

10. Tested (matured) in the wilderness (Midian) for 40 years. (Acts 7:28-30)

Tempted (tested and tried) in the wilderness for 40 days and nights. (Mark 1:12-13)

11. Called and sent by God to deliver the Israelites from Egypt. (Exod. 3:10)

Sent by God the Father to deliver mankind from Satan's dominion. (John 3:16)

12. Spoke the words (the message of deliverance [Exod. 3:15-22]) given him by God... and performed the works which God commanded him to do. (Exod. 4:12-16)

Spoke the words given Him by the Father (the message of salvation). Performed those works which the Father showed Him to do. (John 5:19-20; 8:26-29)

13. Was given miraculous signs to perform so the Israelites would believe. (Acts 4:1-9; Exod 4:17)

Was accredited by God to mankind by miracles, wonders and signs. (Acts 2:22)

14. Foretold that God would in the future raise up a prophet like him (Christ). (Deut. 18:15)

Christ was the prophet "like" Moses. (John 5:45-47; Acts 3:18-23)

From what we have looked at thus far, we can begin to see some of the spiritual relationships to the Christian life that are evidenced in God's dealings with the nation of Israel.

I believe that we are living in the last days. I am convinced that it is a dangerous time for Christians in the sense that we must not be caught unawares and take for granted this salvation that we have received. That is why I believe it is absolutely vital for us to understand and heed the message that is demonstrated through the history of the nation of Israel. It is essential to our Christian well being. I pray that before this book is completed, that message will be clear and will be understood.

The New Testament provides direct evidence that this story is given for our benefit.

> [4]*"For everything that was written in the past was written to teach us, so that through endurance and the encouragement of the Scriptures we might have hope."* (Romans 15:4)

> [6]*"Now these things occurred as examples to keep us from setting our hearts on evil things as they did."* (1 Corinthians 10:6)

> [11]*"These things happened to them as examples and were written down as warnings for us, on whom the fulfillment of the ages has come."* (1 Corinthians 10:11)

I believe then, based on these evidences, that we stand on very good ground in considering the spiritual implications of these Old Testament scriptures for our lives today. However, to avoid error, we will continue to amplify and confirm what is said by reference to the New Testament.

CHAPTER 2

A Message of Hope— The Good News is Preached

The Israelites had been subjugated and put into slavery by Pharaoh and the Egyptians. These descendants of Abraham, Isaac and Jacob, who were only seventy in number when they first came into Egypt at the time of Joseph, had increased in number during their time of slavery in Egypt until they had become a very large group of people[a]. The prophecy previously given to Abraham was being fulfilled...

"Know for certain that your descendants will be strangers in a country not their own, and they will be enslaved and mistreated four hundred years" (Gen. 15:13).

---

[a]Exodus 12:37 and 38:26 indicate that at the time they left Egypt, the men alone numbered slightly over 600,000. With women and children, their numbers would probably have been close to two million.

God had heard the cries of the Israelites and was concerned about them.

MOSES IS GIVEN HIS ASSIGNMENT

[1]*"Now Moses was tending the flock of Jethro his father-in-law, the priest of Midian, and he led the flock to the far side of the desert and came to Horeb, the mountain of God.* [2]*There the angel of the LORD appeared to him in flames of fire from within a bush. Moses saw that though the bush was on fire it did not burn up.* [3]*So Moses thought, 'I will go over and see this strange sight—why the bush does not burn up.'*

[4]*When the LORD saw that he had gone over to look, God called to him from within the bush, 'Moses! Moses!'*
And Moses said, 'Here I am.'

[5]*'Do not come any closer,' God said. 'Take off your sandals, for the place where you are standing is holy ground.'* [6]*Then he said, 'I am the God of your father, the God of Abraham, the God of Isaac and the God of Jacob.' At this, Moses hid his face, because he was afraid to look at God.*

[7]*The LORD said, 'I have indeed seen the misery of my people in Egypt. I have heard them crying out because of their slave drivers, and I am concerned about their suffering.* [8]*So I have come down to rescue them from the hand of the Egyptians and to bring them up out of that land into a good and spacious land, a land flowing with milk and honey– the home of the Canaanites, Hittites, Amorites, Perizzites, Hivites and Jebusites.* [9]*And now the cry of the Israelites has reached me, and I have seen the way the Egyptians are oppressing them.* [10]*So now, go. I am sending you to Pharaoh to bring my people the Israelites out of Egypt.'*

[11]*But Moses said to God, 'Who am I, that I should go to Pharaoh and bring the Israelites out of Egypt?'*

[12]*And God said, 'I will be with you. And this will be the sign to you that it is I who have sent you: When you have brought the people out of Egypt, you will worship God on this mountain.'*

[13]*Moses said to God, 'Suppose I go to the Israelites and say to them, 'The God of your fathers has sent me to you,' and they ask me, 'What is his name?' Then what shall I tell them?'*

[14]God said to Moses, 'I AM WHO I AM.'[b] This is what you are to say to the Israelites: 'I AM has sent me to you.'

[15]God also said to Moses, 'Say to the Israelites, 'The LORD,[c] the God of your fathers—the God of Abraham, the God of Isaac and the God of Jacob—has sent me to you.' This is my name forever, the name by which I am to be remembered from generation to generation.

[16]'Go, assemble the elders of Israel and say to them, 'The LORD, the God of your fathers—the God of Abraham, Isaac and Jacob—appeared to me and said: I have watched over you and have seen what has been done to you in Egypt. [17]And I have promised to bring you up out of your misery in Egypt into the land of the Canaanites, Hittites, Amorites, Perizzites, Hivites and Jebusites—a land flowing with milk and honey'" (Exod. 3:1-17).

"WHAT IF THEY DON'T BELIEVE ME...?"

We see that Moses was to go tell the Israelites that God had sent him to bring them out of Egypt. Can you imagine a man going to tell a people like this that he had come with a message from God to them. I can hear them now...

"You say God appeared to you? ... Uh-huh ...okaaay ... and you're going to lead us out of Egypt? ... Will that be today or tomorrow? You've got to be out of your mind! Go away and don't bother us!"

Even though he was carrying a message that they desperately wanted to hear, it is unlikely they would have believed his story.

Moses considered this, and said to the Lord,

[4]"...What if they do not believe me or listen to me and say, 'The LORD did not appear to you'?'

---

[b]14 Or *I WILL BE WHAT I WILL BE*
[c]15 The Hebrew for *LORD* sounds like and may be derived from the Hebrew for *I AM* in verse 14.

*²Then the LORD said to him, 'What is that in your hand?'
'A staff,' he replied.*

*³The LORD said, 'Throw it on the ground.'
Moses threw it on the ground and it became a snake, and he ran
from it. ⁴Then the LORD said to him, 'Reach out your hand and
take it by the tail.' So Moses reached out and took hold of the
snake and it turned back into a staff in his hand. ⁵"This,' said
the LORD, 'is so that they may believe that the LORD, the God of
their fathers—The God of Abraham, the God of Isaac and the
God of Jacob—has appeared to you.'*

*⁶Then the LORD said, 'Put your hand inside your cloak.' So
Moses put his hand into his cloak, and when he took it out, it
was leprous,ᵈ like snow.*

*⁷"Now put it back into your cloak,' he said. So Moses put his
hand back into his cloak, and when he took it out, it was restored, like the rest of his flesh.*

*⁸Then the LORD said, 'If they do not believe you or pay at-
tention to the first miraculous sign, they may believe the second.
⁹But if they do not believe these two signs or listen to you, take
some water from the Nile and pour it on the dry ground, The
water you take from the river will become blood on the ground'"*
(Exod. 4:1-9).

These miraculous signs would attest to the fact that Moses
was truly carrying a message from God. The signs would also
signify that the God who was now sending Moses, was the same
God who had given the covenant promises to their forefathers, Abraham, Isaac and Jacob. He had not forgotten His
promises to them, but had now come to deliver them and to
bring them to that promised land.

Jesus also came carrying a message from the Father to
the world. Many didn't want to believe what He had to say.
But the miracles, signs and wonders He performed attested
to the authenticity of the message He was carrying, that He
was the Promised One whose coming had been foretold in

ᵈ6 The Hebrew word was used for various diseases affecting the skin—not
necessarily leprosy.

scripture. Philip, Jesus' disciple, was one who believed the Lord's message:

"Philip found Nathanael and told him, 'We have found the one Moses wrote about in the Law, and about whom the prophets also wrote—Jesus of Nazareth, the son of Joseph'" (John 1:45).

Peter, speaking at the day of Pentecost as recorded in the book of Acts said:

[22]"Men of Israel, listen to this: Jesus of Nazareth was a man accredited by God to you by miracles, wonders and signs, which God did among you through him, as you yourselves know" (Acts 2:22).

Jesus spoke of this also when He answered some Jews who had accused Him of blasphemy...

[36]"...Why then do you accuse me of blasphemy because I said, 'I am God's Son'? [37]Do not believe me unless I do what my Father does. [38]But if I do it, even though you do not believe me, believe the miracles, that you may know and understand that the Father is in me, and I in the Father" (John 10:36b-38).

(see also John 10:19-26 and Hebrews 2:3-4)

"BUT LORD, I'M NOT AN ELOQUENT SPEAKER."

Moses also did not feel very good about his ability as a public speaker:

[10]"Moses said to the LORD, 'O Lord, I have never been eloquent, neither in the past nor since you have spoken to your servant. I am slow of speech and tongue.'
[11]The LORD said to him, 'Who gave man his mouth? Who makes him deaf or mute? Who gives him sight or makes him blind? Is it not I, the LORD? [12]Now go; I will help you

speak and will teach you what to say.' [13] But Moses said, 'O Lord, please send someone else to do it.'

[14]Then the LORD's anger burned against Moses and he said, 'What about your brother, Aaron the Levite? I know he can speak well. He is already on his way to meet you, and his heart will be glad when he sees you. [15]You shall speak to him and put words in his mouth; I will help both of you speak and will teach you what to do. [16]He will speak to the people for you, and it will be as if he were your mouth and as if you were God to him. [17]But take this staff in your hand so you can perform miraculous signs with it" (Exod. 4:10-17).

In Stephen's account of Moses' life, which appears in Acts 7, he said:

[22]*"Moses was educated in all the wisdom of the Egyptians and **was powerful in speech and action**"*[e] (Acts 7:22).

Yet in this account of Moses' meeting with God, we find him most reluctant to be the spokesman that God wanted him to be. Moses lived for forty years in Egypt before he ever went to Midian and was raised as part of Pharaoh's family. He undoubtedly had opportunity more than once to speak publicly. Yet tending sheep in Midian for forty years had probably removed a little of his self-confidence. This was not all bad, because it would help Moses to be more dependent upon God than upon his own abilities or eloquence.

Moses was a man of great faith in God as can be seen throughout his life. Yet Moses' lack of trust in this matter of speech displeased God. This is a lesson for us. If we believe that the Lord wants us to perform a particular task, whatever it might be, then we must have the faith to go forward. As we set about to do His will, walking in obedience and dependence upon him, we have every reason to be confident that He will provide the understanding and the strength to do

---

[e]Emphasis added

30

what He wants us to do. We should never be reluctant to step out in obedience.

Moses was not asked to carry his own message, but was to speak the words that God gave. This is a likeness to Jesus who also came proclaiming the message given Him by the Father. Jesus said:

> [49]*"For I did not speak of my own accord, but the Father who sent me commanded me what to say and how to say it. [50]I know that his command leads to eternal life. So whatever I say is just what the Father has told me to say"* (John 12:49-50).

> *"...The words that I say to you are not just my own. Rather, it is the Father, living in me, who is doing his work"* (John 14:10).

Jesus was dependent upon the Father for what He spoke. In similar manner, it is not man's wisdom, ideas and eloquence which will produce the results God desires on this earth. What will truly make a difference in this world, are the words which are spoken with God's anointing and blessing upon them. As the Apostle Paul said,

> [1]*"When I came to you, brothers, I did not come with eloquence or superior wisdom as I proclaimed to you the testimony about God. [2]For I resolved to know nothing while I was with you except Jesus Christ and him crucified. [3]I came to you in weakness and fear, and with much trembling. [4]My message and my preaching were not with wise and persuasive words, but with a demonstration of the Spirit's power, [5]so that your faith might not rest on men's wisdom, but on God's power..."*

Also he said,

> [11]*"...For who among men knows the thoughts of a man except the man's spirit within him? In the same way no one knows the thoughts of God except the Spirit of God. [12]We have not received the spirit of the world but the Spirit who*

is from God, that we may understand what God has freely given us. [13]This is what we speak, not in words taught us by human wisdom but in words taught by the Spirit, expressing spiritual truths in spiritual words" (1 Cor. 2:1-5, 11-13).

Christian witnessing, teaching or preaching is to come from time spent alone with the Lord. How can we truly know the words which are to be spoken unless we spend time in His presence—in reading and meditating on His Word, and in prayer. Also, when we do speak, we must pray that it will be done under the power and anointing of the Holy Spirit, for it is through the Spirit that our words are enabled to bring life to others.

MOSES LEAVES MIDIAN

After his encounter with God at the burning bush, Moses went back to Jethro his father-in-law, and said to him,

[18]"...Let me go back to my own people in Egypt to see if any of them are still alive."
Jethro said, "Go, and I wish you well" (Exod. 4:18).

The Lord revealed to Moses in Midian that all those who formerly sought to kill him were dead. So Moses gathered his family together and departed for Egypt. Meanwhile, the Lord spoke to Aaron, Moses' brother, and told him to go into the desert to meet Moses. So Aaron met Moses at the mountain of God (Horeb). Then Moses told Aaron all the things God had sent him to say and also about all the miraculous signs he had commanded him to perform .

MOSES AND AARON'S FIRST MEETING WITH THE ISRAELITES

[29]"Moses and Aaron brought together all the elders of the Israelites, [30]and Aaron told them everything the LORD had said to Moses. He also performed the signs before the

people, [31]***and they believed**[f]. And when they heard that the LORD was concerned about them and had seen their misery, they bowed down and worshiped"* (Exod 4:29-31).

God has also seen our misery and our inescapable bondage under Satan and this world system, and has sent Jesus with a message of hope and deliverance for us. When we consider the LORD's concern for us and see the way of escape He has provided, we too have every reason to bow down and worship Him in thankfulness.

As Moses performed the miraculous signs, the Israelites believed the words of deliverance he brought from the Lord. It was critical for them to believe this message. How else could the Israelites ever be convinced to leave Egypt unless they believed and received the hope that this message brought. Faith had to be born in their hearts if they were to be delivered from Egypt.

Yet when Jesus came in like manner and proclaimed His message with power and with demonstation of many signs and wonders, most of those to whom He initially came did not believe His message.

> [20]*"Jesus began to denounce the cities in which most of his miracles had been performed, because they did not repent.* [21]*"Woe to you, Korazin! Woe to you, Bethsaida! If the miracles that were performed in you had been performed in Tyre and Sidon, they would have repented long ago in sackcloth and ashes.* [22]*But I tell you, it will be more bearable for Tyre and Sidon on the day of judgment than for you.* [23]*And Capernaum, will you be lifted up to the skies? No, you will go down to the depths.*[g] *If the miracles that were performed in you had been performed in Sodom, it would have remained to this day.* [24]*But I tell you that it will be more bearable for Sodom on the day of judgment than for you"* (Matt. 11:20-24).

(See also John 12:37).

---

[f]Emphasis added
[g]23 Greek *Hades*

33

MOSES AND AARON DELIVER GOD'S
MESSAGE TO PHARAOH

¹"Afterward Moses and Aaron went to Pharaoh and said, 'This is what the Lord, the God of Israel says: 'Let my people go, so that they may hold a festival to me in the desert.'
²Pharaoh said, 'Who is the LORD, that I should obey him and let Israel go? I do not know the LORD and I will not let Israel go.'
³Then they said, 'The God of the Hebrews has met with us. Now let us take a three-day journey into the desert to offer sacrifices to the LORD our God, or he may strike us with plagues or with the sword.'
⁴But the king of Egypt said, 'Moses and Aaron, why are you taking the people away from their labor? Get back to your work!'
⁵Then Pharaoh said, "Look, the people of the land are now numerous, and you are stopping them from working" (Exod. 5:1-5).

Pharaoh made the work of the Israelites more difficult because of the message that Moses and Aaron had brought to him. He said, *"Make the work harder for the men so that they keep working and pay no attention to lies"* (Exod. 5:9). So they were hard pressed by the Egyptians and more was demanded of them.

¹⁵"Then the Israelite foremen went and appealed to Pharaoh: 'Why have you treated your servants this way? ¹⁶Your servants are given no straw, yet we are told 'Make bricks!' Your servants are being beaten, but the fault is with your own people.'
¹⁷Pharaoh said, 'Lazy, that's what you are—lazy! That is why you keep saying, 'Let us go and sacrifice to the LORD.'
¹⁸Now get to work. You will not be given any straw, yet you must produce your full quota of bricks.'
¹⁹The Israelite foremen realized they were in trouble when they were told, 'you are not to reduce the number of bricks required of you for each day.' ²⁰When they left Pharaoh, they found Moses and Aaron waiting to meet them, ²¹and they

said, 'May the LORD look upon you and judge you! You have made us a stench to Pharaoh and his officials and have put a sword in their hand to kill us'" (Exod. 5:15-21).

Before the message of deliverance had much opportunity to register on the minds of the Israelites, Pharaoh acted to destroy it. He did not want that seed of hope to take firm root in their hearts. He knew that once they began to believe in earnest that they could be set free, it would mean trouble for him. So he made their work harder that the word of hope and faith might not take root in their hearts.

Jesus came with a message of salvation for all mankind, but Satan does not sit idly by while this word is proclaimed. He does not want that message to find a place in human hearts, and so he constantly works to keep men from hearing and believing the word of salvation. If they do hear it and do begin to understand and believe it, he then works to destroy that hope of deliverance before it can ever take firm root in the heart. Jesus spoke of this clearly when He explained the parable of the sower...

[18]*"Listen then to what the parable of the sower means:* [19]*When anyone hears the message about the kingdom and does not understand it, the evil one comes and snatches away what was sown in his heart. This is the seed sown along the path.* [20]*The one who received the seed that fell on rocky places is the man who hears the word and at once receives it with joy.* [21]*But since he has no root, he lasts only a short time. When trouble or persecution comes because of the word, he quickly falls away"* (Matt. 13:18-21. See also Matt 13:1-17).

This same principle was at work during the time that Jesus walked on earth when the Pharisees did all they could to keep the people from hearing and believing the Gospel. Satan raises all kinds of smoke and controversy, and uses every trick and deception imaginable to keep men from hearing and heeding the truth.

We may introduce someone to Jesus Christ. They believe the message of deliverance which Jesus offers just as the Israelites believed the message that Moses and Aaron brought to them (Exod. 4:29-30). They ask Jesus to come into their hearts. It seems their response is so wonderful. We rejoice that another person has come to Jesus.

But we may soon detect that the person did not experience the instantaneous turnaround we had expected. Because they have a limited knowledge about this way of salvation offered through Jesus Christ, and about faith in general, the word of hope is snatched from their hearts by the enemy. Just as Pharaoh brought greater hardship and discouragement to the Israelites (and it was very effective), so Satan brings trouble, diversions, lies and added temptations to bear on the one who has heard and received the hope held out in the Gospel. As a consequence, what little faith they have dies and they become discouraged, lose heart and quickly turn back. That seed of hope is taken from them before they are able to fully grasp it.

The Israelites could never be forced to leave Egypt by Moses and Aaron against their will. It would only be as they came to fully trust in that message of deliverance, that God would lead them out.

Because of the discouragement brought on by Pharaoh's actions, the Israelites turned against Moses and Aaron. Even Moses began to question God's intent to deliver them.

> [22]"Moses returned to the LORD and said, 'O LORD, why have you brought trouble upon this people? Is this why you sent me? [23]Ever since I went to Pharaoh to speak in your name, he has brought trouble upon this people, and you have not rescued your people at all'" (Exod. 5:22-23).

Just as Moses became discouraged and failed to understand the ways of deliverance, we may become discouraged too, when we see that there is not an instantaneous victory in the life of a new convert. We become involved in trying to help that one to enter in, and the struggling has an effect on our faith as well.

We see, however, that God was not through with the Israelites and wasn't going to give up on them. So we too must persist through teaching of the scripture, prayer and counselling to help encourage and strengthen the faith of the individual who is sincerely seeking to be free from Satan's grasp. For we know, that Jesus came to set the captives free. He will supernaturally set them free and give them a new heart and life if they can realize, as the Bible says, that they, like all men, are under control of the evil one and need to be set free. If they can but realize that Jesus came to set them free. If they can begin to take hold of this fact by faith and turn their backs on the old way of life in order to take hold of the new life that Jesus is offering them, deliverance can become a reality in their lives.

We who read the account of the Israelites deliverance have wonderful oversight, because we already know the end of the story, but Moses didn't. To him, it appeared that God was somehow not keeping His word. He hadn't rescued His people as He said He would. Knowing the end of the story, we could say to Moses, "Don't be discouraged Moses, just wait, God will deliver the Israelites from Egypt just as He said He would. We know the outcome." God knew in advance the opposition that would arise, but He had every intention to accomplish the deliverance He had promised.

In our own lives, we might have received some promise from God. When we run into a snag, it looks as though God has not come through, and a struggle ensues in our hearts. But we don't see the end of the story. God fully intends to do what He says He will do. His promise is sure. It will be fulfilled. We need to continue on in faith, and leave the rest to him. We can look at Moses and see his concern and identify with it, but we know the outcome—that God did deliver the people out of Pharaoh's grasp. Because we know the outcome, we can take heart in our own situation, that if we have received a call or a promise from God, He will fulfill it in His own way and time. We must continue to stand strong in our faith and be obedient and do what He has asked us to do till we see His promise fulfilled. He will be faithful to His Word.

The Lord reassures Moses:

[1]*"Then the LORD said to Moses, 'Now you will see what I will do to Pharaoh: Because of my mighty hand he will let them go; because of my mighty hand he will drive them out of his country.'*

[2]*God also said to Moses, 'I am the LORD.* [3]*I appeared to Abraham, to Isaac and to Jacob as God Almighty,[h] but by my name the LORD I did not make myself known to them.[i]* [4]*I also established my covenant with them to give them the land of Canaan, where they lived as aliens.* [5]*Moreover, I have heard the groaning of the Israelites, whom the Egyptians are enslaving, and I have remembered my covenant.*

[6]*Therefore, say to the Israelites: 'I am the LORD, **and I will bring you out** from under the yoke of the Egyptians. **I will free you** from being slaves to them, and **I will redeem you** with and outstretched arm and with mighty acts of judgment.* [7]***I will take you as my own people**, and **I will be your God**. Then you will know that I am the LORD your God, who brought you out from under the yoke of the Egyptians.* [8]*And **I will bring you to the land** I swore with uplifted hand to give to Abraham, to Isaac and to Jacob. I will give it to you as a possession. I am the LORD"[j]* (Exod. 6:1-8).

God's Word is true. He is faithful. What He has declared to us in His Word He will do. There is no reason for Him to lie, He doesn't need to.

"God is not a man, that he should lie, nor a son of man, that he should change his mind. Does he speak and then not act? Does he promise and not fulfill?" (Numbers 23:19).

---

[h]3 Hebrew *El-Shaddai*

[i]Or *Almighty,and by my name the LORD did I not let myself be known to them?*

[j]Emphasis added

God was giving His word again, that He would fulfill His promise. The Israelites deliverance was to be accomplished through the power of God. Not through Moses' power, or the power of the Israelites, but by God himself. He would free them from the control of the Egyptians and would take them out of slavery. Not only that, but God would redeem them so that they would belong to him, and become His own people. He would be their God and would bring them to the land promised to them.

This is the kind of salvation that Jesus Christ has made possible for us.

He has come to take us out of Satan's control and out of our slavery to the ways of sin and to the things of this world. Not only that, but Jesus has come to redeem us that we might fully belong to God as His own people. He wants to bring us into the full inheritance He has reserved for us, both in this life and in the one to come. His promise is sure. As we receive this word into our hearts by faith, it becomes a living hope and reality to us.

Moses told the Israelites what God had instructed him to say, but they did not listen to him because of their discouragement and cruel bondage.

> [10]"Then the LORD said to Moses, [11]'Go, tell Pharaoh king of Egypt to let the Israelites go out of his country.'
>
> [12]But Moses said to the LORD, 'If the Israelites will not listen to me, why would Pharaoh listen to me, since I speak with faltering lips[k]?'
>
> [13]Now the LORD spoke to Moses and Aaron about the Israelites and Pharaoh king of Egypt, and he commanded them to bring the Israelites out of Egypt" (Exod. 6:9-12).

Moses was still reluctant to be the spokesman for the LORD, but there was to be no more delay. The Lord "commanded them" to bring the Israelites out of Egypt.

---

[k]12 Hebrew *I am uncircumcised of lips*; also in verse 30.

Moses was right in one sense when he said, *"If the Israelites will not listen to me, why would Pharaoh listen to me...?"* Moses and Aaron did not have the power to deliver anyone from Egypt. They could only speak to Pharaoh by faith in God and His word, and in the authority of His name. They were the Lord's representatives and were presenting themselves to Pharaoh in His name. If they were going to stand in front of Pharaoh on the basis of their own authority or strength, they would be in difficulty in a very short time. Only God could display the power needed to cause Pharaoh to let go of His people.

In the same way, we cannot deliver anyone from Satan's power in our own strength. However, we can reach out to them in the authority of Jesus name and by faith in him. God has given those of us who believe in Him the power to tread on snakes and scorpions (terms representing dangerous forces of spiritual evil) and to overcome all the power of the enemy; nothing will harm us (Luke 10:19). It is the Lord who is doing the work; providing the power for salvation, the power for the sick to be healed, for demons to be cast out and the works of the enemy to be defeated.

Jesus commanded us to go in His name to set the captives free...

> [15]*"He said to them, 'Go into all the world and preach the good news to all creation. [16]Whoever believes and is baptized will be saved, but whoever does not believe will be condemned. [17]And these signs will accompany those who believe: In my name they will drive out demons; they will speak in new tongues; [18]they will pick up snakes with their hands; and when they drink deadly poison, it will not hurt them at all; they will place their hands on sick people, and they will get well'"* (Mark 16:15-18).

We are commanded to tell people about the salvation that God wants to provide them. We are commanded to wage war against the powers of the enemy through faith, witnessing, prayer, casting out of demons, laying hands on the sick, etc., that those who are oppressed by the enemy might be set free. We are to go in Jesus name and by faith in His power to deliver.

As in almost every warfare, the enemy is not about to give up easily. We must stand fast by faith in God and His Word. We must pray diligently, believing that our prayers make a difference. We must live a holy life through the power of the Holy Spirit that the enemy would find no weakness in us to exploit. We must know His Word that we might deliver an accurate message to the lost and that we might know how to stand against the enemy. We must not fear the enemies' words, or be discouraged because the victory does not appear overnight. Surely, as we persist, our labors will bear fruit.

As we walk with the full armor of God, we have no reason to fear Satan or demons of darkness, but we must be aware of his wiles and his trickery which will come to defeat us.

BUT WHAT ABOUT DEMONS?
DO THEY EXIST TODAY?

Demons existed during the time of Jesus, and He dealt with them. So did the apostles. There is no reason to believe that they have gone away although Satan would like us to think they have. There are people in America and around the world who are possessed by demons or are being harrassed by them. The evil that is being manifested in our world today is a testimony to the work of Satan and his beings.

Jesus said that the casting out of demons would be one of the signs to follow believers, and this is occurring today. It is not something we are to go out and look for. But if we find ourselves confronted with such a situation, we have been given the power to deal with it, through the name of Jesus and the power of the Holy Spirit.

Moses and Aaron went to Pharaoh, not in their own name and in their own strength, but in the name of the Lord, representing him. So it is that we too must reach out to others.

It is certainly not in our own authority or our own strength that we can deliver anyone, but we go as Jesus' representatives, in His name and with the authority granted by him.

Peter spoke of this clearly after he had healed a man who had been crippled since birth...

> [16]*"By faith in the name of Jesus, this man whom you see and know was made strong. It is Jesus' name and the faith that comes through him that has given this complete healing to him, as you can all see"* (Acts 3:16).

BUT PHARAOH DID NOT WANT TO GIVE UP EASILY (AND NEITHER DOES SATAN)

> [1]*"Then the LORD said to Moses, 'See, I have made you like God to Pharaoh, and your brother Aaron will be your prophet. [2]You are to say everything I command you, and your brother Aaron is to tell Pharaoh to let the Israelites go out of his country. [3]But I will harden Pharaoh's heart, and though I multiply my miraculous signs and wonders in Egypt, [4]he will not listen to you. Then I will lay my hand on Egypt and with mighty acts of judgment I will bring out my divisions, my people the Israelites. [5]And the Egyptians will know that I am the LORD when I stretch out my hand against Egypt and bring the Israelites out of it.' [6]Moses and Aaron did just as the LORD commanded them. [7]Moses was eighty years old and Aaron eighty-three when they spoke to Pharaoh. [8]The LORD said to Moses and Aaron, [9]"When Pharaoh says to you, 'Perform a miracle,' then say to Aaron, 'Take your staff and throw it down before Pharaoh,' and it will become a snake.' [10]So Moses and Aaron went to Pharaoh and did just as the LORD commanded..."* (Exod 7:1-10).

Moses and Aaron went to Pharoah many times, but each time he refused to let the Israelites go. With each of these refusals, God instructed Moses to bring a specific plague against the

Egyptians. These plagues were devastating to Egypt. They included (in order of occurence):

1. The waters of Egypt—the streams and canals, the ponds and all the reservoirs—were changed into blood. The fish in the Nile died, the river stunk, and the Egyptians could not drink the water.
2. The whole country was plagued with frogs. The Nile teemed with them. They came up into the palace and into the houses of the officials and the people of Egypt.
3. Gnats came on men and animals as thick as the dust of the ground.
4. Dense swarms of flies were sent into Pharaoh's palace and into the houses of his officials, and throughout Egypt the land was ruined by the flies.
5. The livestock in the fields were hit with a plague. Livestock of the Egyptians died.
6. Festering boils broke out on men and animals.
7. The worst hailstorm occurred which had ever fallen on Egypt since the day it was founded. The hail struck every thing in the fields—both men and animals; it beat down everything growing in the fields and stripped every tree.
8. A plague of locusts came upon the land. The Lord made an east wind blow across the land all day and all night. By morning the wind had brought the locusts; they invaded all Egypt and settled down in every area of the country in great numbers.. Never before had there been such a plague of locusts.
9. Total darkness which covered Egypt for four days. It was darkness that could be felt. No one could see anyone else or leave his place for three days.
10. At about midnight on a specific night, every firstborn son in Egypt died, from the firstborn son of Pharoah, to the firstborn son of the slave girl and all the cattle as well.

Pharoah's magicians were able to duplicate the first two plagues by their secret arts, but could not begin to duplicate the rest of the plagues brought by the Lord.

The first three plagues effected the Israelites as well as the Egyptians, but beginning with the fourth plague God spared the Israelites (who were living in the area of Goshen) from any further harm from the plagues.

Meanwhile, Pharoah refused to let the Israelites go. He ignored the first plague, and for each plague thereafter, he gave false promises to let the people go if Moses would only agree to pray to have the plague removed. As soon as Moses prayed and each plague was lifted, Pharaoh would again harden his heart and refuse to allow the Israelites to leave Egypt.

PHARAOH SAID, "GO ... BUT ...
... ONLY A SHORT WAY!

During the plague of flies ...

[28]*"Pharaoh said, 'I will let you go to offer sacrifices to the LORD your God in the desert, but you must not go very far. Now pray for me'"* (Exod. 8:28).

... MEN ONLY!

During the plague of locusts Pharaoh said ...

[11]*"No! Have only the men go; and worship the LORD ..."* (Exod. 10:11).

... NO CATTLE!

During the plague of darkness ...

[24]*"... Pharaoh summoned Moses and said, 'Go, worship the LORD. Even your women and children may go with you; only leave your flocks and herds behind'"* (Exod. 10:24).

Pharaoh knew that the Israelites would never really be free from him if he could keep them from going too far from

Egypt, if he could hold on to their women and children, or if he could hang on to some vital economic interest belonging to them.

> In the same way Satan says to us, "Go ahead and serve the Lord —but, you really don't have to go overboard about it and become a fanatic! You can still enjoy some of the pleasures of Egypt and be a Christian too. God certainly understands. It just doesn't make sense to go too far with this thing!"

Scripture speaks clearly to us, that it is essential, if we desire to come to Christ, that we have repentant hearts. We must be willing to turn away from the ways of this world in order to receive the full forgiveness that He has to offer us. We must not think we can have it both ways.

> [4]*"You adulterous people, don't you know that friendship with the world is hatred toward God? Anyone who chooses to be a friend of the world becomes an enemy of God"* (James 4:4). ... and also ...

> [15]*"Do not love the world or anything in the world. If anyone loves the world, the love of the Father is not in him.* [16]*For everything in the world—the cravings of sinful man, the lust of his eyes and the boasting of what he has and does—comes not from the Father but from the world.* [17]*The world and its desires pass away, but the man who does the will of God lives forever"* (1 John 2:15-17).

"Now hold on a minute," Satan says ...

... you know that your spouse isn't going to go along with your desire to serve Jesus. Why rock the boat at home? Just wait. Maybe he/she will come around one of these days and then you can get serious about Jesus. Then you will be able to really live for him.

But the Lord says ...

[26]*"If anyone comes to me and does not hate[1] his father and mother, his wife and children, his brothers and sisters— yes, even his own life—he cannot be my disciple"* (Luke 14:26).

"Well OK, I understand about that," says Satan, ...

"... but God knows you have to earn a living too, and there are just so many hours in a day, and days in a week. You've been working hard, and you deserve some of the nicer things in life. You need to keep putting in the extra hours just a little longer. Unless you get that advanced degree and that promotion to management, how are you ever going to get that house that you and your wife have been talking about? ... and your car is already over 5 years old. Your friends are all moving up, getting into nicer homes, buying boats, and lots of things, so you had better keep at it. Just a couple of more years and things will settle down. Once you get some of those things out of the way, then you will certainly have more time and money with which to serve the Lord."

Jesus spoke about this in a parable...

[16]*"Jesus replied: 'A certain man was preparing a great banquet and invited many guests. [17]At the time of the banquet he sent his servant to tell those who had been invited, 'Come, for everything is now ready.'"*
[18]*"But they all alike began to make excuses. The first said, 'I have just bought a field, and I must go and see it. Please excuse me.'*
[19]*Another said, 'I have just bought five yoke of oxen, and I'm on my way to try them out. Please excuse me.'"*
[20]*"Still another said, 'I just got married, so I can't come.'*
[21]*"The servant came back and reported this to his master. Then the owner of the house became angry and ordered his ser-*

---

[1]A footnote in the NIV Translation says that *"hate his father"* is a vivid hyperbole, meaning that one must love Jesus even more than his immediate family.

vant, 'Go out quickly into the streets and alleys of the town and bring in the poor, the crippled, the blind and the lame.'

[22]"Sir,' the servant said, 'what you ordered has been done, but there is still room.'

[23]"Then the master told his servant, 'Go out to the roads and country lanes and make them come in, so that my house will be full. [24]I tell you, not one of those men who were invited will get a taste of my banquet"[m] (Luke 14:16-24).

When we come to the Lord, we are making a decision to serve Him whether we have everything or nothing at all. Our motivation is not to have this thing or that thing, but rather to serve (trust and obey) the Lord first, and to let everything else be in response to that first priority. He says that if we will do this, and trust the Lord for the rest, He will meet our needs. In speaking about our basic needs, Jesus said ...

"But seek ye first the kingdom of God, and his righteousness; and all these things shall be added unto you" (Matt 6:33 KJV). (Refer also to the full passage in Matthew 6:25-33)

Other scriptures address this also ...

[6]"But godliness with contentment is great gain. [7]For we brought nothing into the world, and we can take nothing out of it. [8]But if we have food and clothing, we will be content with that. [9]People who want to get rich fall into temptation and a trap and into many foolish and harmful desires that plunge men into ruin and destruction. [10]For the love of money is a root of all kinds of evil. Some people, eager for money, have wandered from the faith and pierced themselves with many griefs" (1 Tim. 6:6-10).

[19]"Do not store up for yourselves treasures on earth, where moth and rust destroy, and where thieves break in and steal. [20]But store up for yourselves treasures in heaven,

---

[m]Emphasis added

47

where moth and rust do not destroy, and where thieves do not break in and steal. [21]For where your treasure is, there your heart will be also.

[22]"The eye is the lamp of the body. If your eyes are good, your whole body will be full of light. [23]But if your eyes are bad, your whole body will be full of darkness. If then the light within you is darkness, how great is that darkness!

[24]"No one can serve two masters. Either he will hate the one and love the other, or he will be devoted to the one and despise the other. You cannot serve both God and Money"[n] (Matt. 6:19-24).

Only when we come to the Lord with our whole heart to give Him our primary devotion and trust, does everything else take its rightful place. When we have placed our whole life in trust with him, even if we lose what we have, we will not panic because we have made Him our strength and can look to Him to sustain us. The things we have do not define us in God's eyes. It is "who we belong to" that is important. If we belong to God through Jesus Christ, then we have all that we need. We have the means to live in peace no matter what our situation may be.

The Bible says that Moses had right thinking on this point...

[24]"By faith Moses, when he had grown up, refused to be known as the son of Pharaoh's daughter. [25]He chose to be mistreated along with the people of God rather than to enjoy the pleasures of sin for a short time."

The next verse is pivotal...

[26]"He regarded disgrace for the sake of Christ as of greater value than the treasures of Egypt, because he was looking ahead to his reward"[o] (Heb. 11:24-26).

---

[n]Emphasis added
[o]Emphasis added

If we want to come to the Lord and be His people, then we must make the kind of choice that Joshua and Elijah placed before subsequent generations of Israelites who lived in their day. Joshua challenged the people and gave them no half-way option when He said:

> [14]*"Now fear the LORD and serve him with all faithfulness. Throw away the gods your forefathers worshiped beyond the River and in Egypt, and serve the LORD. [15]But if serving the LORD seems undesirable to you, then choose for yourselves this day whom you will serve, whether the gods your forefathers served beyond the River, or the gods of the Amorites, in whose land you are living. But as for me and my household, we will serve the LORD"* (Josh. 24:14-15).

The prophet Elijah also asked the people to make the all-important choice to go one way or another ...

> [21]*"Elijah went before the people and said, 'How long will you waver between two opinions? If the LORD is God, follow him; but if Baal is God, follow him.' But the people said nothing"* (1 Kings 18:21).

We cannot successfully live for God if we persist in keeping part of our heart back in the world. That part of our heart which we left behind will serve to snare us and place us in bondage to Satan again, and that was Pharaoh's aim when he suggested to the Israelites that they could go, just so long as they left some part of themselves behind.

However, the Lord says to us ...

> [17]*"... come out from them and be separate, says the Lord. Touch no unclean thing, and I will receive you."*
> [18]*"I will be a Father to you, and you will be my sons and daughters, says the Lord Almighty"* (2 Cor. 6:17-18).

Scripture says (speaking of those who have come to Jesus) that it is possible to become entangled again with the world ...

[20]*"If they have escaped the corruption of the world by knowing our Lord and Savior Jesus Christ and are again entangled in it and overcome, they are worse off at the end than they were at the beginning.* [21]*It would have been better for them not to have known the way of righteousness, than to have known it and then to turn their backs on the sacred command that was passed on to them.* [22]*Of them the proverbs are true: 'A dog returns to its vomit, and, a sow that is washed goes back to her wallowing in the mud.'"* (2 Pet. 2:20-22).

Satan would have us leave some part of ourselves back in his domain where he can again ensnare us and bring us back under his power. There is only one way to be free of his dominion, and that is to wholeheartedly give ourselves to the Lord Jesus Christ, placing Him first, forsaking all that could possibly draw us back.

[1]*"... let us throw off everything that hinders and the sin that so easily entangles, and let us run with perseverance the race marked out for us.* [2]*Let us fix our eyes on Jesus, the author and perfecter of our faith, who for the joy set before him endured the cross, scorning its shame, and sat down at the right hand of the throne of God."* (Heb. 12:1b-2).

CHAPTER 3

Hope Realized— Deliverance Comes

God said that He would lay His hand on Egypt and with mighty acts of judgement would bring out the Israelites (Exod. 7:4). As we have seen, God brought ten plagues to judge Egypt and to secure the release of His people. The first nine plagues had a disastrous effect upon the land, water, animals and people of Egypt. However, the tenth plague, the death of the firstborn, was the most devastating of all.

[1]"*Now the LORD had said to Moses, 'I will bring one more plague on Pharaoh and on Egypt. After that, he will let you go from here, and when he does, he will drive you out completely.* [2]*Tell the people that men and women alike are to ask their neighbors for articles of silver and gold.'* [3]*(The LORD made the Egyptians favorably disposed toward the people, and Moses himself was highly regarded in Egypt by Pharaoh's officials and by the people.)*

[4]*So Moses said, 'This is what the LORD says: 'About midnight I will go throughout Egypt.* [5]*Every firstborn son*

in Egypt will die, from the firstborn son of Pharaoh, who sits on the throne, to the firstborn son of the slave girl, who is at her hand mill, and all the firstborn of the cattle as well. ⁶There will be loud wailing throughout Egypt—worse than there has ever been or ever will be again. ⁷But among the Israelites not a dog will bark at any man or animal.' Then you will know that the LORD makes a distinction between Egypt and Israel. ⁸All these officials of yours will come to me, bowing down before me and saying, 'Go, you and all the people who follow you!' After that I will leave.' Then Moses, hot with anger, left Pharaoh.

⁹The LORD had said to Moses, 'Pharaoh will refuse to listen to you—so that my wonders may be multiplied in Egypt.' ¹⁰Moses and Aaron performed all these wonders before Pharaoh, but the LORD hardened Pharaoh's heart, and he would not let the Israelites go out of his country" (Exod 11:1-10).

God was going to strike down all of the firstborn sons of the Egyptians along with all of the firstborn cattle. It would be a devastating plague and would understandably cause tremendous grief and wailing throughout Egypt. This plague would not discriminate, but would effect all people whether high or low, rich or poor.

The first nine plagues had demonstrated that Egypt's gods and all of the works of its wise men, magicians and sorcerers were impotent to stand against the power of the Lord—their idols were useless and their sorcery inadequate. Now, the tenth and last plague would truly humble Egypt.

The firstborn sons who died in the last plague represented Egypt's present and future hope (the chief of their strength - Ps. 78:51 and 105:36 AMP). They typified Egypt's pride and dependence on their own human wisdom and strength apart from God. But this too would be judged by God. Their disdain for the one true God would be shown to be utter foolishness.

The plague was to occur at midnight, and would mark the end of one era and the beginning of a new. It would be a dark time for Egypt, but would signal a new day for Israel. While it would be the time of Egypt's judgement, it would also be the time of Israel's deliverance. It would be the time at which God would fulfill His covenant promise to Abraham, to bring his descendants out of the land of their slavery that He might bring them into the promised land of Canaan (Genesis 15:1-21).

Egypt rejected the one true God and believed they could defy Him because of their own great strength and the strength of their gods. Yet it was now becoming clear that neither the wisdom and defiance of Egypt or their gods and idols could deliver them from God's judgements. Even after the devastation they had suffered, they were not willing to acknowledge God and bow before him. Pharaoh remained defiant and his people paid the price.

What made the Israelites so special that God would spare them from His judgements? Israel could not boast that Egypt alone was worthy of God's judgements and Israel was not. In fact, it is clearly stated in the book of Ezekiel that God almost destroyed the Israelites in the land of Egypt because of their sin and rebellion.

[5]*"... This is what the Sovereign LORD says: 'On the day I chose Israel, I swore with uplifted hand to the descendants of the house of Jacob and revealed myself to them in Egypt. With uplifted hand I said to them, "I am the LORD your God.'* [6]*On that day I swore to them that I would bring them out of Egypt into a land I had searched out for them, a land flowing with milk and honey, the most beautiful of all lands.* [7]*And I said to them, 'Each of you, get rid of the vile images you have set your eyes on, and do not defile yourselves with the idols of Egypt. I am the LORD your God.'*

[8]*'But they rebelled against me and would not listen to me; they did not get rid of the vile images they had set their eyes on, nor did they forsake the idols of Egypt. So I said I would pour out my wrath on them and spend my anger against them in Egypt.* [9]*But for the sake of my name I did*

what would keep it from being profaned in the eyes of the nations they lived among and in whose sight I had revealed myself to the Israelites by bringing them out of Egypt. [10]Therefore I led them out of Egypt and brought them into the desert" (Ezek. 20:5-10).

A question is posed in the Jewish Passover celebration ...

"Is it for the judgements against the Egyptians that we praise God? No, for God loved the Egyptians even as He loved us. But it is for God's infinite mercies that we praise him."

God showed the Israelites mercy in that He did not give them what they deserved. Israel would be delivered because of the covenant promise which God had made to Abraham and also so that no opportunity would be given to the people of Egypt and others to profane God's name—to declare that God lacked the power to accomplish what He had promised.

God was working to bring a nation unto Himself. A nation through whom He could reveal Himself to the world.

The Israelites were every bit as worthy to suffer judgement as the Egyptians. If they were to be spared from this last judgement, they would have to respond in faith and obedience to certain requirements which God levied upon them.

[1]*"The LORD said to Moses and Aaron in Egypt, [2]"This month is to be for you the first month, the first month of your year. [3]Tell the whole community of Israel that on the tenth day of this month each man is to take a lamb for his family, one for each household. [4]If any household is too small for a whole lamb, they must share one with their nearest neighbor, having taken into account the number of people there are. You are to determine the amount of lamb needed in accordance with what each person will eat. [5]The animals you choose must be year-old males without defect, and you may take them from the sheep or the goats. [6]Take care of them until the fourteenth day of the month, when all the people of the community of Israel must slaughter them at twilight. [7]Then*

they are to take some of the blood and put it on the sides and tops of the doorframes of the houses where they eat the lambs. ⁸That same night they are to eat the meat roasted over the fire, along with bitter herbs, and bread made without yeast. ⁹Do not eat the meat raw or cooked in water, but roast it over the fire—head, legs and inner parts. ¹⁰Do not leave any of it till morning; if some is left till morning, you must burn it. ¹¹This is how you are to eat it: with your cloak tucked into your belt, your sandals on your feet and your staff in your hand. Eat it in haste; it is the LORD's Passover.'

¹²'On that same night I will pass through Egypt and strike down every firstborn—both men and animals—and I will bring judgment on all the gods of Egypt. I am the LORD. ¹³The blood will be a sign for you on the houses where you are; and when I see the blood, I will pass over you. No destructive plague will touch you when I strike Egypt.'

¹⁴"This is a day you are to commemorate; for the generations to come you shall celebrate it as a festival to the LORD—a lasting ordinance. ¹⁵For seven days you are to eat bread made without yeast. On the first day remove the yeast from your houses, for whoever eats anything with yeast in it from the first day through the seventh must be cut off from Israel. ¹⁶On the first day hold a sacred assembly, and another one on the seventh day. Do no work at all on these days, except to prepare food for everyone to eat—that is all you may do.

¹⁷"Celebrate the Feast of Unleavened Bread, because it was on this very day that I brought your divisions out of Egypt. Celebrate this day as a lasting ordinance for the generations to come. ¹⁸In the first month you are to eat bread made without yeast, from the evening of the fourteenth day until the evening of the twenty-first day. ¹⁹For seven days no yeast is to be found in your houses. And whoever eats anything with yeast in it must be cut off from the community of Israel, whether he is an alien or native-born. ²⁰Eat nothing made with yeast. Wherever you live, you must eat unleavened bread."

21Then Moses summoned all the elders of Israel and said to them, "Go at once and select the animals for your families and slaughter the Passover lamb. 22Take a bunch of hyssop, dip it into the blood in the basin and put some of the blood on the top and on both sides of the doorframe. Not one of you shall go out the door of his house until morning. 23When the LORD goes through the land to strike down the Egyptians, he will see the blood on the top and sides of the doorframe and will pass over that doorway, and he will not permit the destroyer to enter your houses and strike you down.

24"Obey these instructions as a lasting ordinance for you and your descendants. 25When you enter the land that the LORD will give you as he promised, observe this ceremony. 26And when your children ask you, 'What does this ceremony mean to you?' 27then tell them, 'It is the Passover sacrifice to the LORD, who passed over the houses of the Israelites in Egypt and spared our homes when he struck down the Egyptians.'" Then the people bowed down and worshiped. 28The Israelites did just what the LORD commanded Moses and Aaron" (Exod. 12:1-28).

Israel would forever mark this historical event on their calendar. The month of their deliverance would become the first month of their year. It represented the beginning of something entirely new, a time when God, through mighty acts of judgement, took a nation of people to be His own.

The instructions given by God to the Israelites through Moses pointed the way for them to be delivered from this last plague. This deliverance would be commemorated by the Passover celebration for generations to come.

God's directions would not seem to make sense. Why must a lamb be slaughtered? What special power did the blood of a lamb have to protect them? What was the significance of all the things they were required to do? Who could explain it? Yet, it was what God required of them if they were to be protected from God's judgements.

We recall it was said that the Israelites believed when they first heard Moses and Aaron's message that God wanted to deliver them from Egypt. They were so overjoyed at the prospect of deliverance that they worshiped the Lord (Exod. 4:29-31). However, when Pharaoh made their work harder (Exod. 5:1-18), they became angry at Moses and Aaron and turned back to despair and unbelief in God's promise to them (Exod. 5:19-23). But now, after they had seen God's mighty acts of judgement poured out on Egypt, their faith was strengthened. They were ready to do what God required of them even if they could not explain it. Doing what God required was essential if their firstborn were not to be killed.

The Israelites knew that they could not deliver themselves from Pharaoh's grasp. Only God could, and He had provided a way for them to be delivered, but it meant that the Israelites had to trust and obey God. They had to do what God said, even when they did not understand it. They would have to respond by faith.

So, as it says in Exod. 12:28, *"the Israelites did just what the Lord commanded Moses and Aaron."*

> [29]*"At midnight the LORD struck down all the firstborn in Egypt, from the firstborn of Pharaoh, who sat on the throne, to the firstborn of the prisoner, who was in the dungeon, and the firstborn of all the livestock as well.* [30]*Pharaoh and all his officials and all the Egyptians got up during the night, and there was loud wailing in Egypt, for there was not a house without someone dead.*
>
> [31]*During the night Pharaoh summoned Moses and Aaron and said, "Up! Leave my people, you and the Israelites! Go, worship the LORD as you have requested.* [32]*Take your flocks and herds, as you have said, and go. And also bless me."*
>
> [33]*The Egyptians urged the people to hurry and leave the country. 'For otherwise,' they said, 'we will all die!'* [34]*So the people took their dough before the yeast was added, and carried it on their shoulders in kneading troughs wrapped in clothing.* [35]*The Israelites did as Moses instructed and*

asked the Egyptians for articles of silver and gold and for clothing. [36]The LORD had made the Egyptians favorably disposed toward the people, and they gave them what they asked for; so they plundered the Egyptians.

[37]The Israelites journeyed from Rameses to Succoth. There were about six hundred thousand men on foot, besides women and children. [38]Many other people went up with them, as well as large droves of livestock, both flocks and herds. [39]With the dough they had brought from Egypt, they baked cakes of unleavened bread. The dough was without yeast because they had been driven out of Egypt and did not have time to prepare food for themselves.

[40]Now the length of time the Israelite people lived in Egypt was 430 years. [41] At the end of the 430 years, to the very day, all the LORD's divisions left Egypt. [42]Because the LORD kept vigil that night to bring them out of Egypt, on this night all the Israelites are to keep vigil to honor the LORD for the generations to come" (Exod. 12:29-42).

As was mentioned earlier, the number of Israelites living in Egypt had probably increased to around two million. But, on the day they went out of Egypt, "many other people went up with them" indicating that perhaps slaves of other nationalities or even some Egyptians made a decision to depart with the Israelites. This large group of people headed toward the Red Sea ...

[17]"When Pharaoh let the people go, God did not lead them on the road through the Philistine country, though that was shorter. For God said, 'If they face war, they might change their minds and return to Egypt.' [18]So God led the people around by the desert road toward the Red Sea. The Israelites went up out of Egypt armed for battle" (Exod. 13:17-18).

But the Lord commanded the Israelites to change direction ...

[1]"Then the LORD said to Moses, [2]'Tell the Israelites to turn back and encamp near Pi Hahiroth, between Migdol

and the sea. They are to encamp by the sea, directly opposite Baal Zephon. ³Pharaoh will think, the Israelites are
wandering around the land in confusion, hemmed in by the
desert. ⁴And I will harden Pharaoh's heart, and he will pursue them. But I will gain glory for myself through Pharaoh
and all his army, and the Egyptians will know that I am the
LORD.' So the Israelites did this.

⁵When the king of Egypt was told that the people had
fled, Pharaoh and his officials changed their minds about
them and said, "What have we done? We have let the Israelites go and have lost their services!" ⁶So he had his chariot
made ready and took his army with him. ⁷He took six hundred of the best chariots, along with all the other chariots of
Egypt, with officers over all of them. ⁸The LORD hardened
the heart of Pharaoh king of Egypt, so that he pursued the
Israelites, who were marching out boldly. ⁹The Egyptians—
all Pharaoh's horses and chariots, horsemen and troops—
pursued the Israelites and overtook them as they camped
by the sea near Pi Hahiroth, opposite Baal Zephon.

¹⁰As Pharaoh approached, the Israelites looked up, and
there were the Egyptians, marching after them. They were
terrified and cried out to the LORD. ¹¹They said to Moses,
'Was it because there were no graves in Egypt that you
brought us to the desert to die? What have you done to us
by bringing us out of Egypt? ¹²Didn't we say to you in Egypt,
'Leave us alone; let us serve the Egyptians'? It would have
been better for us to serve the Egyptians than to die in the
desert!'

¹³Moses answered the people, 'Do not be afraid. Stand
firm and you will see the deliverance the LORD will bring
you today. The Egyptians you see today you will never see
again. ¹⁴The LORD will fight for you; you need only to be still.'

¹⁵Then the LORD said to Moses, 'Why are you crying
out to me? Tell the Israelites to move on. ¹⁶Raise your staff
and stretch out your hand over the sea to divide the water
so that the Israelites can go through the sea on dry ground.
¹⁷I will harden the hearts of the Egyptians so that they will
go in after them. And I will gain glory through Pharaoh and
all his army, through his chariots and his horsemen. ¹⁸The

Egyptians will know that I am the LORD when I gain glory through Pharaoh, his chariots and his horsemen.'

[19]Then the angel of God, who had been traveling in front of Israel's army, withdrew and went behind them. The pillar of cloud also moved from in front and stood behind them, [20]coming between the armies of Egypt and Israel. Throughout the night the cloud brought darkness to the one side and light to the other side; so neither went near the other all night long.

[21]Then Moses stretched out his hand over the sea, and all that night the LORD drove the sea back with a strong east wind and turned it into dry land. The waters were divided, [22]and the Israelites went through the sea on dry ground, with a wall of water on their right and on their left.

[23]The Egyptians pursued them, and all Pharaoh's horses and chariots and horsemen followed them into the sea. [24]During the last watch of the night the LORD looked down from the pillar of fire and cloud at the Egyptian army and threw it into confusion. [25]He made the wheels of their chariots come off so that they had difficulty driving. And the Egyptians said, 'Let's get away from the Israelites! The LORD is fighting for them against Egypt.'

[26]Then the LORD said to Moses, 'Stretch out your hand over the sea so that the waters may flow back over the Egyptians and their chariots and horsemen.' [27] Moses stretched out his hand over the sea, and at daybreak the sea went back to its place. The Egyptians were fleeing toward it, and the LORD swept them into the sea. [28]The water flowed back and covered the chariots and horsemen—the entire army of Pharaoh that had followed the Israelites into the sea. Not one of them survived.

[29]But the Israelites went through the sea on dry ground, with a wall of water on their right and on their left. [30]That day the LORD saved Israel from the hands of the Egyptians, and Israel saw the Egyptians lying dead on the shore. [31]And when the Israelites saw the great power the LORD displayed against the Egyptians, the people feared the LORD and put their trust in him and in Moses his servant" (Exod. 14:1-31). What an awesome spectacle this must have been.

Pharaoh did not want to give up these slaves of his, and although he had let them go, he changed his mind and pursued them toward the Red Sea.

God realized that the Israelites did not yet know how to trust Him very well, but He continued to prod them along. Once more, they cried out in fear when they saw Pharaoh and the Egyptians pursuing them. All faith in God's promises seemed to vanish.

They said to Moses, "Was it because there were no graves in Egypt that you brought us to the desert to die? What have you done to us by bringing us out of Egypt? Didn't we say to you in Egypt, 'Leave us alone; let us serve the Egyptians'? It would have been better for us to serve the Egyptians than to die in the desert!" (Exod. 14:10-12).

We can understand that trusting God in this way was a new thing for the Israelites, and they weren't quite sure how to react. It's no wonder God decided not to lead them through Philistine country where they might have to fight. They were not ready to face warfare. There was much to be learned first.

After reading all of this history (and *it is* actual history), we might begin to wonder, what does all this mean to us?

These events provide insight into things that effect us personally and will effect the world as a whole. Let's look at these things in more detail.

THE PASSOVER

Remember, as we look at these events, that Egypt is a representation of this sinful world, and Pharaoh is a representation of Satan.

The Bible teaches that sin and rebellion against God entered the world through one man, Adam. Because of his rebellion against God, the whole world was plunged into darkness and mankind was separated from a holy God. The whole of mankind, descended from Adam, were declared to be sinners and were made subject to death.

> [12]"Therefore, just as sin entered the world through one man, and death through sin, and in this way death came to all men, because all sinned...
> [14]... death reigned from the time of Adam to the time of Moses, even over those who did not sin by breaking a command, as did Adam ...
> [15]... many died by the trespass of the one man ...
> [16]... The judgment followed one sin and brought condemnation ...
> [17]... by the trespass of the one man, death reigned through that one man ...
> [18]... the result of one trespass was condemnation for all men...
> [19]... through the disobedience of the one man the many were made sinners ... (Extract from Rom. 5:12-19).

These scriptures state (though some may not be willing to accept this fact) that because of the sin of Adam, all mankind stands condemned before God. As a consequence, all who have ever lived have been left in a hopeless, condemned condition, having no way to achieve a reconciliation with God.

> "For all have sinned and fall short of the glory of God..." (Rom. 3:23).

> "For the wages of sin is death..." (Rom. 6:23).

Furthermore, God has given mankind His laws (i.e. the Ten Commandments). These laws were given to Moses at a time following their exodus from Egypt. Mankind not only stands separated from God because of Adam's sin, but also because they have broken God's laws. There are no works that any one of us can do which will bring God's forgiveness and atone for these sins.

"All of us have become like one who is unclean, and all our righteous acts are like filthy rags; we all shrivel up like a leaf, and like the wind our sins sweep us away" (Isa. 64:6).

Another scripture says ...

[9]"What shall we conclude then? Are we any better? Not at all! We have already made the charge that Jews and Gentiles alike are all under sin. [10]As it is written: 'There is no one righteous, not even one;
[11]there is no one who understands, no one who seeks God.
[12]All have turned away, they have together become worthless; there is no one who does good, not even one.'
[13]'Their throats are open graves; their tongues practice deceit.' 'The poison of vipers is on their lips.'
[14]'Their mouths are full of cursing and bitterness.'
[15]'Their feet are swift to shed blood;
[16]ruin and misery mark their ways,
[17]and the way of peace they do not know.'
[18]'There is no fear of God before their eyes.'
[19]Now we know that whatever the law says, it says to those who are under the law, so that every mouth may be silenced and the whole world held accountable to God. [20]Therefore no one will be declared righteous in His sight by observing the law; rather, through the law we become conscious of sin" (Rom. 3:9-20).

A person may say, "Well, I don't curse, I haven't killed someone, or done anything wrong, so I don't believe that I am guilty of any sin."

The Biblical definition of sin is violation of God's commandments. God is the one who created us and has the right to set the standards for what is right and what is wrong. When we rebel against His laws, we are rebelling against Him. Jesus was asked ...

[36]"Teacher, which is the greatest commandment in the Law?"

37Jesus replied: 'Love the Lord your God with all your heart and with all your soul and with all your mind.' 38This is the first and greatest commandment. 39And the second is like it: 'Love your neighbor as yourself.' All the Law and the Prophets hang on these two commandments " (Matt. 22:36-40).

There is no one on this earth who can say that they have not violated these commandments in one way or another by thought, word or deed. The Ten Commandments and all the detailed moral laws given in the Old Testament fall under the umbrella of one or the other of these two commandments.

So, according to scripture, we are all classed as sinners because of Adam's original sin and because we have broken God's laws. We stand guilty before God and therefore are subject to the judgements of God, **but** (and this is a vital message) God has provided a way for our sins to be forgiven that we might be reconciled to him. It is through the means of a sacrifice, a life for a life. (If this bothers you, please don't stop reading here, because what follows is good news!)

We have already considered that the Israelites' deliverance from the tenth and final plague was brought about by what might be deemed "superstitious mumbo-jumbo." Lambs had to be killed at twilight and roasted. There had to be enough lamb for every person to eat. The blood of these lambs had to be placed on the top and sides of the doorpost.

The Bible teaches, and it is a fact, that the life of every creature, whether man or animal, is in its blood. Since blood was the essence of life, God required man to treat it with respect. This is made clear from the very first book of the Bible:

3"Everything that lives and moves will be food for you. Just as I gave you the green plants, I now give you everything. 4'But you must not eat meat that has its lifeblood still in it. 5And for your lifeblood I will surely demand an accounting. I will demand an accounting from every animal. And from

each man, too, I will demand an accounting for the life of his fellow man.'
⁶'Whoever sheds the blood of man, by man shall his blood be shed; for in the image of God has God made man'" (Gen. 9:3-6).

When God gave the Israelites His laws, He amplified this point ...

> *¹⁰"Any Israelite or any alien living among them who eats any blood—I will set my face against that person who eats blood and will cut him off from his people. ¹¹For the life of a creature is in the blood, and I have given it to you to make atonement for yourselves on the altar;* **it is the blood that makes atonement for one's life**.ᵃ *¹²Therefore I say to the Israelites, 'None of you may eat blood, nor may an alien living among you eat blood.'*
> *¹³'Any Israelite or any alien living among you who hunts any animal or bird that may be eaten must drain out the blood and cover it with earth, ¹⁴because the life of every creature is its blood. That is why I have said to the Israelites, 'You must not eat the blood of any creature, because the life of every creature is its blood; anyone who eats it must be cut off'"* (Lev. 17:10-14).

In this passage, it is made clear that the sacrifice of animals as it was performed in the Old Testament days, was intended to make atonement (to bring reconciliation between God and man) for sins committed against God. One life was given for another life. The creature sacrificed may have been a lamb, a bull, a goat, etc., but these are generally representative of a lamb which was a typical sacrifice.

The Bible teaches that the Old Testament sacrifice of animals was only a representation of things that were to come. These animal sacrifices, in and of themselves, had no power to cleanse from sin ...

ᵃEmphasis added

[1]"The law is only a shadow of the good things that are coming—not the realities themselves. For this reason it can never, by the same sacrifices repeated endlessly year after year, make perfect those who draw near to worship. [2]If it could, would they not have stopped being offered? For the worshipers would have been cleansed once for all, and would no longer have felt guilty for their sins. [3]But those sacrifices are an annual reminder of sins, [4]because it is impossible for the blood of bulls and goats to take away sins" (Heb. 10:1-4)"

This scripture may only serve to make these things seem more confusing—until we realize that the lamb (representing all sacrificial animals) finds its ultimate fulfillment in Jesus Christ.

The sacrifice of a lamb and the atonement it provided was a cornerstone of Jewish worship throughout the time of the Old Testament. But without the death and the shed blood of the Lamb of God, Jesus Christ, the sacrifice of lambs could have no meaning or ability to cleanse anyone from sin and keep them from God's judgement. The blood of an animal had no real power to deliver in and of itself. However, *when individuals placed their faith in the ability of that blood to atone for their sins, they were receiving the deliverance paid for by the blood of the one true Lamb Of God, Jesus Christ, whose blood was shed for the sins of all mankind many centuries later when He died on a cross.* John the Baptist identified Jesus for who He truly was when He saw Jesus coming toward him, *"Look, **the** Lamb of God, who takes away the sin of the world."[b]* (John 1:29)

John was looking for Jesus, and understood the significance of His person and His mission. He understood that Jesus was *"**The Lamb**"* of God who had come to give himself as the ultimate sacrifice for sin.

---

[b]Emphasis added

66

⁵"Therefore, when Christ came into the world, he said: 'Sacrifice and offering you did not desire, but a body you prepared for me; ⁶with burnt offerings and sin offerings you were not pleased.

⁷Then I said, 'Here I am—it is written about me in the scroll—I have come to do your will, O God.' ⁸First he said, 'Sacrifices and offerings, burnt offerings and sin offerings you did not desire, nor were you pleased with them''(although the law required them to be made). ⁹Then he said, 'Here I am, I have come to do your will.' He sets aside the first to establish the second. ¹⁰And by that will, we have been made holy through the sacrifice of the body of Jesus Christ once for all.

¹¹Day after day every priest stands and performs his religious duties; again and again he offers the same sacrifices, **which can never take away sins**ᶜ. *¹²But when this priest had offered for all time one sacrifice for sins, he sat down at the right hand of God"* (Heb. 10:5-12).

Christ's death paid the price for the sins of men **of all time**, whether they lived before the time of His death, or after.

"... now he has appeared once for all at the end of the ages **to do away with sin by the sacrifice of himself"**ᵈ (Heb. 9:26).

Jesus became the Lamb of God, the perfect sacrifice, who would, through the one-time sacrifice of himself, become the fulfillment of all the sacrifices ever made since the beginning of time. By this action, He also eliminated the need for any further sacrifices to be offered.

The Bible clearly declares that Jesus is God ...

⁵"Your attitude should be the same as that of Christ Jesus:

ᶜEmphasis added
ᵈEmphasis added

⁶Who, being in very nature God, did not consider equality with God something to be grasped, ⁷but made himself nothing, taking the very nature of a servant, being made in human likeness. ⁸And being found in appearance as a man, he humbled himself and became obedient to death—even death on a cross!" (Phil. 2:5-8).

Jesus died a cruel death on a cross and became the ultimate sacrifice for sins. It is interesting to note that when the Israelites applied the blood of the lamb to the top and sides of the doorpost, the movement of their hands in applying this blood would naturally form the outline of a cross.

Before the coming of Jesus Christ, the Levitical law given to Moses by the Lord required the establishment of a priesthood to offer animal sacrifices for the sins of the people. As it says, "Day after day every priest stands and performs his religious duties; again and again he offers the same sacrifices, which can never take away sin" (Heb. 10:11). But now we see that Jesus has eliminated the need for earthly priests, because he has become our ultimate High Priest through the perfect sacrifice of himself once, and for all. Now there is no longer any need for earthly priests to exist to perform these sacrifices, or to act as mediators between God and mankind. As it says ...

"For there is one God and one mediator between God and men, the man Christ Jesus" (1 Tim. 2:5).

Also ...

"If perfection could have been attained through the Levitical priesthood (for on the basis of it the law was given to the people), why was there still need for another priest (Jesus)ᵉ to come...?" (Heb. 7:11).

Speaking further of that former priesthood ...

ᵉWord in parenthesis added

> [23]*"Now there have been many of those priests, since death prevented them from continuing in office;* [24]*but because Jesus lives forever, he has a permanent priesthood.* [25]*Therefore he is able to save completely those who come to God through him, because he always lives to intercede for them.*
> [26]*Such a high priest meets our need—one who is holy, blameless, pure, set apart from sinners, exalted above the heavens.* [27]*Unlike the other high priests, he does not need to offer sacrifices day after day, first for his own sins, and then for the sins of the people. He sacrificed for their sins once for all when he offered himself.* [28]*For the law appoints as high priests men who are weak; but the oath, which came after the law, appointed the Son, who has been made perfect forever"* (Heb. 7:23-28).

Recognizing that there is only *"one mediator between God and men, the man Christ Jesus,"* we must not seek any other mediator, or mediatrix. Jesus said that when we pray, we are to pray to the Father in Jesus' name. When we do, He will respond. We are not instructed in scripture to go through any other intermediaries. There is no need to.

> [13]*"And I will do whatever you ask in my name, so that the Son may bring glory to the Father.* [14]*You may ask me for anything in my name, and I will do it"* (John 14:13-14).

> *"...I tell you the truth, my Father will give you whatever you ask in my name"* (John 16:23).

The lamb which the Israelites were to offer, was to be a male without blemish. This is also a clear picture of Jesus, who was free from sin and perfect in all His ways ...

> *"God made him **who had no sin** to be sin for us, so that in him we might become the righteousness of God"*[f] (2 Cor. 5:21).

---

[f]Emphasis added

69

Jesus was conceived in Mary of the Holy Ghost. Therefore, He was not infected with the sin of Adam and therefore did not have the fallen nature which plagues us. He was tempted to sin just as we are, but did not succumb to those temptations. When He died on the cross for us, He was without sin, but He took the punishment for our sins upon Himself. He could not have done that had He also been guilty of sin.

As we have seen, the Israelites were to roast the lamb in the fire. One thing which fire represents in scripture is the judgement of God. Jesus has taken our place, and when He died on the cross, He took God's judgement for our sin upon himself and paid the price that we should have paid. (What great love God has for us!) Therefore, when that sacrifice is made applicable to our lives, we are declared to be righteous (no longer guilty of sin) and are placed in right standing with God.

In considering what Jesus has done for us, we can use the example of someone who is pronounced guilty of murder. He is sentenced to die for his crime. Nothing he can do could possibly erase or atone for the crime he has committed. Nothing can bring back the life he has taken.

Then someone else comes along who is innocent of any crime. He offers to give his life in place of the guilty party to pay the penalty that has been meted out. The authorities agree that this is acceptable. The man who is sentenced to die agrees also, and so judgement falls upon the innocent man and the one who was guilty is set free. Because his penalty has been paid, the one who was guilty is no longer subject to the death sentence, but is cleared of all wrongdoing. He is justified—that is, his condition becomes as one who had never committed murder.

In this world, people might still consider the person who has been freed to be guilty. But the death Jesus died on the cross enables a sinner to become, in God's eyes, as one who has never sinned at all. Christ's sacrifice completely pays for the sin and exonerates the guilty one. God remembers his sins no more.

> *"...because by one sacrifice he has made perfect forever those who are being made holy..."* Then he adds: *"Their sins and lawless acts I will remember no more"* (Heb. 10:14,17).

We might ask, is everyone in the world now declared "not guilty" because of what Jesus has done?

No, because God has made it clear to us in scripture that this sacrifice is only effective for those who are willing to repent of their sins and will personally place their trust (have faith and come to depend) upon Jesus, the One who has taken the judgement of God upon Himself in their behalf. Each of us must make this decision.

Let's look at the subjects of repentance and faith in more detail.

First, what does repentance truly mean?

We can see an example of this in our study of the Israelites. The Israelites were instructed to eat the lamb: "with your cloak tucked into your belt, your sandals on your feet and your staff in your hand." They were to partake of the lamb while at the same time being prepared to immediately leave Egypt. The two actions were inseparable.

Those who come to Jesus, the Lamb of God, must at the same time be willing to immediately turn their back on the gods and the ungodly ways of this world. One is not acceptable without the other. That is the true meaning of repentance.

The Apostle Paul spoke of this ...

> *"I have declared to both Jews and Greeks that they must turn to God in repentance and have faith in our Lord Jesus"* (Acts 20:21).

"First to those in Damascus, then to those in Jerusalem and in all Judea, and to the Gentiles also, I preached that they should repent and turn to God and prove their repentance by their deeds" (Acts 26:20).

True repentance brings a complete change in direction and allegiance and is necessary if we want a changed life. Just as the Israelites could not remain in Egypt and at the same time go to the "promised land," so we also cannot expect to hold on to and love the world and our sinful ways, while at the same time trying to love and follow God. We must choose which one we will serve. We can't have it both ways.

Faith was also required. Partaking of the lamb, placing the blood on the doorpost and being prepared to immediately leave Egypt were all acts of faith that were working together to bring deliverance to the Israelites from their former way of life. They had to believe and act by faith upon the instructions that the Lord gave them if they were going to be spared. Because they believed and acted upon God's Word, God honored their faith, and the ultimate death and shed blood of Jesus Christ, the Lamb of God, became effective for them. As a consequence, they were protected from the judgements of God which came against Egypt because of its sins.

When we come to God through this way of faith, we are declared righteous, being forgiven by God and cleansed from all sin. We cannot come any other way than by faith and still be acceptable to God.

"And without faith it is impossible to please God, because anyone who comes to him must believe that he exists and that he rewards those who earnestly seek him" (Heb. 11:6).

[8]*"For it is by grace you have been saved, through faith—and this not from yourselves, it is the gift of God —*[9]*not by works, so that no one can boast"* (Eph. 2:8-9).

Saving faith is the confident commitment and trust of one's life to God. It is not merely believing in the existence of God. That kind of belief will not change a person's life. That is not any more life changing than believing that the earth revolves around the sun.

I am reminded here of a story which illustrates this truth very well:

> A circus performer had placed a high wire all the way across Niagara Falls intending to ride a bicycle on this wire to the opposite side. As he was preparing to go, he looked down at a spectator who was intently watching this feat unfold and asked him, "Do you believe that I can cross on this wire all the way to the other side?
>
> The spectator hesitated a moment and then said, "Sure, I believe that you can do it."
>
> "Okay," the performer said, "Hop on."

This is a humorous story, but its message is very clear. God is not asking us to have a mere mental belief in all the doctrines of salvation. Rather, He is asking us to commit our whole being to Him. We must be ready to place our lives in trust with Him to become His obedient servants through good times as well as times of difficulty. That is the kind of faith that will allow Him to transform our lives.

Along this line, I am also reminded of the pin which was put out by a Christian organization which said "TRY GOD." To just try God, is impossible. We can't sample Christianity like we would sample a can of soda. We can't even become Christians and undergo the transforming power of the Lord until we have made a commitment from our heart to follow Him.

The Israelites couldn't just leave Egypt to see if they would like it. They had to make a decision to stay or leave. It was impossible to have it both ways. It reminds me of a true story I heard once about a pimp who was presented with the message of salvation and decided he wanted to receive Jesus

Christ and be saved. He wanted to receive what Jesus Christ had to offer. But then he was told that he would have to quit his activities as a pimp and let his prostitutes go, he immediately gave up any thought of becoming a Christian. He wanted the good things Jesus had to offer, but he wanted to keep his sinful ways as well. There was no sorrow for sin or true repentance. Therefore he was not able to receive salvation.

Another important point needs to be made here. If we do not believe we are sinners as the Bible says, we are calling God a liar. We must acknowledge that we are sinners in need of the Savior if we would receive the salvation that God offers.

> [8]*"If we claim to be without sin, we deceive ourselves and the truth is not in us.* [9]*If we confess our sins, he is faithful and just and will forgive us our sins and purify us from all unrighteousness.* [10]*If we claim we have not sinned, we make him out to be a liar and his word has no place in our lives"* (1 John 1:8-10).

Abraham was a man who believed God. His actions were consistent with his faith and testified to its reality. This was demonstrated at a time when Abraham was tested by God, and was asked to sacrifice Isaac, the very son who had been promised to him and for whom he and Sarah had waited so many years (Gen. 22:1-18). God had no intention of letting Abraham actually sacrifice his son. However, God was asking for obedience, and Abraham's obedience may have played a very important role in the ultimate redemption of man by Jesus Christ. In any event, Abraham's obedience on that occasion has given us an excellent example of the kind of faith God wants us to have.

> [19]*"You believe that there is one God. Good! Even the demons believe that—and shudder.*

> *20You foolish man, do you want evidence that faith without deeds is useless? 21Was not our ancestor Abraham considered righteous for what he did when he offered his son Isaac on the altar? 22You see that his faith and his actions were working together, and his faith was made complete by what he did. 23And the scripture was fulfilled that says, "Abraham believed God, and it was credited to him as righteousness," and he was called God's friend. 24You see that a person is justified by what he does and not by faith alone"* (James 2:19-24).

God's grace, His unmerited favor, has been given to us through the sacrifice of Jesus Christ. He holds out to us His gift of forgiveness and eternal life, but we must take the action to receive it.

We can become hard-hearted like Pharaoh did, and resist all that God wants to do, or we can humble ourselves before God, repent of our sins and turn to Him with our whole heart. If we choose Pharaoh's path, we can look forward to a day when God will judge us for rejecting the salvation He has so freely offered us in Jesus Christ.[9] However, if we are willing to follow Jesus no matter what the cost and to receive what Jesus has made possible for us through His death and resurrection, we will receive forgiveness for our sins and eternal life.

> *16"For God so loved the world that he gave his one and only Son, that whoever believes in him shall not perish but have eternal life. 17For God did not send his Son into the world to condemn the world, but to save the world through him. 18Whoever believes in him is not condemned, but whoever does not believe stands condemned already because he has not believed in the name of God's one and only Son"* (John 3:16-18).

---

[9]The very name of Jesus means "salvation." "Jesus" is a derivative of the Hebrew word "Joshua" which means "YHVH is salvation" or "the Lord (HE IS) salvation."

"Whoever believes in the Son has eternal life, but whoever rejects the Son will not see life, for God's wrath remains on him" (John 3:36).

If you have never taken the step to put your faith and trust in God, you can do so right at this very moment, by asking Jesus to forgive your sins and by requesting that He come into your life to change you by His power into a person pleasing to Him. Tell Him that you want to give your life to Him, place your trust in Him, turn your back on your old ways and surrender your will to Him.

Enough lamb had to be provided for the Israelites so that every person could partake. So it is today. Jesus' sacrifice is sufficient for all who are willing to come and be reconciled to God. It is up to each person to make the decision to partake. There is no other way. We are not made right with God because our parents are Christians, because we attend church or for any other reason, but only as we individually make the decision to come and put our faith and dependence on Jesus, the Lamb of God who takes away the sin of the world.

The more Pharaoh rejected the word of the Lord, the harder his heart became. So it is with us, too. If we repeatedly reject this message of salvation, we stand in jeopardy of having our hearts become hard. Thus it becomes dangerous for an individual to sit in church and continually hear and reject the salvation message time and time again. Each time the message is rejected, the heart becomes harder and harder until there is no ability to repent.

However, those who do come to God in faith are supernaturally changed. Jesus described this conversion experience as being "born again." It is the supernatural work of the Holy Spirit in a person's life that takes place when they turn to Jesus with their whole heart. The life is transformed. Jesus spoke of this:

[1]"Now there was a man of the Pharisees named Nicodemus, a member of the Jewish ruling council. [2]He came to Jesus at night and said, "Rabbi, we know you are a teacher who has come from God. For no one could perform the miraculous signs you are doing if God were not with him."

*[3]In reply Jesus declared, 'I tell you the truth, **no one can see the kingdom of God unless he is born again.**'*

[4]"How can a man be born when he is old?' Nicodemus asked. 'Surely he cannot enter a second time into his mother's womb to be born!'

*[5]Jesus answered, 'I tell you the truth, no one can enter the kingdom of God unless he is born of water and the Spirit. [6]Flesh gives birth to flesh, but **the Spirit gives birth to spirit**. [7]You should not be surprised at my saying, 'You must be born again.' [8]The wind blows wherever it pleases. You hear its sound, but you cannot tell where it comes from or where it is going. So it is with everyone born of the Spirit"[h]* (John 3:1-8).

We are brought into this world physically as "flesh gives birth to flesh." But there is a second birth available. That is a birth whereby our spirit is reborn by the working of the Holy Spirit of God. This cannot happen unless we meet God's conditions for salvation by faith.

Egypt was to experience God's final judgement. However, the Israelites were being delivered from that impending death and were being brought out into a new life. It is just the same when we come to Christ. We too are taken from the sentence of eternal judgement to a new life in Christ. We become new creations.

"I tell you the truth, whoever hears my word and believes him who sent me has eternal life and will not be condemned; he has crossed over from death to life" (John 5:24).

---

[h]Emphasis added

[17]"Therefore, if anyone is in Christ, he is a new creation; the old has gone, the new has come! [18]All this is from God, who reconciled us to himself through Christ..." (2 Cor. 5:17-18).

When we come to Christ and receive the new birth, we are transformed. Our lives will be changed, and it will become evident to ourselves and to others. We cannot live as God expects us to live it apart from such a transformation— a transformation that is dependent upon the supernatural work of the Holy Spirit of God, who gives us the power to live that new life.

A presidential candidate made the comment during a pre-election debate that he considered himself to be born again because, after all, he attended church. His comment indicated to me, that although he was apparently a church-goer, he did not understand what it meant to be born again.

I believe that there are many who sit in churches today who have never met Jesus in this life changing way. They have never been "born again." They may have attended church for a long time, sung all of the hymns and done many of the things which church people do, and yet they have either not heard or not understood what they need to do to receive true salvation by faith. Others may have heard the message but have not acted upon it. Still others have been unwilling to meet the conditions which God has established.

Being born again is the entry way into the Kingdom of God, eternal life and the place where we are able to receive all that God has for us. It is through this doorway that we receive forgiveness of sins and a new life in Christ. It is here that we gain enthusiasm for the things of God and are given power through the Holy Spirit of God to live the Christian life. We are birthed into the Kingdom by that Holy Spirit of sonship which confirms to our spirit that we truly belong to God.

15"For you did not receive a spirit that makes you a slave again to fear, but you received the Spirit of sonship.[i] And by him we cry, 'Abba,[j] Father.' 16The Spirit himself testifies with our spirit that we are God's children. 17Now if we are children, then we are heirs—heirs of God and co-heirs with Christ, if indeed we share in his sufferings in order that we may also share in his glory" (Rom. 8:15-17).

We know from following the story of the Israelites, that their faith wavered between belief and unbelief. Up one time and down the next, but God was patient while their faith was being established.

New believers sometimes find themselves high in faith one day and down the next. There will be struggles. However, God will confirm and establish the faith of those who continue to diligently seek after Him. Through faith they will see their deliverance from the powers of the enemy.

As Pharaoh pursued the Israelites to the sea and they again began to fear and doubt, Moses spoke to the people:

13 "...'Do not be afraid. Stand firm and you will see the deliverance the LORD will bring you today. The Egyptians you see today you will never see again. 14The LORD will fight for you; you need only to be still.'
15Then the LORD said to Moses, 'Why are you crying out to me? Tell the Israelites to move on'" (Exod. 14:13-15).

This message is for anyone who has come to Jesus for deliverance and begins to doubt the promises he has been given... *"Stand firm and you will see the deliverance the Lord will bring you ... the Lord will fight for you; you need only to be still (to trust and not doubt)."* A struggle for your faith will exist for a time until Satan knows you mean business with God and are not going to be deterred. To maintain a strong faith, it is vital that new believers:

---

[i]Or *adoption*
[j]Aramic for *Father*

1. Become involved in a Bible believing church to worship the Lord, be encouraged in the faith and to be a participant in Christian fellowship and activities.

2. Read the Bible daily to be built up in the faith and to learn more about how to live this new life in Christ.

3. Pray daily (not difficult, just get alone and talk to Him) to seek His help and strength for every situation.

Pharaoh's actions against the Israelites were intended to bring intimidation and fear. But as the Israelites were encouraged to move on with faith in God, they were delivered from Pharaoh's grasp and Pharaoh and his armies were defeated. This same truth applies to Satan. He is a master intimidator who comes to keep us from receiving all that Christ has for us by bringing lies, deception, fear and worry. But those who are born of God can gain the victory as they continue on in faith...

[4]"For everyone born of God overcomes the world. This is the victory that has overcome the world, even our faith. [5]Who is it that overcomes the world? Only he who believes that Jesus is the Son of God" (John 5:4-5).

Jesus has come with this message of deliverance to all who would hear and heed it. As the Lord said to the Apostle Paul:

[17]"I will rescue you from your own people and from the Gentiles. I am sending you to them[18] to open their eyes and turn them from darkness to light, and from the power of Satan to God, so that they may receive forgiveness of sins and a place among those who are sanctified by faith in me" (Acts 26:17-18).

[14]"Since the children have flesh and blood, he too shared in their humanity so that by his death he might destroy him

who holds the power of death—that is, the devil—[15]and free those who all their lives were held in slavery by their fear of death" (Heb. 2:14-15).

We who have come to Jesus are enabled to say:

[13] *"...he has rescued us from the dominion of darkness and brought us into the kingdom of the Son he loves, [14]in whom we have redemption, the forgiveness of sins"* (Col. 1:13-14).

Just as the Israelites fed on the lamb, so we who have been born again need to feed on Jesus. This is accomplished as we read and meditate on the "Word" which is Jesus Christ[k]. As we study the Bible, we partake of Christ, the Lamb of God. We are nourished and built up in Him. Just as we become undernourished and sick if we do not eat physical food, so will we be weak, sick and vulnerable Christians if we do not begin to learn and to meditate on God's truth. We may find that we have many questions at first, and some things may be difficult to understand. However, God's Holy Spirit dwells within the new believer, and we have the promise that through the help of the Holy Spirit we will be enabled to understand the things of God.

When we become Christians by believing and receiving Jesus Christ, we are to commemorate the death of Jesus by partaking of communion. This is a likeness to the Israelite celebration of Passover when they were to remember and mark the events associated with their deliverance from Egypt. Jesus has become our Passover Lamb. It is interesting to note, and one of the confirmations that Jesus was and is the Lamb of God, that Jesus' death in Jerusalem took place at the exact time when many Jews had come into Jerusalem to celebrate the Passover. This was no coincidence. During that week just before His death, some thirteen to fourteen centuries after the Jews' exodus from Egypt, Jesus celebrated

---

[k]See John 1:1,14 and Revelation 19:13

the Passover with His disciples, changing the meaning by indicating that His death would provide the ultimate fulfillment of all that the Passover stood for.

> [19]*"And he took bread, gave thanks and broke it, and gave it to them, saying, 'This is my body given for you; do this in remembrance of me.'* [20]*In the same way, after the supper he took the cup, saying, 'This cup is the New Covenant in my blood, which is poured out for you'"* (Luke 22:19-20).

An important point to note is that *the celebration of communion is not a reenactment of Jesus' death*! Jesus died and was resurrected and is now seated at the right hand of the Father in heaven. The death He died, He died once, and Jesus said at that time, *"It is finished."* He does not die again each time communion is offered. The actual passover for the Israelites occured in Egypt only once. The Passover celebration was therefore a memorial of what had taken place in the past so that they would not forget the deliverance the Lord had provided. In like manner, and as the scripture above says, we are to take Communion *"in remembrance"* of Christ's death on our behalf.

The bitter herbs the Israelites ate during the passover signified both the price paid for their deliverance (the death of the lambs) and the bitterness of the Israelites life of slavery in Egypt. In similar manner, we need to realize the bitter price paid for our deliverance. The sinless Lamb of God, Jesus Christ, bore our sins in His own body on the cross so that we might die to sins and live for righteousness (1 Pet. 2:24). He set us free from the bitterness of a life of sin. The bitterness of that past comes into greater view once a person has tasted of God's goodness and forgiveness and has entered into the new life in Christ. Who could possibly want to go that way again, to once more be enslaved? It was through great suffering and agony that Jesus provided the way for us to be free. In the commemoration of the communion, we must therefore consider with much thankfulness the bitter price that Jesus paid for our deliverance. The protection of His shed blood is over our lives and delivers us from the eternal death that would otherwise have been ours. Certainly we need to follow Jesus wholeheartedly that His death for us might not be in vain.

Participation in communion is reserved for those who have come to Jesus by faith and have been born again. We are not saved (born again) by taking communion, but rather we take communion because we are saved. We can see this pictured in the qualifications stipulated by God for those who could partake in the Passover celebration:

> [48]*"An alien living among you who wants to celebrate the LORD's Passover must have all the males in his household circumcised; then he may take part like one born in the land. No uncircumcised male may eat of it.* [49]*The same law applies to the native-born and to the alien living among you"* (Exod. 12:48-49).

The Passover was to be commemorated by those who bore the mark of circumcision. Circumcision was an identifying sign or mark of those who were participants in the covenant which God had initiated through Abraham many years before.

> [9]*"Then God said to Abraham, 'As for you, you must keep my covenant, you and your descendants after you for the generations to come.* [10]*This is my covenant with you and your descendants after you, the covenant you are to keep: Every male among you shall be circumcised.* [11]*You are to undergo circumcision, and it will be the sign of the covenant between me and you.* [12]*For the generations to come every male among you who is eight days old must be circumcised, including those born in your household or bought with money from a foreigner—those who are not your offspring.*

[13]*Whether born in your household or bought with your money, they must be circumcised. My covenant in your flesh is to be an everlasting covenant.* [14]*Any uncircumcised male, who has not been circumcised in the flesh, will be cut off from his people; he has broken my covenant"* (Gen. 17:9-14).

All Israelite males and any alien, including all the males in his household, had to first receive the mark of circumcision in the flesh signifying their entry into this covenant relationship to God. Then they could participate in the Passover celebration.

Circumcision is a cutting away of flesh. While it did have it's advantages from a health standpoint, it was also intended to illustrate a spiritual truth spoken of in the New Testament which becomes effective for those who come to God through faith in Jesus Christ. This spiritual truth is discussed by the Apostle Paul in the book of Colossians:

[11]*"In him [Christ][1]* **you were also circumcised, in the putting off of the sinful nature**[m], *not with a circumcision done by the hands of men but with the circumcision done by Christ,* [12]*having been buried with him in baptism and raised with him through your faith in the power of God, who raised him from the dead.* [13]*When you were dead in your sins and in the uncircumcision of your sinful nature, God made you alive with Christ. He forgave us all our sins*[n] ..." (Col. 2:11-13).

A Christian supernaturally receives a changed (circumcised) heart when they are born again. A transformation occurs and the individual is loosed from the power of sin which formerly held them captive. This changed heart is the mark of those who are truly born again, and it becomes evident to those around them. They have an inborn desire to

---

[l][]Information in brackets has been added
[m]Or *the flesh*
[n]Emphasis added

live for the Lord and to walk free from sin. Old things pass away, and all things become new (2 Cor. 5:17). This is truly a remarkable thing to behold.

The advent of a time when this kind of personal transformation would take place in a believer was foretold before the time of Christ by the prophet Ezekiel:

> [26]"I will give you a new heart and put a new spirit in you; I will remove from you your heart of stone and give you a heart of flesh. [27]And I will put my Spirit in you and move you to follow my decrees and be careful to keep my laws" (Ezek. 36:26-27).

So then, anyone who desires to partake of communion must first come to Christ to receive Him by faith as Savior and Lord and receive that new "circumcised" heart. Communion does not provide the means for a person to come to Christ and be saved, and is not a means to preserve that salvation, but rather is a commemoration of Christ's death by those who have already received Him as their Savior and Lord.

With the death and resurrection of Christ, the Old Covenant was made obsolete. Through His death and shed blood, Jesus established a "New Covenant" or "New Testament" which replaced the covenant made earlier with Abraham and Israel. Those who come to Jesus by faith receive the mark of this New Covenant, which is a transformed (circumcised) heart. The Lord spoke through Old Testament prophets declaring that a New Covenant would come:

> [31]"'The time is coming,' declares the Lord, "when I will make a New Covenant with the house of Israel and with the house of Judah. [32]It will not be like the covenant I made with their forefathers when I took them by the hand to lead them out of Egypt, because they broke my covenant, though I was a husband to them,' declares the Lord" (Jer. 31:31-32).

Jesus is the mediator of that New Covenant, having established the means to effect a reconciliation between God and man. Through Jesus, we are enabled to enter into this New Covenant with God:

> [14]*"How much more, then, will the blood of Christ, who through the eternal Spirit offered himself unblemished to God, cleanse our consciences from acts that lead to death, so that we may serve the living God!* [15]*For this reason Christ is the mediator of a New Covenant, that those who are called may receive the promised eternal inheritance—now that he has died as a ransom to set them free from the sins committed under the first covenant"* (Heb. 9:14-15).

(The *"sins committed under the first covenant"* refers to mans violation of the laws, i.e. the ten commandments, which were given by God as a part of that first covenant).

The Israelites were instructed at the time of their deliverance to eat bread made without leaven (yeast). Yeast is something that works very slowly and somewhat imperceptibly. Yet it has a pronounced effect on the end product. Leaven represents sin. After we have been cleansed from sin through faith in Jesus Christ, we are not to live in sin any longer. We are asked to put away sin (the leaven) from our lives. We put away sin because we are redeemed, our hearts have been circumcised and the Holy Spirit of Christ living within us gives us the power to conquer the sin that formerly held us captive. Just as leaven is somewhat sour, so sin makes our lives sour. Jesus has cleansed us from our sin, and now He wants us to walk free from that sin, that the sweetness of His presence will flow through us. It doesn't take much yeast to effect the whole loaf of bread. So it is, that just a little bit of sin can spoil our walk with God. The Israelites were to search out and get rid of the leaven in their homes. We also are to search our hearts regarding sin in our lives and be rid it— that we might be holy (walk in purity) before the Lord.

6"Your boasting is not good. Don't you know that a little yeast works through the whole batch of dough? 7Get rid of the old yeast that you may be a new batch without yeast— as you really are. For Christ, our Passover lamb, has been sacrificed. 8Therefore let us keep the Festival, not with the old yeast, the yeast of malice and wickedness, but with bread without yeast, the bread of sincerity and truth" (1 Cor. 5:6-8).

When we recognize that we have sinned against God, we are to sincerely turn from it and ask God's forgiveness that we might be set right again:

"If we confess our sins, he is faithful and just and will forgive us our sins and purify us from all unrighteousness" (1 John 1:9).

For a person to be qualified to partake of communion, the remembrance of Jesus death, he must first be a Christian bearing the mark of a circumcised heart. Then, each time he comes to communion, he must also evaluate his current condition and if there is any sin (leaven) in his life that has not been dealt with, he must come to the Lord to receive forgiveness. If he has wronged others, he must set that right. Then he may partake of communion with a clear conscience. Paul makes this very clear in his writings:

23"For I received from the Lord what I also passed on to you: The Lord Jesus, on the night he was betrayed, took bread, 24and when he had given thanks, he broke it and said, "This is my body, which is for you; do this in remembrance of me." 25In the same way, after supper he took the cup, saying, "This cup is the New Covenant in my blood; do this, whenever you drink it, in remembrance of me." 26For whenever you eat this bread and drink this cup, you proclaim the Lord's death until he comes.
27Therefore, whoever eats the bread or drinks the cup of the Lord in an unworthy manner will be guilty of sinning against the body and blood of the Lord. 28A man ought to

examine himself before he eats of the bread and drinks of the cup. [29]For anyone who eats and drinks without recognizing the body of the Lord eats and drinks judgment on himself. [30]That is why many among you are weak and sick, and a number of you have fallen asleep. [31]But if we judged ourselves, we would not come under judgment. [32]When we are judged by the Lord, we are being disciplined so that we will not be condemned with the world" (1 Cor. 11:23-32).

As the Israelites approached the Red Sea, the angel of God and the pillar of cloud (signifying the Lord's presence), went behind them, coming between the armies of Egypt and the people of Israel. Their final separation from Egypt was to be accomplished this night. The Israelites, who had been slaves to Pharaoh and Egypt, were leaving all of that behind. As they went down into the Red Sea, the enemy pursued them, but the Israelites would come up out of that sea into a new life, whereas their enemy would be drowned behind them.

When we come to Jesus, and receive Him as our Savior and Lord, it is then that we are to participate in water baptism. The meaning of water baptism is wonderfully demonstrated by this passage of the Israelites through the Red Sea. When Israel went down into the Sea, it represented a death on their part to all that Egypt had meant to them—all of the despair, slavery, false worship, false gods and idols—everything that had held them captive. They would be coming up out of that death and despair to a new life in which God would be their guide, their hope and their strength. They would be embarking on a journey whereby they might obtain all that God had promised to them.

When Jesus died on the cross, He laid down His own desires that the Father might be glorified and that sin might be paid for and conquered. In like manner, when we come to Christ, our sinful nature is crucified with Christ. Going down into the waters of baptism symbolizes this death to sin and our old nature.

But, praise God, it doesn't end there, for just as Christ was resurrected from the dead, so too is the believer "resurrected" into a new life to be lived in the power of God. This resurrection is depicted as we come up out of the waters of baptism.

[1]"What shall we say, then? Shall we go on sinning so that grace may increase? [2]By no means! We died to sin; how can we live in it any longer? [3]Or don't you know that all of us who were baptized into Christ Jesus were baptized into his death? [4]We were therefore buried with him through baptism into death in order that, just as Christ was raised from the dead through the glory of the Father, we too may live a new life.

[5]If we have been united with him like this in his death, we will certainly also be united with him in his resurrection. [6]For we know that our old self was crucified with him so that the body of sin might be done away with, that we should no longer be slaves to sin—[7]because anyone who has died has been freed from sin.

[8]Now if we died with Christ, we believe that we will also live with him. [9]For we know that since Christ was raised from the dead, he cannot die again; death no longer has mastery over him. [10]The death he died, he died to sin once for all; but the life he lives, he lives to God.

[11]In the same way, count yourselves dead to sin but alive to God in Christ Jesus. [12]Therefore do not let sin reign in your mortal body so that you obey its evil desires. [13]Do not offer the parts of your body to sin, as instruments of wickedness, but rather offer yourselves to God, as those who have been brought from death to life; and offer the parts of your body to him as instruments of righteousness. For sin shall not be your master..." (Rom. 6:1-14a).

Baptism is an act which follows a person's commitment to Jesus Christ and symbolizes the new believer's deliverance from sin. Some people, who have been sprinkled or baptized when they were infants, may believe that they received salvation through that infant baptism. Yet nowhere is this taught in the Bible. A person can only receive salvation as they make a choice to come to God in repentance and faith. Then they are to be baptized as an act of obedience to their Lord and as an open confession of their faith and salvation.

Water baptism should be more than a symbolic act. I believe it should also be a time for the new believer to take hold of certain vital truths which are represented in the Israelites' deliverance through the Red Sea. When the Israelites passed through the sea, the powers of Egypt which had held them captive were defeated. Pharaoh's army was drowned, and the Israelites were now delivered and set apart from Egypt by the Red Sea. They had come up out of the water to live a completely new life through the power of God.

As a person participates in water baptism, it would be helpful for them to picture this deliverance of the Israelites. They need to realize as they go down into the water, that the power of Satan, sin and every destructive habit which has held them in bondage has been broken. Just as Christ died, so they should receive by faith the fact that they have been crucified with Christ and as a consequence are now dead to the ways of sin. But it does not end there. As they are brought out of the water, it signifies that just as Christ was raised to life by the power of God, so they have been raised by the power of God to live a completely new life—a life lived under the power, guidance and care of a loving heavenly Father.

As it says in the scripture we have just read, "... count yourselves dead to sin but alive to God in Christ Jesus." The believer is to lay hold of this truth by faith, and is to reckon (or consider) that he has been (past tense) set free from the power of sin and Satan. We cannot deliver ourselves from the power of sin, but Jesus has, and will. We may on occasion struggle against old habits and sins and find ourselves trying to overcome them in our own strength, but this is not

God's way. God's power is available to deliver us from sin, but we must take hold of that deliverance by faith. We must commit or give these areas of difficulty to Him and by faith ask and expect Him to provide the victory that we seek

Our attention and desires must now be directed toward Him. Just as it says, *"the death he died, he died to sin once for all; but the life he lives, he lives to God,"* so we are to offer ourselves to God, as those who have been brought from death to life; and we are to offer the parts of your bodies to Him as instruments of righteousness. The Israelites were no longer to turn back, look back, or head back to Egypt, but were to set themselves to go a new direction. They were to go on to take and possess the land and receive that inheritance that the Lord has promised them. Their hearts and minds were to be diligently directed toward God and the new life He had given them. I believe that the greatest help to walking in the way of holiness, is for us to be turned fully toward the Lord— to follow after Him with all our heart, soul, mind and strength. Then God's resurrection power will be at work in us to give us victory over any temptation and sin which would come to take us captive. As we wholeheartedly seek first His kingdom and His righteousness, sin will not have dominion over us, but we will be defeated if we continue to turn back to dabble in the sinful ways of this world, and we will never know the joy and victory that God longs to give us.

Jesus came to John the Baptist to be baptized in water also:

> [13]*"Then Jesus came from Galilee to the Jordan to be baptized by John.* [14]*But John tried to deter him, saying, 'I need to be baptized by you, and do you come to me?'*
> [15]*Jesus replied, 'Let it be so now; it is proper for us to do this to fulfill all righteousness.' Then John consented"* (Matt. 3:13-15).

As we can see from this passage, water baptism after our salvation is not an option. It is proper for us to do this to fulfill all righteousness and is the first step, in what should be a life of obedience to the Lord.

The Israelites had been delivered from Egypt and Pharaoh. Their enemy had been defeated. God had brought them out of the Sea into a new life. He would go before them to bring them into the inheritance promised to them.

Jesus has become our Passover Lamb. He has paid the price for our total deliverance from sin and the power of Satan. Now, through Him, we have received circumcised hearts and the power to live transformed lives pleasing to God. Sin should no longer be our master. We have died to the past. We have been raised to a new life by the same power that raised Jesus Christ from the dead. And we have been equipped with His power to walk victoriously in this life and to attain to the eternal inheritance promised us in Jesus Christ.

CHAPTER 4

Surprise!!!—Now Where's Your Trust?

The Israelites had much to be thankful for as they surveyed the scene at the Red Sea where their enemies lay dead on the shore. They had been delivered from Egypt. God had been faithful to His word to deliver them from their oppressors. When they considered all God had done for them, ...

> "...the people feared the Lord and put their trust in him and in Moses his servant" (Exod. 14:31).

This was certainly a cause for celebration and a time to come before the Lord with singing and dancing.

> [1]"Then Moses and the Israelites sang this song to the LORD:
>
> 'I will sing to the LORD, for he is highly exalted. The horse and its rider he has hurled into the sea. [2]The LORD is my strength and my song; he has become my salvation. He is my God, and I will praise him, my father's God, and I will exalt him. [3]The LORD is a warrior; the LORD is his name. [4]Pharaoh's chariots and his army he has hurled into the sea.

The best of Pharaoh's officers are drowned in the Red Sea. ⁵The deep waters have covered them; they sank to the depths like a stone... ⁶"Your right hand, O LORD, was majestic in power. Your right hand, O LORD, shattered the enemy...

¹¹"Who among the gods is like you, O LORD? Who is like you—majestic in holiness, awesome in glory, working wonders? ¹²You stretched out your right hand and the earth swallowed them. ¹³"In your unfailing love you will lead the people you have redeemed. In your strength you will guide them to your holy dwelling'" (Exod. 15:1-6,11-13).

So it was that they praised the Lord for the deliverance He had provided from their enemies. But they also praised Him in anticipation of the fear and trembling that the news of their deliverance would cause in the hearts of the peoples and nations they would meet as they continued on to the promised land.

¹⁴"The nations will hear and tremble; anguish will grip the people of Philistia. ¹⁵The chiefs of Edom will be terrified, the leaders of Moab will be seized with trembling, the people of Canaan will melt away; ¹⁶terror and dread will fall upon them. By the power of your arm they will be as still as a stone—until your people pass by, O LORD, until the people you bought pass by. ¹⁷You will bring them in and plant them on the mountain of your inheritance the place, O LORD, you made for your dwelling, the sanctuary, O Lord, your hands established. ¹⁸The LORD will reign for ever and ever" (Exod. 15:14-18).

²⁰"Then Miriam the prophetess, Aaron's sister, took a tambourine in her hand, and all the women followed her, with tambourines and dancing. ²¹Miriam sang to them: "Sing to the LORD, for he is highly exalted. The horse and its rider he has hurled into the sea" (Exod. 15:20-21).

Could anything stop them? The Lord their God was mighty. He had won an awesome victory over Pharaoh and his armies and had kept His promise to deliver them from their bondage in Egypt. Certainly He would also bring them into the land which had long been promised to them, and they would be victorious over all of their enemies. Now that they had been set free from Pharaoh and Egypt, everything looked rosy. From here on in, who could stop them, how could they fail? Certainly they had every right and obligation to sing to the Lord their praises, for He had surely done great things.

This time of rejoicing reminds me of newlyweds who are extremely joyous in their new relationship. Their eyes are filled with stars and everything is coming up roses. Certainly everything about their marriage is going to be absolutely wonderful. There are no problems on the horizon that they can't handle. And yet, those of us who have been married know that as newlyweds they probably have a very limited understanding of the trials and problems they are going to face and the effort they must apply in their marriages to keep them loving and warm and to make them work. If their marriage is to be successful, they will have to commit themselves to work at it through good times and bad times without any thought of giving up.

So Israel at this point may be likened to newlyweds. Everything was wonderful, but they had no clue as to the difficulties that lay ahead. We have already seen just how fragile their faith in God had been. We have seen that they believed when they were first told by Moses that they would be delivered from Egypt, but they had returned to a state of despair when Pharaoh brought additional hardships upon them to discourage them. Their faith was again strengthened when they saw the plagues God brought against Egypt, but then once again, they succumbed to fear when Pharaoh pursued them after they had left Egypt. One minute they were on top rejoicing and the next minute they were down in despair as their hearts wavered between faith in God, and fear and doubt.

This is a picture of us too. We say we believe in God, yet how quickly we forsake our trust in Him when our senses cry "danger," even though in the midst of it all He has not left us.

It would be good at this point to look again to the promise of God which Moses delivered to the Israelites while they were still in Egypt.

> [7]*"The LORD said, 'I have indeed seen the misery of my people in Egypt. I have heard them crying out because of their slave drivers, and I am concerned about their suffering. [8]So I have come down to rescue them from the hand of the Egyptians and to bring them up out of that land into a good and spacious land, a land flowing with milk and honey—the home of the Canaanites, Hittites, Amorites, Perizzites, Hivites and Jebusites'"* (Exod. 3:7-8).

God told the Israelites that He would deliver them from Egypt and would take them to a land of milk and honey. It should be noted, however, that in all the times God had stated that He would bring the Israelites into the promised land, He never discussed the wilderness. We can expect that they knew something about the journey that would be required because their forefathers had come from Canaan to Egypt and certainly many traders regularly passed that way also. Yet, in light of the final significance that this journey would have on their lives, it is amazing that it was never mentioned to them in advance. It was going to be in that wilderness that God would prove their faith and trust in Him and their willingness to obey Him.

When we come to Christ by faith, we also are not anticipating the wilderness experiences we will have to face. We certainly will have them. They will come to prove our faith and trust in God. They will prove our willingness to obey, and they will serve to test, teach and mature us.

What God promised the Israelites was truly wonderful—deliverance from their bondage in Egypt and entry into a new land that would be theirs, where they could live in freedom and prosperity. However, in all of this, God had a much larger objective in mind: the reconciliation of mankind to Himself. He was not just arbitrarily blessing this one nation. Rather, He was establishing a nation through whom He could reveal Himself to the world and bring about a reconciliation between God and man. It was through this nation that Jesus Christ the Son of God would be revealed. He would be the One who would pay the price necessary to make this reconciliation possible.

As we have seen, many other people went up with the Israelites as they left Egypt. The King James translation refers to the group who left Egypt as a mixed multitude. There were those who undoubtedly came along just for what they could get out of it. Certainly slavery in Egypt was no picnic, and who wouldn't want to have a "land flowing with milk and honey," but the wilderness would ultimately test their motives and the depth of their commitment to God. The promises of God were intended for a people who would submit themselves to Him—who would love, trust and obey Him above all else. As they did so, they would become His ambassadors (priests) to the whole world. This was promised to the Israelites in a covenant which God made with them just a little later ...

> [4]*"You yourselves have seen what I did to Egypt, and how I carried you on eagles' wings and brought you to myself.* [5]*Now if you obey me fully and keep my covenant, then out of all nations you will be my treasured possession. Although the whole earth is mine,* [6]*you will be for me a kingdom of priests and a holy nation"* (Exod. 19:4-6).

As it states "...*if you obey me fully and keep my covenant, then...*" These were the conditions God established for blessing the nation of Israel. It would be in the wilderness that God would prove this large group of people whom He had delivered from Egypt and would find out what was really in their hearts—whether they would, or would not submit themselves to follow Him without reservation.

Today, we have many people who attend church and who sing songs which are very similar to the song which Israel sang upon their deliverance from Egypt, but it is very clear that those who sing these songs are a mixed multitude. Some truly know God and continue to grow and mature in Him. Others do not, never seeming to come to maturity or to the victory which they sing about. The wilderness experiences come to determine the genuiness of each person's faith, and their ability to persevere.

If we individually are to be victorious in Christ, then we need to come to know God—His character, His promises, and His faithfulness—through reading and meditating on His Word, and by learning to trust and obey Him in our daily experiences. We place our Christian lives in jeopardy if our faith and obedience to Christ does not develop and mature. When difficulties and temptations arise, we may find that we do not have the strength to stand. We could perish from lack of true spiritual knowledge of this God we serve. This will be particularly true as we approach a future time of great difficulty on this planet which Daniel refers to as *a time of distress such as has not happened from the beginning of nations until then* (Dan. 12:1b).

It is in this life that we face our wilderness of testing. Are we willing to follow God through thick and through thin? Do we really love Him and trust Him? Are we willing to obey Him in all things?

God expects us to grow, and to learn how to find our strength in Him alone. He wants us to walk in obedience and to have a faith that does not waver with each trial but that can stand no matter what difficulties may come our way. The strength we need to make it through our Christian journey depends on more than our songs and the prayers of others.

Giving praise to God is important and the prayers and encouragement of pastors and saints is certainly not harmful and should be sought when we need it. However, if difficulties in our lives have been brought about because we are walking in sin, or we are failing to trust in God and His Word, then we need to confess our sin, repent and do what the Bible tells us to do. It is then that we will obtain true victory in Christ. Prayer to obtain deliverance from problems which are caused because we are walking in sin will not be effective.

The Bible says that the Lord does not want us to walk in fear and doubt. We do not need to pray for what God's Word says is already ours. We just need to take hold of it by faith. In all of these things, the Lord wants us to mature to the point that we might minister to others instead of being those who constantly need ministry. We must strive to become strong in faith and obedience to Christ.

The wilderness is the place of growth for us as it was to be for the Israelites. It is a place of change...

- from trusting in Egypt to trusting in God.
- from trusting in that which is seen, to a trust and obedience to God's Word.
- from worrying about tomorrow, to living one day at a time, trusting God to guide and provide.
- from a mere mental belief in God, to a full trust, reliance and dependence upon God... a full commitment to Him.

Even though the Israelites did not like their existence in Egypt, they had grown to trust in Egypt. God had now taken them away from that source of trust to a place where they could learn dependence upon Him. God wanted to be everything to the Israelites—their sole source of strength.

In the events that had taken place with Abraham, Isaac, Jacob, Moses and now the people of Israel, God was giving a greater and greater revelation of Himself. It is important that we digress from our story at this point to consider these progressive revelations because it will have a bearing on what follows.

We saw earlier that in His conversations with Moses, God made reference to himself in various ways. He said to Moses that He had appeared to Abraham, to Isaac and to Jacob as God Almighty (Exod. 6:2). As we saw in Exod. 3:14, He had told Moses, *"I AM WHO I AM. **This is what you are to say to the Israelites: 'I AM has sent me to you.'"*** Then in Exod. 6:2-6, He reveals himself as the ***LORD***. The One who was revealed as God Almighty to their forefathers Abraham, Isaac and Jacob, now wanted to reveal himself as LORD to the Israelites. What is the significance of these various names of God and what are their meanings to us?

Undoubtedly there is considerable depth of meaning in these different names for God going beyond what we can comprehend at this time. I believe the Bible provides insights which can help us to better understand their meaning for us.

GOD ALMIGHTY
(reference Exod. 6:3)

The name God Almighty gives a rather clear indication of its meaning. There is no one higher than Him in the heavens or on earth. He is the omnipotent (all powerful) omniscient (all knowing), omnipresent (everywhere present) God, the Creator of heaven and earth. He is the absolute universal Sovereign, supreme in position and authority. There is none who is His equal.

I would think that this is the way we first picture God to be. When we consider the one who created the universe and all living things, who manages the movements of the planets, and keeps all things in their proper course, we cannot help but envision an incomprehensibly great and mighty being. A being who is so great and so far beyond our comprehension as to render any personal communion with Him or access to Him impossible.

When we see the sky, stars, planets, the earth and all that is in them, we cannot help but come to the conclusion that there is a God who has created it all.

The fool says in his heart, *"There is no God"* (Ps. 14:1; 53:1).

The Almighty God says ...

"...There is no God apart from me, a righteous God and a Savior; there is none but me" (Isaiah 45:21).

[1]*"The heavens declare the glory of God; the skies proclaim the work of his hands.* [2]*Day after day they pour forth speech; night after night they display knowledge.* [3]*There is no speech or language where their voice is not heard.* [4]*Their voice goes out into all the earth, their words to the ends of the world..."* (Psalms 19:1-4).

[18]*"The wrath of God is being revealed from heaven against all the godlessness and wickedness of men who suppress the truth by their wickedness,* [19]*since what may be known about God is plain to them, because God has made it plain to them.* [20]*For since the creation of the world God's invisible qualities—his eternal power and divine nature—have been clearly seen, being understood from what has been made, so that men are without excuse"* (Rom.1:18-20).

This great and incomprehensible God, creator of heaven and earth, broke through the barrier and communicated with man. He said to Abram, *"I am God Almighty...,"* and it says, *"Abram fell face down"* (Gen. 17:1-3). What an awesome thing to consider. This is the name, *"God Almighty"*, by which God introduced himself to Abraham, Isaac and Jacob. It was but a beginning.

I AM WHO I AM
(reference Exod. 3:13-14)

In the Amplified Translation, Exod. 3:14 reads,

[14]*"And God said to Moses, **I AM WHO I AM** and **WHAT I AM**, and **I WILL BE WHAT I WILL BE**; and He said, you shall say this to the Israelites, **I AM** has sent me to you!*[a] *"*

In the book of John is recorded a conversation that Jesus had with a group of Jews who were disputing Jesus' claims about himself. Jesus said,

[51]*"I tell you the truth, if anyone keeps my word, he will never see death."*
[52]*At this the Jews exclaimed, "Now we know that you are demon-possessed! Abraham died and so did the prophets, yet you say that if anyone keeps your word, he will never taste death.* [53]*Are you greater than our father Abraham? He died, and so did the prophets. Who do you think you are?"*
[54]*Jesus replied, "If I glorify myself, my glory means nothing. My Father, whom you claim as your God, is the one who glorifies me.* [55]*Though you do not know him, I know him. If I said I did not, I would be a liar like you, but I do know him and keep his word.* [56]*Your father Abraham rejoiced at the thought of seeing my day; he saw it and was glad."*
[57]*"You are not yet fifty years old," the Jews said to him, "and you have seen Abraham!"*
[58]*"I tell you the truth," Jesus answered, "before Abraham was born, **I am!**"*[b] *At this, they picked up stones to stone him, but Jesus hid himself, slipping away from the temple grounds"* (John 8:51-58).

God's name, "***I AM***," had been known to the Jews from the time of the exodus from Egypt. Jesus' statement, *"before*

---

[a]Emphasis added
[b]Emphasis added

*Abraham was, **I am!**,"* meant to the Jews that he was declaring himself to be God. They did not believe Him and in fact wanted to stone Him for speaking blasphemy.

The name I AM and Jesus' use of it, speaks to the fact that God (and Jesus **is** God) is ageless, timeless, eternal and self existent. He is always in the present in every age and stands independent of time. Jesus also used "I am" in declaring other things about himself. In speaking of himself, Jesus said, *"**I am** the bread of life"*; *"**I am** the light of the world"*; *"**I am** the gate for the sheep"*; *"**I am** the good shepherd"*; *"**I am** the resurrection and the life"*; *"**I am** the way, the truth and the life"*; *"**I am** the true vine"*. These statements are found in the book of John.

What this reveals is that the Almighty God has many attributes and in Him is the ultimate embodiment of all good things. 1 John 4:16 says, *"...God is love."* Psalms 99:9 says, *"...the LORD our God is holy."* John 1:1 says, *"In the beginning was the Word, and the Word was with God, and the Word was God."* He has many attributes.

It says in the book of Romans ...

"For from Him and through Him and to Him are all things. For all things originate with Him and come from Him; all things live through Him, and all things center in and tend to consummate and to end in Him..." (Rom. 11:36 AMP).

So I believe that we can safely say that the *I AM* (God) in addition to being Almighty, and ageless and timeless, is also the embodiment of absolute wisdom, knowledge, truth, life, light, holiness, love, joy, peace, patience, kindness, gentleness, strength, power, provision, protection, etc., etc. God's identification of himself as *I AM* was a greater revelation of himself than He had previously given.

THE LORD

We see that God's next declaration to Moses was:

15"...Say to the Israelites, 'The LORD,c the God of your fathers—the God of Abraham, the God of Isaac and the God of Jacob has—sent me to you.' This is my name forever, the name by which I am to be remembered from generation to generation" (Exod. 3:15).

I want to repeat Exodus 6:2-8 here also:

2"God also said to Moses, "I am the LORD. 3I appeared to Abraham, to Isaac and to Jacob as God Almighty,d but by my name the LORD I did not make myself known to them.e 4I also established my covenant with them to give them the land of Canaan, where they lived as aliens. 5Moreover, I have heard the groaning of the Israelites, whom the Egyptians are enslaving, and I have remembered my covenant. 6"Therefore, say to the Israelites: 'I am the LORD, and I will bring you out from under the yoke of the Egyptians. I will free you from being slaves to them, and I will redeem you with and outstretched arm and with mighty acts of judgment. 7I will take you as my own people, and I will be your God. Then you will know that I am the LORD your God, who brought you out from under the yoke of the Egyptians. 8And I will bring you to the land I swore with uplifted hand to give to Abraham, to Isaac and to Jacob. I will give it to you as a possession. I am the LORD'"f (Exod. 6:2-8).

"LORD" in the Hebrew is YHWH ("Yahweh"). The four consonants forming the Hebrew name of the supreme being are known as the "tetragrammaton." The true pronunciation of

---

cEmphasis added
d3 Hebrew *El-Shaddai*
eOr *Almighty, and by my name the LORD did I not let myself be known to them?*
fEmphasis added

the name has been lost over time. For a period of time it was the belief of the Jews that it was wrong to say this name of God out loud. As a result, the correct pronunciation is no longer known.

A study note in the NIV Study Bible for Exodus 3:15 says that Yahweh is often incorrectly spelled "Jehovah." Vowels have been placed between the letters "YHWH" to form "YaH-WeH," and "Jehovah" is a variation of this.

The same NIV study note for Exodus 3:15 also indicates that the word **LORD** means "He is" or He will be" and is the third-person form of the verb translated "I will be" and "I AM" When God speaks of himself He says, "I AM," and when we speak of Him we say, LORD ("He is").

God first said, "I am **God Almighty**..." and revealed His awesomeness in authority and power. Then we see that He desired to reveal himself as the **I AM**, the embodiment of all things. This revelation of himself would be unfolded in all that was to happen to the Israelites. Through this revelation of Himself, they would begin to see His love, faithfulness, mercy, holiness, wisdom, power, and the many other facets and attributes of His being extended on their behalf. They needed to recognize that they were the object of God's attributes. They were the objects of God's love, His mercy, His grace, His faithfulness. He was in essence saying, "**I WILL BE** all of these things to you... **I will** bring you out... **I will** free you... **I will** redeem you... **I will** take you as my own people and **I will** be your God..." Then before continuing with two more "I will's," He says, "**then you will know that I am "the LORD" "your" God**, who brought you out from under the yoke of the Egyptians.

In God was all that was needed for every situation that the Israelites could ever face. God was saying to them, **I will** do all, and be all, for you ... then YOU will begin to know me as **LORD**, that is, you will begin to know that **I AM** all you need and will begin to confess, **HE IS** my hope, **HE IS** my strength, **HE IS** my provider, **HE IS** my way, **HE IS** my truth,

HE IS my life, ... and you will begin to walk in that fact daily. As soon as the Israelites could come to understand that, and begin to walk and live and act on that truth by faith, they would begin to know it in reality and would be victorious no matter what their physical circumstances might be.

God desired that the Israelites would say, *LORD (HE IS)*, and in so doing would identify with Him, trust Him and obey Him. He desired that each of them would individually come to know this Almighty God, the Creator, as their personal God and be able to declare *HE IS* my God and *HE IS* all I need. With the Almighty God as their LORD (HE IS), there would be no need for fear and doubt.

Some of the ways that the Lord (YHWH) is identified in the Old Testament are:

JEHOVAH TSIDKENU	THE LORD MY RIGHTEOUSNESS[g]
JEHOVAH M'KADESH	THE LORD WHO MAKES ME HOLY[h]
JEHOVAH SHALOM	THE LORD WHO IS MY PEACE[i]
JEHOVAH SHAMMAH	THE LORD WHO IS THERE[j]
JEHOVAH RAPHA	THE LORD WHO HEALS ME[k]
JEHOVAH JIREH	THE LORD WHO PROVIDES[l]
JEHOVAH NISSI	THE LORD MY BANNER[m]
JEHOVAH ROHI	THE LORD MY SHEPHERD[n]
JEHOVAH TSEBAHOTH	THE LORD ALMIGHTY (OF HOSTS)[o]
JEHOVAH HELEYON	THE LORD MOST HIGH[p]

---

[g]"The Lord our righteousness" Jer 33:15-18
[h]"The Lord who makes you holy (who sanctifies you)" Exod 31:13;Lev 20:7-8; 21:8; 22:9,15-16,31-32
[i]"The Lord is peace" Judg 6:22-24
[j]"The Lord is there" (Name of the holy city) Ezek 48:35
[k]"I am the Lord who heals you" Exod 15:26
[l]"The Lord will provide" Gen 22:14
[m]"The Lord is my Banner" Exod 17:15-16
[n]"The Lord is my Shepherd" Ps 23:1
[o]"The Lord of Hosts" or "The Lord Almighty" 1 Sam 1:3
[p](as stated) Ps 7:17; 47:2; 97:9

We need to fully grasp what this means. Egypt was not Israel's security, rather God wanted them to learn to say with full confidence, **HE IS**. It is the same with me. He wants me to know that my job and my bank account are not my security, **HE IS**. This world is not my security, **HE IS**. **HE IS ALL** I will ever truly need. Everything may collapse around me, but **HE IS** mine. If everything else fails, He will not. And that is the way God wants it. How can He fail? He is the Creator of all things and has all power.

He is not an aloof and inaccessible God. He created us that we might have fellowship with Him and truly belong to Him. It is foolishness to spend our whole lives seeking after things but not after God because He is truly the source of all that we need. All of this may be difficult to believe because it is so utterly fantastic, and yet I am hopeful that these truths will become clearer to us as we continue in our study of the Israelites.

It is essential to know, and it is entirely scriptural, that unbelief limits God's power to move on our behalf. Jesus died on the cross to pay for our salvation and to free us from sin, but He cannot give that salvation to us except as we believe it and receive it by faith.

> [8]*"For it is by grace you have been saved, **through faith**—and this not from yourselves, it is the gift of God—*
> [9] *not by works, so that no one can boast*[q] (Eph. 2:8-9).

God does not want our faith to stop there. Unbelief in other areas can prevent God's fullest blessings from coming to us. There is power released to meet our many needs as we choose to believe and trust God. It is true that God causes the sun to rise on the evil and the good, and sends rain on the righteous and unrighteous (Matthew 5:45) and yet I believe God's power can be cut off from us in many ways when we

---

[q]Emphasis added

turn to unbelief in God's Word, or turn to doubt and fear. We become unable to receive what He wants to give us.

The power of God is able to work where faith is present, but is hindered where unbelief abounds. When Jesus came to His home town of Nazareth, they couldn't believe that He (who was a son of Joseph the carpenter, and whose earthly brothers and sisters lived among them) could possibly be anyone special. So they took offense at Him and created an atmosphere of unbelief. Matthew 13:58 says, *"And He did not do many miracles there because of their lack of faith."* Their unbelief hindered the flow of God's power.

A very clear example of this principle is found in the life of Peter at the time he was enabled to supernaturally walk on water...

> [25]*"During the fourth watch of the night Jesus went out to them, walking on the lake. [26]When the disciples saw him walking on the lake, they were terrified. 'It's a ghost,' they said, and cried out in fear.*
>
> [27]*But Jesus immediately said to them: 'Take courage! It is I. Don't be afraid.'*
>
> [28]*'Lord, if it's you,' Peter replied, 'tell me to come to you on the water.'*
>
> [29]*'Come,' he said.*
> *Then Peter got down out of the boat, walked on the water and came toward Jesus. [30]But when he saw the wind, he was afraid and, beginning to sink, cried out, 'Lord, save me!'*
>
> [31]*Immediately Jesus reached out his hand and caught him. 'You of little faith,' he said, 'why did you doubt?'*
>
> [32]*And when they climbed into the boat, the wind died down"* (Matt. 14:25-32).

Peter came out of the boat and walked on the water. The supernatural power of God was present because of Peter's faith. However, it then says, "But when he saw the wind, he was afraid *and, beginning to sink*[r] ..."

---

[r]Emphasis added

Immediately, as soon as he began to fear (to doubt), the supernatural power that had allowed him to walk on the water was cut off, and Peter sank.

What is important here, is not the idea of physically walking on water. The sea and the turmoil that arises on it, is a picture of the turmoil and turbulence of life. It is by our trust in Him that we are enabled to be victorious over the trials and tribulations of this life, for it is then, as we walk by faith, that God's power is manifested to enable us to walk victoriously through it all. It is then that He can freely work in our lives and circumstances.

That turbulence was under Peter's feet so long as he walked by faith, but he fell into that turbulence when he turned from his trust in the Lord. He was overcome by the waves.

We need God's power that our needs might be met, and that we might live victoriously. When we turn to fear and doubt (symptoms of unbelief), we are forsaking our own salvation.

> *"Those who cling to worthless idols forfeit the grace that could be theirs"* (Jonah 2:8).

When we turn to place our trust in someone or something other than the Lord, we are in fact clinging to a worthless object and are forfeiting the grace that could be ours in the Lord.

In the middle of our difficulties, we often turn to unbelief. Instead of trusting in the Lord, we are overcome by feelings of helplessness. We wonder where God is, and why He doesn't help us, not realizing that He has been waiting for us to just trust and rest in Him. We start paddling furiously because we do not believe that we can look to God. We know of no other way to handle it than to try and save ourselves in our own strength, and so our faith in God is weakened. There is an excellent scripture passage in Isaiah which speaks directly to this problem...

[15]*"This is what the Sovereign LORD, the Holy One of Israel, says: 'In repentance and rest is your salvation, in quietness and trust is your strength, but you would have none of it.* [16]*You said, 'No, we will flee on horses.' Therefore you will flee! You said, 'We will ride off on swift horses.' Therefore your pursuers will be swift!* [17]*A thousand will flee at the threat of one; at the threat of five you will all flee away, till you are left like a flagstaff on a mountaintop, like a banner on a hill."* [18]*Yet the LORD longs to be gracious to you; he rises to show you compassion. For the LORD is a God of justice.* **Blessed are all who wait for him!**[s]*"* (Isa. 30:15-18).

In repentance and rest is our salvation. In quietness and trust is our strength. We are blessed when we wait for Him. Instead of "fleeing" because of fear and unbelief.

The Amplified Bible (AMP) says in Heb. 4:16 ...

"Let us then fearlessly and confidently and boldly draw near to the throne of grace—the throne of God's unmerited favor [to us sinners]; that we may receive mercy [for our failures] and find grace to help in good time for every need—appropriate help and well timed help, coming just when we need it.[t]*"*

Also, in Heb. 13:5-6 (AMP) ...

"Let your character or moral disposition be free from love of money—[including] greed, avarice, lust and craving for earthly possessions—and be satisfied with your present [circumstances and with what you have]; for He (God) Himself has said, I will not in any way fail you nor give you up nor leave you without support. [I will] not, [I will] not, [I will] not in any degree leave you helpless, nor forsake nor let [you] down, [relax My hold on you]—Assuredly not!

---

[s]Emphasis added
[t]Emphasis added

110

*So we take comfort and are encouraged and confidently and boldly say, **The Lord is my Helper**, I will not be seized with alarm—I will not fear or dread or be terrified ...[u]"*

Jesus came that He might deliver us from bondage. He desires that we would come to **know** Him. Some know **of** him, others know **about** him, and still others know Him perhaps as Savior from sin, but yet in very limited ways beyond that.

I believe that we limit God by the extent to which we know Him as the *HE IS* in our lives. He can be our Savior from sin and the one who gives us eternal life, and so we can say, "*HE IS* my savior from sin and I have eternal life in Him." By faith we receive and believe Him to be our Savior and we walk with that confession on our lips. His power acts in response to our faith and He powerfully changes us and makes us the recipients of His saving grace.

However, we may still have difficulty believing that *HE IS* our Helper in the time of trouble, or believe that *HE IS* our Healer, or that *HE IS* our Provider, etc., etc., and so we find ourselves living in dependence on something else, i.e., ourselves, our job, our retirement plan, our doctor, or our health insurance plan, etc. I am not saying that these things are bad. They are not, but they must not become the things that we trust in.

God is greater than everything that has happened, is happening and will happen in our lives. A health insurance plan can be a help to us, but if we can't afford one, or our job does not provide one, has God been caught off guard and has He been rendered powerless so that we should now live in fear?

God has ordained that work is good and scripture admonishes us not to be idle, but if we lose our job, does God not know it? Is He rendered powerless to help us?

What if retirement money that we have counted on is squandered or pilfered away by the company we have worked

---

[u]Emphasis added

111

for many years? We suddenly find ourselves with no retirement money to fall back on. Has God been caught off guard and is He now rendered powerless to help us, ...or can we continue to rest and have confidence in Him?

Who knows what will happen to the Social Security System in the years to come. If it falls apart, can I still trust in God? Of course!

We must know God in these areas, and He must be the One in whom we trust. Then, if our world seems to fall apart, we will not be shaken. Why? Because we know (have true faith) that as long as we trust and walk in obedience before Him, He will meet our every need. He not only knows our every need, but will meet our every need, and "will never leave us nor forsake us." That is His promise to us. Therefore, we will have no reason to fear! The *I AM* (Jesus) is **all we need** (in this life and for the one to come) to meet **all of our needs** (spiritual, material and physical) no matter what they may be.

As it says ...

9"For in Christ all the fullness of the Deity lives in bodily form, 10and you have been given fullness in Christ, who is the head over every power and authority" (Col. 2:9-10).

... and again ...

*13"**His divine power has given us everything we need for life and godliness through our knowledge of him** who called us by his own glory and goodness. 4Through these he has given us his very great and precious promises, so that through them you may participate in the divine nature and escape the corruption in the world caused by evil desires.ᵛ"*

IT IS ALSO TRUE, that the more we have of the various kinds of worldly security, the less opportunity we will have of

---

ᵛEmphasis added

living in dependence upon Him and of seeing His faithfulness toward us. So while wealth and prosperity may be a blessing to some, in the long run, it may be a curse to the growth of our faith and thus a curse to our spiritual lives. James 2:5 speaks about this ...

> *"Listen, my dear brothers:* **Has not God chosen those who are poor in the eyes of the world to be rich in faith** *and to inherit the kingdom he promised those who love him?*ʷ *"*

The poor who follow Jesus become rich in faith because they are given plenty of opportunity to turn to God and to trust Him for their needs and to see His hand work in their lives. They do not have all the "securities" of this world in which to put their trust and so they learn to depend on the Lord.

Scripture says that when we do not put our faith and trust in Jesus in all situations, we displease Him...

> *"But my righteous one will* **live by faith.** *And if he shrinks back, I will not be pleased with him"*ˣ (Heb. 10:38).

That's a little scary! Other scriptures back this up ...

> *"... everything that does not come from faith is sin"* (Rom. 14:23).

> *"... it is by faith you stand firm"* (2 Cor. 1:24).

> *"The Lord is good, a refuge in times of trouble. He cares for those who trust in him..."* (Nah. 1:7).

How do we have access to all the attributes of the **LORD (HE IS)** in our lives? Even when we understand the principles involved, we do not enter in overnight, but we begin

---

ʷEmphasis added
ˣ38 Hab. 2:3-4

to make progress. We gain greater knowledge of it as we meditate on the Word and He begins to reveal himself and His truth to us. Then as we act on that Word daily by faith, we come to know His attributes and to experience His operation in every aspect of our lives. We begin to see His power atwork and our faith is strengthened.

These attributes are also present to help us overcome the power of sin in our lives and to make us more like Christ. However, the attributes of the **LORD (HE IS)** will not be apparent in us if we are in the way. We are to be like Christ and yet we have no power in and of ourselves to be like Him. If we seek to do in our own strength what He came to do in us and through us, then we will not see His power in it. What we must do instead is step out of the way, and by faith let the life of Christ and His attributes and His power be revealed in us. The Apostle Paul said in Gal. 2:20:

> *"I have been crucified with Christ and I no longer live, but Christ lives in me. The life I live in the body, I live by faith in the Son of God, who loved me and gave himself for me*[y]*"* (Gal. 2:20).

Our old life and our own strength to do good must be crucified within us. So long as we hang on to the world, our own righteousness, our own strength to do good, our own plans, our own security, our own god's of any kind, etc., to that extent, Christ will not be revealed in us.

This is what Paul was talking about when he said,

> [7]*"But we have this treasure in jars of clay to show that this all-surpassing power is from God and not from us.* [8]*We are hard pressed on every side, but not crushed; perplexed, but not in despair;* [9]*persecuted, but not abandoned; struck*

---

[y]Emphasis added

114

down, but not destroyed. ¹⁰We always carry around in our body the death of Jesus, so that the life of Jesus may also be revealed in our body. ¹¹For we who are alive are always being given over to death for Jesus' sake, so that his life may be revealed in our mortal bodyᶻ" (2 Cor. 4:7-11).

Our walk is perfected in the wilderness. This is where we come to know God. We can duck what God wants to teach us if, through lack of knowledge or through unbelief, we choose to substitute our own works for God's works, our own escape for God's victory. If we do, we will never see God's power manifest as we would desire. We will miss it. This is the message of this book. I believe this will become clearer as we continue.

The Israelites had the faith to leave Egypt and to begin their journey. As their song indicates, they believed that the promised land was theirs. Now would come the testing of their faith and of their understanding of God.

The Apostle Paul has urged us to take heed in our lives to the example laid down by the Israelites in their wilderness journey. He says ...

"These things happened to them as examples and were written down as warnings for us, on whom the fulfillment of the ages has come" (1 Cor. 10:11).

God had promised the Israelites wonderful things, but that generation would not attain to that promise unless they were willing to trust and obey the Lord at all cost. That land of milk and honey was far superior to the land of Egypt and everything that Egypt had to offer. However, in the midst of the difficulties that lay ahead, they needed to keep their eyes on the goal and to be prepared to do all that God required of them. They had to be willing to pay the price.

This is certainly the case with those who have come to Christ for salvation. We must count the cost of following

---

ᶻEmphasis added

Jesus and make up our minds that we are not going to be deterred by the attractions of this life, nor by any hardships that might come our way. Jesus spoke about the cost of following Him...

■   **What we seek is a treasure. All that we may consider to be valuable in this life cannot compare with that treasure ...**

[44]"The kingdom of heaven is like treasure hidden in a field. When a man found it, he hid it again, and then in his joy went and sold all he had and bought that field.

[45]"Again, the kingdom of heaven is like a merchant looking for fine pearls. [46] When he found one of great value, he went away and sold everything he had and bought it. (Matt. 13:44-46)

■ **We need to carefully consider the cost of following Jesus...**

[26]"If anyone comes to me and does not hate his father and mother, his wife and children, his brothers and sisters— yes, even his own life—he cannot be my disciple. [27]And anyone who does not carry his cross and follow me cannot be my disciple.

[28]"Suppose one of you wants to build a tower. Will he not first sit down and estimate the cost to see if he has enough money to complete it? [29]For if he lays the foundation and is not able to finish it, everyone who sees it will ridicule him, [30]saying, 'This fellow began to build and was not able to finish.'

[31]"Or suppose a king is about to go to war against another king. Will he not first sit down and consider whether he is able with ten thousand men to oppose the one coming against him with twenty thousand? [32]If he is not able, he will send a delegation while the other is still a long way off and will ask for terms of peace. [33]In the same way, any of you who does not give up everything he has cannot be my disciple" (Luke 14:26-33).

116

(As a side note here, a disciple is a person who is a Christian. As it says in Acts 11:26, "*... The disciples were called Christians first at Antioch.*")

■ **Jesus gave us an example to follow ...**

[2]"*Let us fix our eyes on Jesus, the author and perfecter of our faith, who for the joy set before him endured the cross, scorning its shame, and sat down at the right hand of the throne of God.* [3]*Consider him who endured such opposition from sinful men, so that you will not grow weary and lose heart*" (Heb. 12:2-3).

■ **In like manner, we must be willing to deny ourselves ...**

[23]"*Then he said to them all: "If anyone would come after me, he must deny himself and take up his cross daily and follow me.* [24]*For whoever wants to save his life will lose it, but whoever loses his life for me will save it.* [25]*What good is it for a man to gain the whole world, and yet lose or forfeit his very self?*" (Luke 9:23-25).

■ **We are to press on toward the goal. The Apostle Paul recognized this as related to his own life ...**

[7]"*But whatever was to my profit I now consider loss for the sake of Christ.* [8]*What is more, I consider everything a loss compared to the surpassing greatness of knowing Christ Jesus my Lord, for whose sake I have lost all things. I consider them rubbish, that I may gain Christ* [9]*and be found in him, not having a righteousness of my own that comes from the law, but that which is through faith in Christ—the righteousness that comes from God and is by faith.* [10]*I want to know Christ and the power of his resurrection and the fellowship of sharing in his sufferings, becoming like him in his death,* [11]*and so, somehow, to attain to the resurrection from the dead.* [12]*Not that I have already obtained all this, or*

have already been made perfect, but I press on to take hold of that for which Christ Jesus took hold of me.

¹³Brothers, I do not consider myself yet to have taken hold of it. But one thing I do: Forgetting what is behind and straining toward what is ahead, ¹⁴I press on toward the goal to win the prize for which God has called me heavenward in Christ Jesus.

¹⁵All of us who are mature should take such a view of things. And if on some point you think differently, that too God will make clear to you. ¹⁶Only let us live up to what we have already attained" (Phil. 3:7-16).

The Israelites had to be done with Egypt, harboring no illusions that anything in Egypt was worth going back for. We also must look at this world and all it has to offer in a similar way. This life is just a fleeting dot on the endless line of eternity. What foolishness it would be to cherish this world so much that we would forfeit the eternal inheritance which God has laid up for us in Jesus Christ. We must be prepared to run the race through to completion no matter what the hardship, no matter what the difficulty—trusting and being obedient to our Lord all the way through.

CHAPTER 5

One Day at a Time, There's No Other Way

The Israelites departed from their place of rejoicing beside the Red Sea and headed into the wilderness...

> *²²"Then Moses led Israel from the Red Sea and they went into the Desert of Shur. For three days they traveled in the desert without finding water. ²³When they came to Marah, they could not drink its water because it was bitter. (That is why the place is called Marah[a] .) ²⁴So the people grumbled against Moses, saying, "What are we to drink?"*
>
> *²⁵Then Moses cried out to the LORD, and the LORD showed Him a piece of wood. He threw it into the water, and the water became sweet.*
>
> *There the LORD made a decree and a law for them, and there he tested them"* (Exod. 15:22-25).

The Israelites were now in a place where they could not readily provide for themselves. They had some sources of food with them (e.g. cattle) but certainly not enough to sustain

---

[a]Marah means *bitter.*

119

them for very long, and their supply of water was very limited. They had never travelled this way before, so they were at the mercy of God to provide their basic necessities. When they finally came to water after travelling for three days, they must have been delighted until they realized that they couldn't drink it. Then they did what many of us would have done in the same situation, they grumbled against their leader Moses, saying, *"What are we to drink?"* Considering their circumstances, this would certainly seem to be a valid question.

It is interesting to note that Jesus addressed this very question in the Sermon on the Mount. What He had to say was nothing less than astounding ...

> [24]*"No one can serve two masters. Either he will hate the one and love the other, or he will be devoted to the one and despise the other. You cannot serve both God and Money.*
>
> [25]*"Therefore I tell you, do not worry about your life, what you will eat or drink; or about your body, what you will wear. Is not life more important than food, and the body more important than clothes?* [26]*Look at the birds of the air; they do not sow or reap or store away in barns, and yet your heavenly Father feeds them. Are you not much more valuable than they?* [27]*Who of you by worrying can add a single hour to his life?[b]*
>
> [28]*"And why do you worry about clothes? See how the lilies of the field grow. They do not labor or spin.* [29]*Yet I tell you that not even Solomon in all his splendor was dressed like one of these.* [30]*If that is how God clothes the grass of the field, which is here today and tomorrow is thrown into the fire, will he not much more clothe you, O you of little faith?* [31]**So do not worry, saying, 'What shall we eat?' or 'What shall we drink?' or 'What shall we wear?'** [32]*For the pagans run after all these things, and your heavenly Father knows that you need them.* [33]*But seek first his kingdom and his righteousness, and all these things will be given to you as well[c] "*
> (Matt. 6:24-33)

---

[b]Or *single cubit to his height*
[c]Emphasis added

I am sure that many have looked at this particular passage in the Sermon on the Mount and considered that there must be some kind of spiritual truth here, but certainly nothing that could be applied in a practical sense. But I believe that this passage means just what it says. Those who don't know the Lord (the pagans) seek after the necessities of life as their first priority, but Jesus said not to do that. Rather, He tells us to be continually absorbed in seeking God, in doing His will and in acquiring and walking in the righteousness that comes from Him. This is to be our first priority. He promises that when we do that, our basic necessities will be provided. So Jesus says in response to those who would ask the question the Israelites asked, "... do not worry saying, 'What shall we eat?' or 'What shall we drink?' or 'What shall we wear?.' But seek first the kingdom and his righteousness, and all these things will be given you as well."

A scripture which many, many people have memorized is John 3:16...

"For God so loved the world, that he gave his only begotten Son, that whosoever believeth in Him should not perish, but have everlasting life" (John 3:16 KJV).

The word "believe" in the English language is a rather weak word to convey the underlying meaning that exists in the Greek. To illustrate, I can believe that the earth revolves around the sun, but that doesn't change my life. I can believe that certain facts are true, but it doesn't necessarily mean that I have acted on those beliefs in such a way that they have made a real difference in my life. I can believe that Jesus lived, died and rose from the dead, but it may not change my life.

The Greek word that is translated 'believe' in John 3:16 actually has a greater depth of meaning. To get the deeper meaning behind the word 'believe' as it is translated in most Bibles, we can go to a Greek Dictionary of New Testament words, or to the Amplified Bible, or to Vine's Expository Dictionary, or other like sources.

The Amplified Bible is a wonderful Bible translation. The purpose for which it was established was to "reveal, together with the single word English equivalent to each key Hebrew and Greek word, any other clarifying shades of meaning that may be concealed by the traditional word-for-word method of translation." When we look at John 3:16-18 in the Amplified Bible, we see the following ...

> *16"For God so greatly loved and dearly prized the world that He [even] gave up His only-begotten (unique) Son, so that whoever believes in (trusts, clings to, relies on) Him shall not perish—come to destruction, be lost—but have eternal (everlasting life).*
> *17For God did not send the Son into the world in order to judge—to reject, to condemn, to pass sentence on—the world; but that the world might find salvation and be made safe and sound through Him.*
> *18He who believes on Him—who clings to, trusts in, relies on Him—is not judged (he who trusts in Him never comes up for judgment; for Him there is no rejection, no condemnation; he incurs no damnation). But he who does not believe (not cleave to, rely on, trust in Him) is judged already; (he has already been convicted; has already received his sentence) because he has not believed on and trusted in the name of the only begotten Son of God.—He is condemned for refusing to let his trust rest in Christ's name"* (John 3:16-18 AMP).

The question can be asked: You believe that Jesus is the Son of God, that He came to die for you, He rose from the dead and is now seated at the right hand of God, and you believe that you have eternal life... BUT, HAVE YOU GIVEN YOURSELF OVER TO TRUST, CLING TO AND RELY ON HIM FOR ALL THINGS IN THE HERE AND NOW? This is the issue being addressed by this book.

Vine's Expository Dictionary of Biblical Words says of the Greek word *pisteuo* which is translated as 'believe' in John 3:16...

pisteuo, "to believe," also "to be persuaded of," and hence, "to place confidence in, to trust," signifies, in this sense of the word, reliance upon, not mere credence.

Again we see a deeper meaning than the single word 'believe' normally conveys to us. Here we see it means to place confidence in, to trust, signifying reliance upon, **not mere credence**.

The question the Israelites asked (what are we to drink?) actually implied a lack of trust in God's faithfulness and in His promise to lead them on to the promised land. Some of Jesus' hearers were like that, and He indicated they were of "little faith." Lack of faith or trust in God is the root cause of worry, and Jesus is telling us that if we are seeking the Lord and His ways first, we have no need to worry or fear.

The consequence of having that kind of "little faith" is that we will act like the pagan world, making the acquisition of the basic necessities our first priority. We will be placing our trust in the securities of this world rather than in God. If the bottom suddenly drops out of the economy, we become very ill and can't work, or some other major crisis hits us, we might very will be devastated because the source of our security has been taken from us. Will we then blame God for letting us down? Will we suddenly see that we have been placing our trust in the wrong things and be able to establish the trust in Him that we should have had in the beginning?

To place our trust in the securities of this world is to build the foundation of our lives on shifting sand. This is what Jesus said in concluding His Sermon on the Mount ...

24"Therefore everyone who hears these words of mine and puts them into practice is like a wise man who built his house on the rock. 25The rain came down, the streams rose, and the winds blew and beat against that house; yet it did not fall, because it had its foundation on the rock. 26But everyone who hears these words of mine and does not put them

into practice is like a foolish man who built his house on sand. ²⁷The rain came down, the streams rose, and the winds blew and beat against that house, and it fell with a great crash" (Matt. 7:24-27)

WE MUST BELIEVE AND BASE OUR LIVES ON GOD'S WORD! ANY OTHER FOUNDATION WILL NOT STAND WHEN THE TESTS COME!

If we are seeking first and trusting in other things rather than the Lord, we will without a doubt be living a lukewarm Christian life. That is a dangerous place to be also. In the book of Revelation, Jesus speaks to the church in Laodicea (and to us) and says ...

¹⁴"To the angel of the church in Laodicea write: These are the words of the Amen, the faithful and true witness, the ruler of God's creation. ¹⁵I know your deeds, that you are neither cold nor hot. I wish you were either one or the other! ¹⁶So, because you are lukewarm—neither hot nor cold—I am about to spit you out of my mouth" (Rev. 3:14-16).

Jesus instruction to seek first the Kingdom of God that our needs might be supplied does not mean that we should not work. The Bible clearly teaches that we must not be idle (2 Thes. 3:6-15)...

1. That we might earn the bread we eat (2 Thes. 3:12) and provide for daily necessities (Titus 3:14).
2. That we will not be dependent on anybody (1 Thes. 4:12).
3. That we might have something to share with those in need (Eph. 4:28).
4. That we might gain the respect of non-Christians (1 Thes. 4:12).

A scriptural rule is *"If a man will not work, he shall not eat"* (2 Thes. 3:10). Yes, we are to work, but we are not to put our trust in our income, in our jobs, in our retirement plans, social security, etc., but in God, for it is He who will not fail us.

There is something liberating about this also. How many individuals have compromised their principles because they were afraid of losing their jobs or of not making enough money to meet their needs? Certainly many dishonest or even immoral things have been done under the justification that it was necessary to gain a job or avoid losing one. Principles which Christians would like to uphold (e.g. not working on Sunday) have been violated for the same reasons (I speak from experience here). This is not meant to invoke legalism, but rather to say that when we begin to give other things higher priority, the things of God will gradually be crowded out and our Christian walk will suffer.

I recently heard of some pastors who confessed to watering down what they preached from the pulpits because of their economic concerns. They had become fearful that were they to speak God's truth too forcefully they might drive away tithing parishioners, might lose their pastorship, their pensions, etc., and so they had allowed the Word of God to be compromised. As a consequence their churches had become dead and lifeless.

When we compromise, we are denying God's Word and walking in unbelief. The difficulties of this life loom larger than our God and so we make wrong decisions and take wrong actions which are the fruits of our unbelief. Taking a stand may cost someone their job or something else of importance, but, do we believe God's Word? Do we really believe that when we do God's will first He will meet our needs? Do we believe that our circumstances are greater than our God, or is our God greater than our circumstances? It is a certainty, that when we start making these hard choices it will also drive us to a closer walk with God. That is what God wants, that we might be totally obedient and dependent upon Him.

Christians must never compromise because of financial fears. We have no basis for such fears if we are seeking Him first, but that does not mean we won't be tested. God could have provided the Israelites water on the first day out, or the second day, but He waited until the third day. When they finally did find water, they couldn't drink it. Their lack of faith in God was revealed by their grumbling at Moses.

It might be the same with us. The Lord might test our faith and our patience by not providing what we need just when we think we may need it. We may then run to have someone pray for us that God will take the problem away. There is nothing wrong with prayer, but what we need most is to trust and to base our actions on what God has said to us in His Word. If we haven't taken time to know Him and His Word to us, then we will not know how to respond in the time of crisis.

As we saw in Exod. 14:31, the Israelites had feared the Lord and put their trust in Him when they saw what God had done to Pharaoh's army when He delivered them. Now the *genuineness* or *validity* of that faith would be tested and proved as they made their way through the wilderness. He had brought them to a place where they could not provide the essential things of life that they needed, nor could they obtain them from others. Were they ready to trust that He would provide what they needed, or would their lack of faith cause them to grumble and complain?

Are there two kinds of faith: One that believes God's promises for salvation and eternal life and another that may optionally believe God in relation to the other things He promises? It is easy to believe God for eternal life, but more difficult to believe and act that faith out on a daily basis with respect to God's provision for us. *Is a partial faith acceptable to God?* This is what the testing in the wilderness was all about. Did the Israelites truly trust God or not? They may have believed for the promised land, but *if they didn't believe God for everything else, they might never get to the promised land at all!*

It is in the time of impatience that our faith is liable to be shaken and we make the choice to either trust God, or to complain and take matters into our own hands. In this regard I would like to quote from the book, Answers to Prayer,

126

published by Moody Press, which contains a number of narratives by George Mueller.

George Mueller was born in Prussia in 1805, but in his later life went to England and there opened and ran orphanages. He was a man of unusual faith who believed that God was able to provide all that was needed to establish and sustain the homes and to provide for the children. He did not plead with others to supply the needs of the children and the orphanage, but instead he took these needs to God in prayer. Sometimes food and other necessities did not arrive until the very day it was required. For the years the orphanages were in operation under George Mueller's direction, God never failed to provide all that was needed.

In his narratives he writes:

"... faith with every fresh trial of it either increases by trusting God, and thus getting help, or it decreases by not trusting Him; and then there is less and less power of looking simply and directly to Him, and a habit of self-dependency is begotten or encouraged. One or the other of these will always be the case in each particular instance. Either we trust in God, and in that case we neither trust in ourselves, nor in anything besides; or we DO trust in one or more of these, and in that case do NOT trust in God.

If we, indeed, desire our faith to be strengthened, we should not shrink from opportunities where our faith may be tried, and, therefore, through the trial, be strengthened. In our natural state we dislike dealing with God alone. Through our natural alienation from God we shrink from Him, and from eternal realities. This cleaves to us more or less, even after our regeneration. Hence it is, that more or less, even as believers, we have the same shrinking from standing with God alone—from depending upon Him alone—from looking to Him alone:—and yet this is the very position in which we ought to be, if we wish our faith to be strengthened. The more I am in a position to be tried in faith with reference to my body, my family, my service for the Lord, my business, etc., the more shall I have opportunity of seeing God's help and deliverance; and every fresh instance, in which He helps and delivers me, will tend towards the increase of my faith. On this account, therefore, the believer should not shrink from situations, positions, circumstances, in which his faith may be tried; but should cheerfully embrace them as opportunities where he may see the hand of God stretched out on his behalf, to help and deliver him, and whereby he may thus have his faith strengthened.

The last important point for the strengthening of our faith is, that we let God work for us, when the hour of the trial of our faith comes, and do not work a deliverance of our own. Wherever God has given faith, it is given, among other reasons, for the very purpose of being tried.

Yea, however weak our faith may be, God will try it; only with this restriction, that as in every way, He leads on gently, gradually, patiently, so also with reference to the trial of our faith. At first our faith will be tried very little in comparison with what it may be afterwards; for God never lays more upon us than He is willing to enable us to bear. Now when the trial of faith comes, we are naturally inclined to mistrust God, and to trust rather in ourselves, or in our friends, or in circumstances.

We will rather work a deliverance of our own somehow or other, than simply look to God and wait for His help. But if we do not patiently wait for God's help, if we work a deliverance of our own, then at the next trial of our faith it will be thus again, we shall again be inclined to deliver ourselves; and thus with every fresh instance of that kind, our faith will decrease; whilst on the contrary, were we to stand still, in order to see the salvation of God, to see His hand stretched out on our behalf, trusting in Him alone, then our faith would be increased, and with every fresh case in which the hand of God is stretched out on our behalf in the hour of the trial of our faith, our faith would be increased yet more.

Would the believer, therefore, have his faith strengthened, he must especially, give time to God, who tries his faith in order to prove to His child, in the end, how willing He is to help and deliver Him the moment it is good for him."[d]

---

[d]Taken from the book, "Answers to Prayer" from George Mueller's narratives, compiled by A.E.C. Brooks as published by Moody Press, Chicago

This is the kind of testing that the Israelites would experience in the wilderness. It would either result in their faith being strengthened or their unbelief being revealed.

The Israelites wanted water, and had finally found it after three days, but couldn't drink it. Moses threw the piece of wood into the bitter water, and the water became sweet. Yet, God was behind it all. Did the Israelites recognize this as the hand of God, or did they think it was brought about by Moses only, or by some magic? Was their faith strengthened at all here?

We have opportunities to see God's provision also. Unfortunately, we seldom pay attention as we should to what God does for us and make a note of it, and so our faith in God is not strengthened. Perhaps we have received a good job, or obtained a bonus, or gained some other good thing which we either needed or wanted, and God has provided, but we have given ourselves or someone else credit, without seeing God's hand behind it all. We certainly should thank those through whom such blessings come, but we must also thank the Lord who is the ultimate source of all we obtain.

Or perhaps we have not experienced the calamities that have come on many others, and just chalk it up to our good fortune. Certainly we need to thank God for the mercy He grants us.

The words of the doxology fit in here...

> *Praise God from Whom **all** blessings flow;*
> *Praise Him all creatures here below;*
> *Praise Him above ye heavenly hosts;*
> *Praise Father, Son and Holy Ghost!*[e]

The Israelites had received their water. Did they recognize the faithfulness of God or did they attribute it to someone or something else? Had they already forgotten all He had done for them? Psalm 106 speaks about this forgetfulness ...

[e]Emphasis added

[7]"When our fathers were in Egypt, they gave no thought to your miracles; they did not remember your many kindnesses, and they rebelled by the sea, the Red Sea. [8]Yet he saved them for his name's sake, to make his mighty power known. [9]He rebuked the Red Sea, and it dried up; he led them through the depths as through a desert. [10]He saved them from the hand of the foe; from the hand of the enemy he redeemed them. [11]The waters covered their adversaries; not one of them survived. [12]Then they believed his promises and sang his praise. [13]But they soon forgot what he had done and did not wait for his counsel. [14]In the desert they gave in to their craving; in the wasteland they put God to the test" (Ps. 106:7-14).

While they were at Marah, God also made a decree and a law for the Israelites ...

[25]"... There the LORD made a decree and a law for them, and there he tested them.
[26]He said, 'If you listen carefully to the voice of the LORD your God and do what is right in his eyes, if you pay attention to his commands and keep all his decrees, I will not bring on you any of the diseases I brought on the Egyptians, for I am the LORD, who heals you'" (Exod. 15:25-26).

God gave the Israelites a law which included a right or privilege. If they would do all that the Lord required of them, then He would not bring on them any of the diseases which He brought on the Egyptians. For He would be to them Jehovah Rapha, "The LORD who heals you."

This passage states that God brought diseases on the Egyptians. Whether God brought them directly, or indirectly by allowing Satan to inflict the Egyptians is not discussed. But in any event, the Lord makes it clear, that if the Israelites would do what God desired of them, they would not be afflicted with any of these diseases.

This may be difficult to understand, that a God of love could afflict people with diseases. However, when God provided the Ten Commandments, He revealed a prescription for living that He would bless. Just as an automaker provides a manual that specifies how a car is to be cared for if it is to provide good service, so the Lord has provided an owners manual for mankind which gives the requirements for a successful life. When we violate the conditions which God has laid down, we lay ourselves open to all kinds of difficulties. One of the difficulties can be disease.

Today we see venereal diseases, AID's, etc., which have come about as a consequence of the violation of God's laws. If the people of this planet were to do what God has prescribed, these diseases would disappear. Because they will not, the diseases are spreading. If the Bible says that God brought diseases upon the Egyptians, I believe it was because of the things they were doing which were contrary to God's ways, and they reaped the results of their sin.

We who have come to Jesus, and have given our lives to Him can expect that we will not be afflicted with such diseases. But also, He has given us the ability to bring any other health problem to Him, that we might be healed. Can I say that we see all Christians healed of health problems? No! However, we have been given authority to come into the presence of Jehovah Rapha to receive healing.

After the Israelites had their water replenished, they continued on ...

> [27]"Then they came to Elim, where there were twelve springs and seventy palm trees, and they camped there near the water" (Exod. 15:27).

The journey up to this point had not been too long, but some difficulties had been encountered. Now God brings them to an oasis in the desert, a place of refreshment and shade from the heat. Here there were twelve springs for their tribes, which provided enough water for all with plenty of shade. The number seven in scripture often is symbolic of completeness or perfection, but at Elim they came to seventy palm trees which implies a perfection amplified.

131

The Lord was going to bring them through many tests and trials in order to reveal what was in their hearts. Yet He longed to be gracious to them and so brings them to a place of blessed rest and refreshing. God knows our frailties too, and so brings to us those special times of rest and refreshing where He can minister to our needs and deal with the stresses we experience as we walk through this life.

[5]"The LORD watches over you—the LORD is your shade at your right hand; [6]the sun will not harm you by day, nor the moon by night. [7]The LORD will keep you from all harm—he will watch over your life; [8]the LORD will watch over your coming and going both now and forevermore" (Ps. 121:5-8).

[5]"Blessed are those whose strength is in you, who have set their hearts on pilgrimage. [6]As they pass through the Valley of Baca, they make it a place of springs; the autumn rains also cover it with pools" (Ps. 84:5-6).

As we follow the Lord, we set our hearts on our pilgrimage to attain the goal and the inheritance that He has set before us. Even though our walk through the wilderness of this life can at times be very difficult, we are enabled to make it a place of springs because we have made God our joy and our strength. God is gracious and loving and longs to bless us and will not give us more than we can bear, and He delights to show us His kindness and favor at times and in ways which we never could have anticipated or imagined.

[4]"Sing to the LORD, you saints of his; praise his holy name. [5]For his anger lasts only a moment, but his favor lasts a lifetime; weeping may remain for a night, but rejoicing comes in the morning" (Ps. 30:4-5).

The Israelites were given the opportunity to camp in a place of blessed rest and refreshment where the stresses of all that had happened to them could be washed away and where they could be strengthened for what lay ahead.

But this oasis, as nice as it was, was not the object of their journey. Once again it came time to travel on...

> [1]*"The whole Israelite community set out from Elim and came to the Desert of Sin, which is between Elim and Sinai, on the fifteenth day of the second month after they had come out of Egypt.* [2]*In the desert the whole community grumbled against Moses and Aaron.* [3]*The Israelites said to them, 'If only we had died by the LORD's hand in Egypt! There we sat around pots of meat and ate all the food we wanted, but you have brought us out into this desert to starve this entire assembly to death'"* (Exod. 16:1-3).

Even though they addressed their gripes to Moses and Aaron, it was God who they were really complaining against. All of the works which God had performed, were now once again forgotten. They remembered Egypt instead of *"...forgetting that which lay behind ... and straining to go on to what lay ahead"* (Phil. 3:13-14).

The questions could logically be asked: What was the reason the Israelites left Egypt? Why did Egypt still hold any kind of attraction for them? Why was their attention not focused on their objective instead of the momentary afflictions of their journey? What was lacking?

Did they not realize that in whatever ways life in Egypt might have appeared to be attractive or glamorous or secure, it was nonetheless, in fact, a place of bondage and slavery? Could they not remember Pharaoh's cruelty and hatred for them? Certainly they did not have any kind of real life under his tyranny. Did they not see what a great deliverance God had won for them? He had led them out of Egypt as He had promised and taken them through the Red Sea. He had not failed them in any way but had been true to His Word.

There are some who reach out to Jesus Christ because of what they think He can offer them—insulation from any problems, the promise of eternal life, prosperity, quick solutions to their life's difficulties, etc.—a God who will be available to them when they need Him, and doesn't ask them to walk through any difficulties. They are not ready to give themselves fully to Jesus because they want to hold on to their own agenda and the sinful pleasures of this world.

It is in the wilderness that such heart attitudes are identified and exposed. When God doesn't come through for such individuals in the way they think He should, they lose interest, and their hearts are quickly turned back to embrace the "wonderful" things in this world because they have never died to them. There has been no real heart repentance or turning away from the things that have held them captive, and so they quickly fall away.

They do not realize that it is only as we begin to see this world for what it is, and repent of our past ways and die to our own sinful desires that we can come to God with an earnest heart. It is only as our hearts turn away completely from the ways of sin and death that we are able to be transformed by the power of God. It is realizing that whatever God would have us go through is nothing compared to the life and hope He offers us both now and for eternity. As it says in 2 Corinthians ...

[16]*"Therefore we do not lose heart. Though outwardly we are wasting away, yet inwardly we are being renewed day by day.* [17]*For our light and momentary troubles are achieving for us an eternal glory that far outweighs them all.* [18]*So we fix our eyes not on what is seen, but on what is unseen. For what is seen is temporary, but what is unseen is eternal"* (2 Cor. 4:16-18).

There is nothing worth going back for. God's best is ours as we continue on the path of His choosing. What we left behind is worthless and will someday be burned up. Again we should consider Psalm 84:5 ...

[5]*"Blessed are those whose strength is in you, who have set their hearts on pilgrimage."*

How different it could have been for the Israelites if they would have set their hearts on pilgrimage and allowed themselves only one thought, and that to reach their inheritance, the promised land. In the same way, we who believe in Jesus Christ are called to find our strength in God and to set our hearts on pilgrimage, to reach that eternal destiny promised to those who persevere in following the Lord Jesus Christ. When we have set our hearts in this way, there can be no looking back. Going back is not an option available for our consideration.

God is with us and will never leave us or forsake us. We will face tests and trials of all kinds, and yet we know that it is in the middle of those difficulties that we are enabled to learn obedience to the Lord. This was true for Jesus ...

8"Although he was a son, he learned obedience from what he suffered..." (Heb. 5:8).

Jesus counted the cost and submitted Himself to the Father that He might be obedient in all things. Likewise, there have been many other saints identified in scripture and throughout history whose faithfulness and perseverance in following the Lord have provided a wonderful testimony to us.

1"Therefore, since we are surrounded by such a great cloud of witnesses, let us throw off everything that hinders and the sin that so easily entangles, and let us run with perseverance the race marked out for us. 2Let us fix our eyes on Jesus, the author and perfecter of our faith, who for the joy set before Him endured the cross, scorning its shame, and sat down at the right hand of the throne of God. 3Consider Him who endured such opposition from sinful men, so that you will not grow weary and lose heart.

4In your struggle against sin, you have not yet resisted to the point of shedding your blood. 5And you have forgotten that word of encouragement that addresses you as sons:

"My son, do not make light of the Lord's discipline,
and do not lose heart when he rebukes you,

135

*⁶because the Lord disciplines those he loves,
and he punishes everyone he accepts as a son."*

⁷Endure hardship as discipline; God is treating you as sons. For what son is not disciplined by his father? ⁸If you are not disciplined (and everyone undergoes discipline), then you are illegitimate children and not true sons. ⁹Moreover, we have all had human fathers who disciplined us and we respected them for it. How much more should we submit to the Father of our spirits and live! ¹⁰Our fathers disciplined us for a little while as they thought best; but God disciplines us for our good, that we may share in his holiness. ¹¹No discipline seems pleasant at the time, but painful. Later on, however, it produces a harvest of righteousness and peace for those who have been trained by it" (Heb. 12:1-11).

If we are going to follow Jesus, we must come to that place where we make a commitment to ourselves and to the Lord that we are going to follow Him all the way—no turning back.

If we have committed to go all the way with Jesus no matter what the cost, then it can be helpful to view the moment of that transaction as a time and place when we placed a marker in the ground. Behind the marker lays the place we have come from. The opposite way is the way of the Lord. Should we ever become discouraged and turn to look back on the way we have come, our eyes would fall upon that marker whereon is written...

HALT !!!

THIS PATH LEADS BACK TO EGYPT.
IT IS NO LONGER OPEN TO YOU
YOU ARE CALLED TO PRESS ON
WITH JESUS.

Egypt, that place of slavery and degradation had somehow become wonderful to the Israelites in retrospect. One thing about

136

Egypt, it didn't require them to apply any faith. God, the creator of the universe and everything in it, including all human beings, all cattle, birds and all plant life that man could eat, had promised them that He would take them to a promised land—a land flowing with milk and honey. Implied in this was the fact that He would provide for all of their needs. How else would He be able to get them to that land? But they could not bring themselves to trust in Him. Instead they remembered the 'wonderful food' of Egypt.

The book of Psalms speaks about this incident ...

[17]*"But they continued to sin against him, rebelling in the desert against the Most High.* [18]*They willfully put God to the test by demanding the food they craved.* [19]*They spoke against God, saying, "Can God spread a table in the desert?"* (Ps. 78:17-19).

The Israelites did not have an attitude of surrender to God, of thankfulness and trust in Him, but rather arrogance and rebellion which is sin. They were calling into question the Lord's unswerving loyalty and love for them, and were doubting His faithfulness and His power to provide for them.

God provides for us too. But instead of being grateful in our hearts, perhaps we complain and say, "Boy, I hate that food. Why do we always have to have that?" Yet, what is provided is nourishing and good for us. Maybe we think our various complaints in life are just to our parents or our wife, husband or some other person. But God is the ultimate source of what we have. Our complaints come before Him. Is this not the lesson here? The Israelites grumbling complaints were heard by God. Aren't ours also? Isn't He the true source of all things?

God can save our souls from hell and give us eternal life, but can He provide for us? ... Does He see what we are going through? Yes he does. He calls us to trust and rely upon Him and to be thankful for all that He has done for us.

> *"...Give thanks in all circumstances, for this is God's will for you in Christ Jesus"* (Thes. 5:18).

> [19]*"Speak to one another with psalms, hymns and spiritual songs. Sing and make music in your heart to the Lord,* [20]*always giving thanks to God the Father for everything, in the name of our Lord Jesus Christ"* (Eph. 5:19-20).

God heard the grumbling of the Israelites, yet He showed His patience toward them. He knew their frailties and that they had never had to walk this way before. It was never His plan to leave them helpless or without the water and food that they certainly needed.

> [4]*"Then the LORD said to Moses, 'I will rain down bread from heaven for you. The people are to go out each day and gather enough for that day. In this way I will test them and see whether they will follow my instructions.* [5]*On the sixth day they are to prepare what they bring in, and that is to be twice as much as they gather on the other days.'*
>
> [6]*So Moses and Aaron said to all the Israelites, 'In the evening you will know that it was the LORD who brought you out of Egypt,* [7]*and in the morning you will see the glory of the LORD, because he has heard your grumbling against him. Who are we, that you should grumble against us?"* [8]*Moses also said, 'You will know that it was the LORD when he gives you meat to eat in the evening and all the bread you want in the morning, because he has heard your grumbling against him. Who are we? You are not grumbling against us, but against the LORD.'*
>
> [9]*Then Moses told Aaron, 'Say to the entire Israelite community, 'Come before the LORD, for he has heard your grumbling.'*
>
> [10]*While Aaron was speaking to the whole Israelite community, they looked toward the desert, and there was the glory of the LORD appearing in the cloud.*

[11]The LORD said to Moses, [12]'I have heard the grumbling of the Israelites. Tell them, 'At twilight you will eat meat, and in the morning you will be filled with bread. Then you will know that I am the LORD your God'" (Exod. 16:4-12).

The word "grumbling" appears seven times in Exodus 16:2-11. There is no mistaking that this was their attitude. Their grumbling became evident whenever they faced a crisis. As we have already said, and as it is confirmed in verse 8, their grumbling was not against Moses and Aaron, but against the Lord, and the Lord heard it. Their grumbling came about because of a failure to believe that God would or could provide what they needed.

If we walk in fear and unbelief, we are much more apt to grumble and complain. In times of difficulty, we believe that God has failed us. We do not continue to submit to the Lord and to believe that He will be faithful to us. Yet that is the exact time that we must turn to Him with trust in our hearts, *"because God has said, 'Never will I leave you; never will I forsake you'"* (Heb. 13:5).

God was going to provide food for the Israelites. He would test them to see if they would follow His instructions to them as to how they were to gather and use this bread from heaven. Each day they were to go out and gather only enough for that day, but on the sixth day they were to gather and prepare twice as much. As we shall see, they were not to go out and gather any on the seventh day.

[13]"That evening quail came and covered the camp, and in the morning there was a layer of dew around the camp. [14]When the dew was gone, thin flakes like frost on the ground appeared on the desert floor. [15]When the Israelites saw it, they said to each other, "What is it?" For they did not know what it was.

Moses said to them, "It is the bread the LORD has given you to eat. [16]This is what the LORD has commanded: 'Each one is to gather as much as he needs. Take an omer for each person you have in your tent.'"

139

[17]*The Israelites did as they were told; some gathered much, some little.* [18]*And when they measured it by the omer, he who gathered much did not have too much, and he who gathered little did not have too little. Each one gathered as much as he needed.*

[19]*Then Moses said to them, 'No one is to keep any of it until morning.'*

[20]*However, some of them paid no attention to Moses; they kept part of it until morning, but it was full of maggots and began to smell. So Moses was angry with them.*

[21]*Each morning everyone gathered as much as he needed, and when the sun grew hot, it melted away.* [22]*On the sixth day, they gathered twice as much—two omers for each person—and the leaders of the community came and reported this to Moses.* [23]*He said to them, 'This is what the LORD commanded: 'Tomorrow is to be a day of rest, a holy Sabbath to the LORD. So bake what you want to bake and boil what you want to boil. Save whatever is left and keep it until morning.'*

[24]*So they saved it until morning, as Moses commanded, and it did not stink or get maggots in it.* [25]*'Eat it today,' Moses said, 'because today is a Sabbath to the LORD. You will not find any of it on the ground today.* [26]*Six days you are to gather it, but on the seventh day, the Sabbath, there will not be any.'*

[27]*Nevertheless, some of the people went out on the seventh day to gather it, but they found none.* [28]*Then the LORD said to Moses, 'How long will you refuse to keep my commands and my instructions?* [29]*Bear in mind that the LORD has given you the Sabbath; that is why on the sixth day he gives you bread for two days. Everyone is to stay where he is on the seventh day; no one is to go out.'* [30]*So the people rested on the seventh day.*

[31]*The people of Israel called the bread manna. It was white like coriander seed and tasted like wafers made with honey'"* (Exod. 16:13-31).

Quail came in and covered the camp of the Israelites. They were going to have meat at night and bread in the morning. If you were hungry and needed food, and quail suddenly started landing down around you, how long would it take you to believe that Divine Providence was watching over you? Yet I suppose that in some kind of blindness you could say, "My ... what a remarkable coincidence!"

You may think that this story of the Israelites is too far fetched to believe, but is there anything too hard for the One who created all things? It was the Creator of the universe who was watching over them.

> *"I am the LORD, the God of all mankind. Is anything too hard for me?"* (Jer. 32:27).

In the morning, thin flakes that looked like frost lay on the ground all around them. It was called "manna." Manna is a Hebrew word meaning "what is it?" (see verse 15). That is what the Israelites asked, because they had never seen this kind of food before.

What God desired to teach the Israelites is marvelous. Our natural tendency as humans is to store away what we need so that we don't have any worries about tomorrow. But we see that God required the Israelites to get their "bread" from Him one day at a time with no stockpiling allowed. It would be a test to see if they had sufficient faith to obey Him.

This is a difficult thing to do, and some of the Israelites tried to save their daily ration of manna so that they could make sure that they had enough for the next day. However, it wouldn't keep beyond one day. It got maggots in it and began to smell.

Is it not very clear what God wanted to teach them and us? He desires that we trust Him for each day as it comes. We are not to be worried (anxious, troubled) by what may come about tomorrow (or the next day, or the day after that). This requires us to submit all of our tomorrows to the Lord. It does not mean that we cannot plan ahead, but only that we are not to fear or be alarmed about the future. IF ONE DAY WE HAVE LOTS OF MONEY, BUT THE NEXT DAY HAVE NONE,

HE HAS NOT CHANGED AND NEITHER HAVE HIS PROMISES TO US. This does not mean we are to be careless with what He has given us, it only means that no situation can come upon us which He does not foresee and make allowance for.

All we need to do is trust and obey Him. If we can only believe this, what a wonderful peace will be ours. It is in this environment of faith that we will receive what we need. We need not live in bondage to fear.

In Egypt the Israelites were slaves to fear, but God wanted to set them free from that bondage. What the Lord did for them is spoken of in Psalms 81...

> He says, *"I removed the burden from their shoulders; their hands were set free from the basket"* (Ps. 81:6).

They did not need to be encumbered with fear about the necessities of this life, for God would be their provider. As long as they lived for Him they needed to fear nothing. As He has already said to us, "seek first his kingdom and his righteousness, and all these things will be given to you as well" (Matt. 6:33). In the very next verse (Matt. 6:34) Jesus said ...

> *"Therefore do not worry about tomorrow, for tomorrow will worry about itself. Each day has enough trouble of its own"* (Matt. 6:34).

What is worry anyway? It is gathering up all the "what if's" that could possibly relate to our lives in the future, and bringing them into the present moment so that we can be fearful about them. Most of these "what if's" will never come to pass. When we ponder and worry about them, they only serve to give us ulcers. If we have submitted our lives to the Lord and are trusting in Him, we do not need to worry about these things, because God will see us through as we trust in Him for each day as it comes. Worry and fear are rooted in unbelief.

The things the Israelites went through are not just stories but actual history. It is very clear that the lessons which the Lord was teaching the Israelites are meant for us also. Jesus confirmed it by the words which He spoke as we have seen in Matthew chapter 6, and we have already noted (and will note again) Paul's statement that "*... these things happened to them as examples and were written down as warnings for us, on whom the fulfillment of the ages has come*" (1 Cor. 10:11).

It had to be miraculous that the manna which would not keep overnight the first five days of the week, could be gathered on the sixth day and kept for the seventh day (the Sabbath) without getting maggots in it. The Israelites would have no excuse for not observing the Sabbath rest which God had commanded (Exod 16:29-30). His commandment would not have been issued to them if it was impossible to observe.

Later, God gave the Ten Commandments. The fifth commandment says ...

"Remember the Sabbath day by keeping it holy" (Exod. 20:8).

The Sabbath day was to be kept "holy" or set apart to the Lord and thereby was to be different from the other days of the week. As we have seen in our story of the Israelites, it was not to be just another work day like all of the others. The Hebrew word for Sabbath means "to rest, cease or desist." It was to be a day of rest from labor and a turning away from the day-to-day concerns of planting, harvesting, buying, selling, etc., a cessation from everyday activities.

That the seventh day was a sacred day was noted before the law was given through Moses...

[2]"By the seventh day God had finished the work he had been doing; so on the seventh day he rested from all his work. [3]And God blessed the seventh day and made it holy, because on it he rested from all the work of creating that he had done" (Gen. 2:2-3).

The fact that God declared the seventh day to be holy, before it was ever made a law with the giving of the Ten Commandments, gives evidence that observance of this day was not to be limited to the Jewish people.

Jesus never said anything to abrogate the requirement that we should set aside one day in seven to cease from normal work so that we might give ourselves to rest and the worship of the Lord. The New Testament Church set aside the first day of the week (still one day in seven) to worship and to commemorate the resurrection of Christ. This has continued to be observed as the "Lord's day."

When God gave the commandment regarding the Sabbath, He fully understood our need for food, clothing, and the other necessities of life. Yet He declared that one day each week was to be free from the labor associated with obtaining such things. As we observe this day, we reaffirm that our trust and delight is truly in the Lord and not in all of the other things that would take our attention.

It was never the Lord's intent to make the observance of this day of rest a legalistic nightmare as was later to become the practice of the Pharisees. When Jesus healed on the Sabbath, or the disciples picked grain from the stalks to put directly into their mouth, the Pharisees accused them of working on the Sabbath. Jesus showed that such an approach to the Sabbath was clearly wrong (Matt. 12:1-13; Luke 13:10-17). We need to consider that if we go to church on Sunday morning because we feel we must keep some legalistic requirement or just because we may feel it is expected of us, then we miss the whole point.

Every seventh day was to be more than just a day of rest. It was to be a Sabbath to the Lord. So while they would turn aside from their labors, they were to direct their attention to the Lord. A scripture from the book of Isaiah gives us good insight into this thought...

[13]"If you keep your feet from breaking the Sabbath and from doing as you please on my holy day, if you call the Sabbath a delight and the LORD's holy day honorable, and if you honor it by not going your own way and not doing as you please or speaking idle words, [14]then you will find your joy in the LORD, and I will cause you to ride on the heights of the land and to feast on the inheritance of your father Jacob." The mouth of the LORD has spoken" (Isa. 58:13-14).

This scripture more clearly shows the direction that the Sabbath observance was to take—certainly a turning away from the day-to-day labors, but also a turning to the Lord in a special way. In my life I have done many things on the Lord's day, including going to ball games, going fishing, boating, shopping, etc., etc. But I have come to believe that these activities most logically would be considered as "doing as I please" and "going my own way." I have engaged in idle chit-chat which is not uplifting in the Lord. If I do these other things on the Lord's day, I may not be committing a sin, but when I do these things, if I understand the words of Isaiah, I will not be finding my joy in the Lord, but in something else and I will not receive the blessing that the Lord desires to provide. Jesus made it very clear that the Sabbath was made for man and not the other way around (Mark 2:27). It was meant to bless us. Going to church on Sunday is part of this when we set our hearts on seeking the Lord and worshipping Him. I believe that we can be blessed in a special way if we will continue with activities throughout the day which keep our hearts and minds focused upon Him in reverence, praise, worship and prayer.

This is not a matter of doing some legalistic thing. It is rather a matter of the heart. God does not desire to force us to come into His presence, but He blesses us when we do. If our foremost desire is to live for the Lord and please Him, then we will not be offended by the thought of devoting this day to the Lord. Certainly it can be a time when family members are together, sharing in food and in activities which do

145

not take you away from the realization that this is the Lord's day. I have found greater joy this last year in being in the presence of the Lord on Sunday than I can ever remember. As my wife and I have begun to give the majority of each Sunday after morning worship to fellowship with other believers around food and then to rest and to the reading of scripture, Christian books, music and prayer, we have been blessed. We have not started treating Sunday this way because it is a legalistic requirement, but because we want to be in the presence of the Lord. We find that we delight to go to church, to take our place in working in Sunday school with the children, to enter into praise and worship in the morning service and to hear what He wants to say to us. We find that we do not miss the other things that are going on in the world.

God did the miraculous to assure that the people of Israel were able to observe the Sabbath. I believe that He will honor us in like manner as we observe the Lord's day in His presence. This is illustrated with regard to another practice that the Israelites were to observe. The Lord instituted a requirement upon the Israelites that when they entered the land of Canaan, they were to plant crops in six out of every seven years. The seventh year they were to give the land rest. (Crop rotation is now commonly observed to perform this function.)

[1]"The LORD said to Moses on Mount Sinai, [2]"Speak to the Israelites and say to them: 'When you enter the land I am going to give you, the land itself must observe a sabbath to the LORD. [3]For six years sow your fields, and for six years prune your vineyards and gather their crops. [4]But in the seventh year the land is to have a sabbath of rest, a sabbath to the LORD. Do not sow your fields or prune your vineyards. [5]Do not reap what grows of itself or harvest the grapes of your untended vines. The land is to have a year of rest. [6]Whatever the land yields during the sabbath year will be food for you—for yourself, your manservant and maidservant, and the hired worker and temporary resident who live among you, [7]as well as for your livestock and the wild ani-

mals in your land. Whatever the land produces may be eaten" (Lev. 25:1-7).

The soil would be replenished through a year of "Sabbath" rest. But you can imagine, that some would question God and wonder how they would survive or make a living if they gave the land this year of rest. God knew this in advance and answered this question ...

[18]"Follow my decrees and be careful to obey my laws, and you will live safely in the land. [19]Then the land will yield its fruit, and you will eat your fill and live there in safety. [20]You may ask, "What will we eat in the seventh year if we do not plant or harvest our crops?" [21]I will send you such a blessing in the sixth year that the land will yield enough for three years. [22]While you plant during the eighth year, you will eat from the old crop and will continue to eat from it until the harvest of the ninth year comes in" (Lev. 25:18-22).

God would make a way for the Israelites to observe this sabbatical year by sending a special blessing upon them in the sixth year—the land would yield enough food to last for three years.

This is an illustration for us I believe as relates to the observance of the Lord's day. He will bless us in it. However, there may be more than one reason why some Christians feel they are unable to observe this day. Perhaps their company requires them to work on Sunday. Certainly this world does not desire to honor the Lord or to be in His presence on this day and so more and more businesses are remaining open on Sunday. There was a time in this United States when businesses were required to be closed on Sunday unless they were providing certain essential services. I recall an election which was held to change the laws in the Seattle area to allow additional stores and other businesses to be open. The argument for making this change was that those who opposed the change certainly did not have to use these services, but their beliefs should not prevent others from having access to them on Sunday. The change was instituted, and now we have many stores and businesses open on Sunday. The change has affected many Christians who are employed by these companies. Sunday work has become for many, a requirement of employment.

My wife had to take a stand at her place of employment to be free from Sunday work. It was not an easy thing to achieve. I also have been frequently required to work on Sunday. I took steps to change this practice. Since that time there is no question that I have been blessed, blessed, blessed by the Lord and have been drawn much closer to Him.

Certainly there are some types of work which must continue on Sunday (e.g., caregivers in nursing homes, doctors and nurses, etc.). Christians who work in these occupations need the benefits of the Lord's day also. If you are in this type of situation, I would encourage you to prayerfully seek a way that you might be relieved of work on Sunday, at least some of the time, that you would be able to enter into the day of rest that God has designed for your benefit.

God told the Israelites that they did not need to go out and look for food on the seventh day because what they gathered on the sixth day could be carried over. I believe that God is saying to us also that He will provide for us and bless us as we seek to observe the holy day which He has instituted. He will bless business owners who take a stand to shut down on Sundays to give their employees the day off, and to other individuals who take steps to observe this day of worship and rest. If we do not believe this, we may find that even when we work on the seventh day there may not be enough to meet our needs.

The questions we need to consider are, "DO WE TRULY BELIEVE GOD'S WORD?" ARE WE GOING TO ALLOW OUR FEARS AND UNBELIEF TO RULE US AND CAUSE US TO REJECT WHAT GOD SAYS—OR, WILL WE ACT ON HIS WORD BY FAITH EVEN WHEN IT RUNS CONTRARY TO OUR

NATURAL REASONINGS? This is an important issue. I believe that much of our disobedience to the Lord comes because we do not believe His Word and so we fail to act upon it as we should. As was said earlier, it is easy to trust for heaven, but not so easy to trust when our daily living is at stake. Yet if we want to know success with God, we must honor Him with our full trust and obedience in every aspect of our lives.

The Lord continued to provide opportunities for the Israelites to learn these lessons as they again moved on in their travels ...

> [1]*"The whole Israelite community set out from the Desert of Sin, traveling from place to place as the LORD commanded. They camped at Rephidim, but there was no water for the people to drink.* [2]*So they quarreled with Moses and said, 'Give us water to drink.'*
>
> *Moses replied, 'Why do you quarrel with me? Why do you put the LORD to the test?'*
>
> [3]*But the people were thirsty for water there, and they grumbled against Moses. They said, 'Why did you bring us up out of Egypt to make us and our children and livestock die of thirst?'*
>
> [4]*Then Moses cried out to the LORD, 'What am I to do with these people? They are almost ready to stone me.'*
>
> [5]*The LORD answered Moses, 'Walk on ahead of the people. Take with you some of the elders of Israel and take in your hand the staff with which you struck the Nile, and go.* [6]*I will stand there before you by the rock at Horeb. Strike the rock, and water will come out of it for the people to drink.' So Moses did this in the sight of the elders of Israel.* [7]*And he called the place Massah and Meribah because the Israelites quarreled and because they tested the LORD saying, 'Is the LORD among us or not?'"* (Exod. 17:1-7).

God continued to use the essentials of life (food, water) to test their trust in Him. As we have seen, He wanted to meet their need for these things one day at a time.

We have to ask ourselves, if the Israelites put the Lord to the test by asking for water when they were thirsty, what should they have done? I believe there is only one response that would have pleased the Lord, and it was to continue on without complaining or murmuring, believing the Lord would provide in sufficient time all that was needed.

This is clearly God's instruction to us and was confirmed by Jesus when he said, "do not worry, saying, 'What shall we eat?' or 'What shall we drink?' or 'What shall we wear?' ... your heavenly Father knows that you need [these things]" (Matt. 6:31-32). It is God's will for us that we go forward without worry, without fear, believing God will provide as we are obedient and place our trust in Him.

Though God was now feeding them with manna on a daily basis and had provided for their needs up to this point, yet they refused to acknowledge that He was with them. They refused to believe. Instead of becoming stronger in faith in each instance in which the Lord helped them, their hearts were becoming harder. They were continuing to be contentious, rebellious and ungrateful for all the Lord had done for them. These are the fruits of unbelief.

The Israelites said (verse 3) ...

"Why did you bring us up out of Egypt to make us and our children and livestock die of thirst?"

This statement was directed to Moses but was an absolute rejection of God. It perhaps could have been stated ...

"Why did you bring us up out of Egypt (the place of real security) to the wilderness (the place of insecurity) where all we have to trust in now is Moses and God? We could see our security in Egypt, now we can't see it."

This is a big lie. In the world there is no true lasting security. Only in God is there true security.

"The world and its desires pass away, but the man who does the will of God lives forever" (1 John 2:17).

"So we fix our eyes not on what is seen, but on what is unseen. For what is seen is temporary, but what is unseen is eternal" (2 Cor. 4:18).

It is important to again mention that our whole life is to be lived by faith once we have made the initial step to receive Jesus as our Lord and Savior. We don't just enter into the door of salvation by faith and then forget faith from that moment on. No, as we have seen, we are to **LIVE by faith** ...

"...But my righteous one will live by faith. And if he shrinks back, I will not be pleased with him" (Heb. 10:38).

"...We live by faith, not by sight" (2 Cor. 5:7).

It is to be our way of life. We may not have difficulty believing God for heaven in the by-and-by, yet somehow we find it difficult to exercise faith in the important issues of our daily lives. God seems too far away to trust Him for our daily needs. However, when we receive Jesus as our personal Savior, we are to surrender our whole lives to Him. It is clearly God's intent that we trust Him for everything, and not just for heaven. If we do not do this, we will continue to fret and stew whenever anything does not appear to be working out as we think it should. This is displeasing to God.

When difficult circumstances come into our lives, do we trust God ... or quarrel and complain? For example, we may get uptight over our income and go to our boss and say "How come ...

> Why didn't I get a raise?
> Joe gets more hours than me?
> I never get any overtime?
> I get all the dirty work?
> etc., etc., etc.

(I know, I've been there...) It's easy to do when we are not walking in faith and submission to the Lord.

I don't believe that God wants us to strive. Certainly we can talk about some of these things in a civil way with those we work for, but our attitudes should reflect the fact that our trust is not in these things, but in God. Matthew 6:33 does **not** say ... "Seek first to harass your boss and he will supply all your needs." No, it says ..."Seek first the kingdom of God and his righteousness (his way of doing and being right) and all these things will be added unto you."[f]

How can we come to that faith that trusts God in, and for, all things?

1. **We must read and meditate on the scriptures.** Our faith is increased as we study the Bible. In the scriptures...

    a. We see the promises that God has given to all who will place their trust in Him. We need to believe and act upon these promises.

    b. We see examples of individuals who exercised faith in God in various situations and how God responded to that faith. We also see those who turned away from faith and the results they reaped because of their unbelief.

2. **We must take steps to exercise our faith in God.** To trust, or not to trust in God is a decision we make. It is an act of our will, something we can choose to do or not do. When we make the choice to trust in God in any particular situation and commit ourselves to Him, we will have the opportunity to see the results of standing by faith in God, and our faith will be strengthened. We must be careful however that we give Him the freedom to bring a different outcome than what we may

be anticipating. God provided for the Israelites in His way and according to His schedule. When things did not come to the Israelites in the way and at the time they thought it should, they turned to grumbling and complaining. A key for us is that we must trust God even when things don't seem to be happening as we think they should. Though everything may look bleak and the outcome questionable, yet we must commit all into the hands of the Lord and just trust in Him.

3. **We must walk in obedience to the Lord.** We must never pursue the necessities of life at the expense of obedience to God. When we do we sin. If we take matters into our own hands and go our own way without regard for what God would have us to do, we will miss God's best for our lives. How can we trust God if we are disobeying Him and going our own way? How can we be confident in Him if we are rejecting His will for us?

4. **We need to fellowship with other believers** in church and elsewhere that we might be strengthened by preaching, teaching and the testimonies of God's workings in the lives of others.

The Lord was clearly with the Israelites. Yet they could not see Him any more than we can see Him in our times of testing. They needed to consciously make the choice to trust the Lord. Likewise, we also need to stand fast in Him when our time of difficulty comes. We must be willing to commit all into His hands and believe that He will see us through. If we do not stand on the Word of God and live out our faith on a day-by-day basis we will be tempted to say as the Israelites did in their time of trial, "Is the Lord among us or not?"

We need to look for God behind our circumstances. He knew everything that was going on with the people of Israel

153

and He knows everything that is going on in our lives. He has our best interests at heart.

IF THE ISRAELITES PUT GOD TO THE TEST BY THE THINGS THAT THEY DID, DO WE NOT ALSO PUT GOD TO THE TEST WHEN WE DO THE SAME THINGS? God had been merciful and patient with these people and spoke no word of rebuke even though they had failed to fully commit themselves to Him in trust and obedience. He now instructed Moses to strike the rock that all the water they needed might be supplied. This miraculous act was performed before the elders of Israel that they might see God's power and believe.

CHAPTER 6

Let's Make a Deal

¹"In the third month after the Israelites left Egypt—on the very day—they came to the Desert of Sinai. ²After they set out from Rephidim, they entered the Desert of Sinai, and Israel camped there in the desert in front of the mountain" (Exod. 19:1-2).

The desert of Sinai and Mt. Sinai are located in the southern portion of the triangular shaped Sinai Peninsula which lies between Egypt and Palestine. The peninsula extends down between the northern arms of the Red Sea. The remainder of the book of Exodus, beginning with Exodus chapter 19, and all of Leviticus and Numbers 1:1—10:10 record the events that took place at Mt. Sinai, the laws given to Moses and the Israelites, and the initiation of God's covenant with them.

There is much to be gained from a careful study of the events, laws and instructions given to the Israelites at Mt. Sinai. Though many spiritual insights and parallels are contained in these passages, we will only touch on them briefly.

Upon their exodus from Egypt, the Israelites had been given God's commandments regarding circumcision and the keeping of the Passover celebration, but not very much beyond that. We have seen how deliverance for the Israelites came because of God's grace and power and the shed blood of sacrificial lambs. The Israelites, by placing their faith in God's Word and the blood of the lambs, and by turning their backs on Egypt, had been delivered by the power of God out of their life of misery in Egypt. Now they would learn how they were to live for this God and become the people that He desired them to be. It would be through them that God would be enabled to reveal His righteous laws to a fallen world.

At Mt. Sinai, God first gave the people the Ten Commandments. These He spoke directly to the people and also wrote on tablets of stone. More detailed moral and ethical laws were also given (which consisted largely of expansions on and expositions of the Ten Commandments) as well as laws pertaining to worship. These laws are recorded in the book of Exodus, beginning in Exodus 20:22 and continuing through the books of Leviticus and Numbers. The whole of the requirements given to the Israelites included 1) the Ten Commandments, 2) laws for civil and social behavior, and 3) regulations governing worship (levitical law).

While some of the subordinate civil and social laws may be considered unique to their day and to the nation of Israel, they give us an understanding of the morality, justice, honesty and respect for others which God expects of us.

The regulations regarding worship provided the means for the Israelites to be forgiven for their sins (the breaking of God's laws) and to be reconciled to God. This reconciliation could only be accomplished through the shedding of blood. The ministry of the priests, and the offering of the various animal sacrifices prescribed by the levitical law met this need up to the coming of Jesus Christ. The levitical law with all of its sacrifices and rituals is now obsolete having found its fulfillment in Jesus Christ who has become our sacrificial Lamb and our High Priest. There is now no longer any need for animal sacrifices and a priesthood to offer them for the people.

At Mt. Sinai, God was going to enter into a covenant with the people of Israel. This covenant would include the Ten Commandments and the civil and levitical laws. Shortly after reaching Mt. Sinai, Moses went up to speak with God ...

> [3]*"Then Moses went up to God, and the LORD called to him from the mountain and said, 'This is what you are to say to the house of Jacob and what you are to tell the people of Israel:* [4]*"You yourselves have seen what I did to Egypt, and how I carried you on eagles' wings and brought you to myself.* [5]*Now if you obey me fully and keep my covenant, then out of all nations you will be my treasured possession. Although the whole earth is mine,* [6]*you will be for me a kingdom of priests and a holy nation.' These are the words you are to speak to the Israelites.'*
> [7]*So Moses went back and summoned the elders of the people and set before them all the words the LORD had commanded him to speak.* [8]**The people all responded together, 'We will do everything the LORD has said[a].'** *So Moses brought their answer back to the LORD"* (Exod. 19:3-8).

The Israelites were to honor and obey the Lord and keep this covenant which He was establishing with them. If they would do that, then out of all nations they would be a unique and special people, a kingdom of priests and a holy nation. For them to be a kingdom of priests would imply that they would be a nation that would represent God to the peoples of the earth, becoming His emissaries and spokesmen to all other nations on the earth.

Up to this point, the Israelites had not heard all that God would require of them since He had not yet given them His commandments, but they vowed to obey God fully and to keep His covenant with them. The first step for their entrance into the covenant had been taken. Now, the more specific provisions and laws of the covenant would be forthcoming.

> [10]*"And the LORD said to Moses, 'Go to the people and consecrate them today and tomorrow. Have them wash their clothes* [11]*and be ready by the third day, because on that day*

---

[a]Emphasis added

the LORD will come down on Mount Sinai in the sight of all the people. *12*Put limits for the people around the mountain and tell them, 'Be careful that you do not go up the mountain or touch the foot of it. Whoever touches the mountain shall surely be put to death. *13*He shall surely be stoned or shot with arrows; not a hand is to be laid on him. Whether man or animal, he shall not be permitted to live.' Only when the ram's horn sounds a long blast may they go up to the mountain.'

*14*After Moses had gone down the mountain to the people, he consecrated them, and they washed their clothes. *15*Then he said to the people, 'Prepare yourselves for the third day. Abstain from sexual relations.'

*16*On the morning of the third day there was thunder and lightning, with a thick cloud over the mountain, and a very loud trumpet blast. Everyone in the camp trembled. *17*Then Moses led the people out of the camp to meet with God, and they stood at the foot of the mountain. *18*Mount Sinai was covered with smoke, because the LORD descended on it in fire. The smoke billowed up from it like smoke from a furnace, the whole mountain trembled violently, *19*and the sound of the trumpet grew louder and louder. Then Moses spoke and the voice of God answered him.

*20*The LORD descended to the top of Mount Sinai and called Moses to the top of the mountain. So Moses went up *21*and the LORD said to him, 'Go down and warn the people so they do not force their way through to see the LORD and many of them perish. *22*Even the priests, who approach the LORD, must consecrate themselves, or the LORD will break out against them.'

*23*Moses said to the LORD, 'The people cannot come up Mount Sinai, because you yourself warned us, 'Put limits around the mountain and set it apart as holy.'

*24*The LORD replied, 'Go down and bring Aaron up with you. But the priests and the people must not force their way through to come up to the LORD, or he will break out against them.'

*25*So Moses went down to the people and told them" (Exod. 19:10-25).

The people were instructed to cleanse and consecrate themselves. This outward cleansing was a picture of the inward cleansing that God requires of His people. The Israelites, who were sinners and unclean in many respects were going to stand before a holy and awesome God. If they even so much as touched the mountain where God's presence would descend, they would perish.

God is a holy God, completely free from sin, completely pure. I am convinced that because we live in a fallen world, we cannot fully appreciate what the holiness of God is like. To illustrate, we live in a world of noise, and it is wonderful to us when we can escape to a place of quiet. We may feel that we know what silence is—but do we really?

An article was written in The Boeing Company internal newspaper a few years back about a room that they built to block out all external noise. Because of the silence in that room, any person who went into that room and sat quietly could hear their heartbeat, the blood flowing through their veins and the many noises that existed in the normal functioning of their bodies—sounds that normally cannot be heard even in the places that we consider quiet because there is still too much noise.

I am sure, that while the individuals who went into that room thought that they had experienced silence before, they now gained a new appreciation for the word. It is the same with respect to the holiness of God. I believe that we are unable to fully comprehend the holiness of God because we have been defiled by our knowledge of evil in this sinful world. Because God is completely holy and pure, He cannot allow man to come into His presence while in his sinful state, and so the Israelites were warned that they would be destroyed if they broke through and even touched the foot of the mountain. The mountain was set apart as holy.

Many years after the Israelites came into the promised land, the prophet Isaiah wrote that he saw the Lord seated in heaven in all of His holiness, and the vision he experienced had a tremendous effect upon him...

> [1]*"In the year that King Uzziah died, I saw the Lord seated on a throne, high and exalted, and the train of his robe filled the temple.* [2]*Above him were seraphs, each with six wings: With two wings they covered their faces, with two they covered their feet, and with two they were flying.* [3]*And they were calling to one another:*
>
> *"Holy, holy, holy is the LORD Almighty; the whole earth is full of his glory."* [4]*At the sound of their voices the doorposts and thresholds shook and the temple was filled with smoke.*
>
> [5]*"Woe to me!" I cried. "I am ruined! For I am a man of unclean lips, and I live among a people of unclean lips, and my eyes have seen the King, the LORD Almighty"* (Isa. 6:1-5).

Isaiah was a man of God, yet he realized his own sinfulness in a way that he had never before experienced when he came face to face with the holiness of God.

It was in the awesome display of God's presence that the Ten Commandments were spoken to the Israelites. The Israelites needed to understand the seriousness of the covenant they would be making with God and of the laws that would be included in this covenant.

> [18]*"When the people saw the thunder and lightning and heard the trumpet and saw the mountain in smoke, they trembled with fear. They stayed at a distance* [19]*and said to Moses, 'Speak to us yourself and we will listen. But do not have God speak to us or we will die.'*
>
> [20]*Moses said to the people, 'Do not be afraid. God has come to test you, so that the fear of God will be with you to keep you from sinning'"* (Exod. 20:18-20).

It was important that the Israelites gain an appreciation and a healthy respect for God and not take this covenant lightly. As it says, *"The fear of the LORD is the beginning of wisdom ..."* (Ps. 111:10); *"the fear of the LORD is a fountain of life, turning*

160

a man from the snares of death (Pr. 14:27); and "*... through the fear of the LORD a man avoids evil*" (Pr 16:6).

Moses then went up before the Lord and received from Him the more detailed laws of the covenant. After he had received them, Moses again returned to the people...

> [3]"*When Moses went and told the people all the LORD's words and laws, they responded with one voice, 'Everything the LORD has said we will do.'* [4]*Moses then wrote down everything the LORD had said.*
>
> *He got up early the next morning and built an altar at the foot of the mountain and set up twelve stone pillars representing the twelve tribes of Israel.* [5]*Then he sent young Israelite men, and they offered burnt offerings and sacrificed young bulls as fellowship offerings to the LORD.* [6]*Moses took half of the blood and put it in bowls, and the other half he sprinkled on the altar.* [7]*Then he took the Book of the Covenant and read it to the people. They responded, 'We will do everything the LORD has said; we will obey.'"*[b]
>
> [8]*Moses then took the blood, sprinkled it on the people and said, 'This is the blood of the covenant that the LORD has made with you in accordance with all these words'"* (Exod. 24:3-8).

We have seen that at three different times, the Israelites pledged themselves to be obedient to God's requirements, stating, **"We will do everything the LORD has said; we will obey"** (Exod. 19:8; 24:3,7). Moses took the blood of the sacrificed animals and sprinkled it on the people. By their oaths and the sprinkling of blood upon them, the people entered into a solemn and binding covenant with God. In this covenant God promised that Israel would be His treasured possession and would be for God a kingdom of priests and a holy nation. In return, Israel had agreed to keep all the requirements of the covenant and obey God fully.

---

[b]Emphasis added

161

Some time later Moses told the Israelites...

> [5]*"See, I have taught you decrees and laws as the LORD my God commanded me, so that you may follow them in the land you are entering to take possession of it. [6]Observe them carefully, for this will show your wisdom and understanding to the nations, who will hear about all these decrees and say, 'Surely this great nation is a wise and understanding people.' [7]What other nation is so great as to have their gods near them the way the LORD our God is near us whenever we pray to him? [8]And what other nation is so great as to have such righteous decrees and laws as this body of laws I am setting before you today?*
>
> [9]*Only be careful, and watch yourselves closely so that you do not forget the things your eyes have seen or let them slip from your heart as long as you live. Teach them to your children and to their children after them'"* (Deut. 4:5-9).

God promised tremendous benefits to the Israelites if they would live for Him and keep the covenant they had entered into...

> [20]*"See, I am sending an angel ahead of you to guard you along the way and to bring you to the place I have prepared. [21]Pay attention to him and listen to what he says. Do not rebel against him; he will not forgive your rebellion, since my Name is in him. [22]If you listen carefully to what he says and do all that I say, I will be an enemy to your enemies and will oppose those who oppose you. [23]My angel will go ahead of you and bring you into the land of the Amorites, Hittites, Perizzites, Canaanites, Hivites and Jebusites, and I will wipe them out. [24]Do not bow down before their gods or worship them or follow their practices. You must demolish them and break their sacred stones to pieces. [25]Worship the LORD your God, and his blessing will be on your food and water. I will take away sickness from among you, [26]and none will miscarry or be barren in your land. I will give you a full life span.*

*²⁷'I will send my terror ahead of you and throw into con-
fusion every nation you encounter. I will make all your enemies turn their backs and run. ²⁸I will send the hornet ahead
of you to drive the Hivites, Canaanites and Hittites out of
your way. ²⁹But I will not drive them out in a single year,
because the land would become desolate and the wild animals too numerous for you. ³⁰Little by little I will drive them
out before you, until you have increased enough to take possession of the land.'*

*³¹'I will establish your borders from the Red Sea to the Sea of
the Philistines, and from the desert to the River. I will hand over
to you the people who live in the land and you will drive them
out before you. ³²Do not make a covenant with them or with
their gods. ³³Do not let them live in your land, or they will cause
you to sin against me, because the worship of their gods will
certainly be a snare to you'"* (Exod. 23:20-33).

God promised the Israelites that if they did what He required,
His blessing would be upon them. The God of heaven and earth
would care for them in every way. God clearly revealed the blessings that would come on the Israelites if they would but keep
the requirements of the covenant, but also forewarned them of
the curses that would come if they rejected Him (see blessings -
Deut. 28:1-14; curses - Deut 28:15-68).

When God's ways are adhered to by faith and obedience,
there is a wall of God's protection built up around us. When we
violate His laws, then the wall is broken down and the enemy
gains access to us.

Israel was to be a kingdom of priests and a holy nation.
However, the Old Testament clearly shows how Israel ultimately
violated and rejected God's covenant with them. God was
faithful to keep all His promises, but the Israelites hearts became hard and they turned away from Him. Therefore, the
terrible consequences of their disobedience—the curses of the
law —came upon them and they were scattered over the whole
earth. While scripture still contains many promises which
pertain to the nation of Israel which are being, and are yet to

be fulfilled, yet they have suffered terribly as a consequence of their rejection of God's covenant with them.

With the death and resurrection of Jesus Christ, God established a New Covenant—a "New Testament" in His blood which is not meant for the people of a single nation, but to all on this earth—Jews and Gentiles alike—who will come to God through faith in Jesus Christ.

> *"Here there is no Greek or Jew, circumcised or uncircumcised, barbarian, Scythian, slave or free, but Christ is all, and is in all"* (Col. 3:11).

This New Covenant has made the old one obsolete (Heb. 8:13). Whereas God had called Israel to be a kingdom of priests and a holy nation, He now gives this distinction to all who come to HIm by faith in Jesus Christ. God now makes a wonderful declaration to all who enter into this New Covenant...

> [9]*"...you are a chosen people, a royal priesthood, a holy nation, a people belonging to God, that you may declare the praises of him who called you out of darkness into his wonderful light.* [10]*Once you were not a people, but now you are the people of God; once you had not received mercy, but now you have received mercy"* (1 Pet. 2:9-10).

The New Covenant is based upon better promises (Heb. 8:6). As we enter into this New Covenant, we are sanctified by the blood of Jesus, and God's laws are written upon our hearts and minds (Heb. 8:10). We are to live lives of faith and obedience to the Lord Jesus Christ. We are now part of a "royal priesthood" that is to declare the praises of God. But we will be wise to consider the tragedy which befell the Israelites as a consequence of their rebellion. We are warned to see to it that none of us has a sinful unbelieving heart that turns away from the living God (Heb. 3:12). We have been purchased by the blood of Christ and therefore our lives no longer belong to us ...

[19]*"Do you not know that your body is a temple of the Holy Spirit, who is in you, whom you have received from God? You are not your own;* [20]*you were bought at a price. Therefore honor God with your body"* (1 Cor. 6:19-20).

So we are no longer to live just to please ourselves, but to please Him who purchased us by His own blood...

[1]*"Therefore, I urge you, brothers, in view of God's mercy, to offer your bodies as living sacrifices, holy and pleasing to God—this is your spiritual act of worship.* [2]*Do not conform any longer to the pattern of this world, but be transformed by the renewing of your mind. Then you will be able to test and approve what God's will is-- his good, pleasing and perfect will"* (Rom. 12:1-2).

[14]*"For Christ's love compels us, because we are convinced that one died for all, and therefore all died.* [15]*And he died for all, that those who live should no longer live for themselves but for him who died for them and was raised again"* (2 Cor. 5:14-15).

When we come to Jesus Christ to be saved, we do not come just to receive an eternal life insurance policy. Rather, we come to begin a new life which has Christ at its center. Our aim must now be to please Him in everything we do. We must not think that our salvation is so eternally secured that we can live any way we want and still be acceptable in the eyes of God. If anyone thinks that way, there is room for reasonable doubt as to whether he has truly repented of his sin and come to know Christ at all.

[26]*"If we deliberately keep on sinning after we have received the knowledge of the truth, no sacrifice for sins is left,* [27]*but only a fearful expectation of judgment and of raging fire that will consume the enemies of God.* [28]*Anyone who rejected the law of Moses died without mercy on the testimony of two or three witnesses.* [29]*How much more severely do you think a man deserves to be punished who has trampled the Son of God under foot, who has treated as an*

unholy thing the blood of the covenant that sanctified him, and who has insulted the Spirit of grace? [30]For we know him who said, 'It is mine to avenge; I will repay,' and again, 'The Lord will judge his people.' [31]It is a dreadful thing to fall into the hands of the living God'" (Heb. 10:26-31).

Also ...

[18] *"You have not come to a mountain that can be touched and that is burning with fire; to darkness, gloom and storm; [19]to a trumpet blast or to such a voice speaking words that those who heard it begged that no further word be spoken to them, [20]because they could not bear what was commanded: 'If even an animal touches the mountain, it must be stoned.' [21]The sight was so terrifying that Moses said, 'I am trembling with fear.'"*

[22]*But you have come to Mount Zion, to the heavenly Jerusalem, the city of the living God. You have come to thousands upon thousands of angels in joyful assembly, [23]to the church of the firstborn, whose names are written in heaven. You have come to God, the judge of all men, to the spirits of righteous men made perfect, [24]to Jesus the mediator of a new covenant, and to the sprinkled blood that speaks a better word than the blood of Abel.*

[25]*See to it that you do not refuse him who speaks. If they did not escape when they refused him who warned them on earth, how much less will we, if we turn away from him who warns us from heaven? [26]At that time his voice shook the earth, but now he has promised, 'Once more I will shake not only the earth but also the heavens.' [27]The words once more indicate the removing of what can be shaken—that is, created things—so that what cannot be shaken may remain.*

[28]*Therefore, since we are receiving a kingdom that cannot be shaken, let us be thankful, and so worship God acceptably with reverence and awe, [29]for our 'God is a consuming fire'"* (Heb. 12:18-29).

God came down on the mountain to test the Israelites that the fear of God might keep them from sinning (Exod.

20:20). So we too must "worship God acceptably with reverence and awe, for our God is *"a consuming fire."*

In the book of Deuteronomy, at the time they were finally going to enter the promised land, Moses talked with the people about obeying the voice of the Lord their God, keeping His commandments and His statutes, and turning to the Lord their God with all their heart, mind and strength. He said that all of this was not too hard for them to do. It was within their grasp. It was not some kind of secret laid up in heaven that someone would need to go and bring it down to them. It was not beyond the sea, that they should say, Who shall go over the sea for us, and bring it to us, that we may hear and do it? But rather, the Word (what God requires) is very near you, in your mouth, and in your mind and in your heart, so that you can do it (Deut. 30:11-15). It is the same with us. God has clearly delineated in His Word what He desires of us. It is not too hard for us to understand. For those who have never come to Jesus by faith, the Word of salvation is near and is yours to receive.

8"...The Word (God's message in Christ) is near you, on your lips and in your heart; that is, the Word—the message, the basis and object—of faith, which we preach. 9Because if you acknowledge and confess with your lips that Jesus is Lord and in your heart believe (adhere to, trust in and rely on the truth) that God raised Him from the dead, you will be saved. 10For with the heart a person believes (adheres to, trusts in and relies on Christ) and so is justified (declared righteous, acceptable to God), and with the mouth he confesses—declares openly and speaks out freely his faith—and confirms [his] salvation. 11The Scripture says, No man who believes in Him—who adheres to, relies on and trusts in Him—will [ever] be put to shame or be disappointed. 12[No one,] for there is no distinction between Jew and Greek. The same Lord is Lord over all [of us] and He generously bestows His riches upon all who call upon Him [in faith]. 13For every one who calls upon the name of the Lord [invoking Him as Lord] will be saved" (Rom. 10:8-13 AMP).

If you have previously received Christ as Lord but have wandered away from Him or have not lived for Him as you should, then that Word is also standing before you—that Word of repentance and restoration. It is available for you to act upon. Each one of us must set our hearts to do what He desires; to turn to Him with all of our heart, soul, mind and strength.

When we follow the Lord with all of our being we will find the blessing of the Lord which brings no sorrow or trouble with it. His blessing will eventually come if we persist in doing good and are patient in waiting upon the Lord. If we turn away in impatience from the Lord's path or we allow ourselves to be attracted by the glitter, glamour or sensuousness of what Satan has to offer and partake of it, it may satisfy for a short time but will ultimately bring the emptiness, bitterness and the sorrow that always accompanies sin—a sorrow and pain that can last a lifetime. He sets before us the choice: to receive through His hand that which will make life rich, full and productive, or to reject what He offers and to continue living a life that will ultimately bring only sorrow, pain and regret.

Faith and obedience to God are inseparable. If we do not believe in Him, we will not obey Him. Even if we know that He exists, we may still not obey Him unless we are convinced of His love for us. The single most important factor which will motivate our obedience to the Lord is a knowledge of the genuineness and depth of that love. If we are convinced that all that God requires of us is based in His love for us, we will be quick to do what He asks. Once we come to Christ by faith, we are enabled to grow in that knowledge of His love.

[16]"*I pray that out of his glorious riches he may strengthen you with power through his Spirit in your inner being,* [17]*so that Christ may dwell in your hearts through faith. And I pray that you, being rooted and established in love,* [18]*may have power, together with all the saints, to grasp how wide and long and high and deep is the love of Christ,* [19]*and to*

know this love that surpasses knowledge—that you may be filled to the measure of all the fullness of God" (Eph. 3:16-19).

When Moses went up on Mt. Sinai to meet with the Lord, the Lord declared His love ...

[5]*"Then the LORD came down in the cloud and stood there with him and proclaimed his name, the LORD.* [6]*And he passed in front of Moses, proclaiming, 'The LORD, the LORD, the compassionate and gracious God, slow to anger, abounding in love and faithfulness,* [7]*maintaining love to thousands, and forgiving wickedness, rebellion and sin. Yet he does not leave the guilty unpunished; he punishes the children and their children for the sin of the fathers to the third and fourth generation.'* [8]*Moses bowed to the ground at once and worshiped"* (Exod. 34:4-8).

Compassionate, gracious, slow to anger, abounding in love and faithfulness, maintaining love to thousands, forgiving wickedness, rebellion and sin are characteristics of this God who loves us with a deep and steadfast love that is beyond our comprehension. However, it also says that He does not leave the guilty unpunished. He expects us to choose the right path, and to turn away from that which is evil.

In the book of Deuteronomy, the nature of God's love is expressed many times. Among those passages is the following:

[7]*"The LORD did not set his affection on you and choose you because you were more numerous than other peoples, for you were the fewest of all peoples.* [8]*But it was because the LORD loved you and kept the oath he swore to your forefathers that he brought you out with a mighty hand and redeemed you from the land of slavery, from the power of Pharaoh king of Egypt.* [9]*Know therefore that the LORD your God is God; he is the faithful God, keeping his covenant of love to a thousand generations of those who love him and keep his commands"* (Deut. 7:7-9).

The covenant which God established with the Israelites is referred to here as His "covenant of love." Strict laws were made a part of this covenant. These laws were not meant to be burdensome, but were an expression of His love. The keeping of these laws would provide a blessing for them. If the Israelites could but understand that all God asked of them was rooted in His deep love for them, it would bring their wholehearted obedience.

"...O LORD, God of Israel, there is no God like you in heaven above or on earth below—you who keep your covenant of love with your servants who continue wholeheartedly in your way" (1 Kings 8:23).

Satan works to convince us that God doesn't exist or doesn't love us, has forsaken us and only wants to punish us. He comes to convince us that if we follow the Lord wholeheartedly we will miss out on "the good stuff" in this life. However, Satan's purpose is to keep us from following the Lord wholeheartedly. To the extent we depart from obedience to the Lord, to that extent we will be prevented from receiving the best God has for us.

For example, there should be no reason for a Christian couple to have a bad marriage, although we know that every marriage will have its difficulties to overcome. God has given instructions for living and for marriage, that if followed, will provide strong, happy marriages. As couples work within God's principles to overcome the difficulties they face, their marriages will become stronger and more satisfying. However, to the extent that either or both individuals choose to go their own selfish way instead of God's way, to that extent their marriage will have problems.

This same principle applies in every area of our lives. We must come to the place where we will follow the Lord wholeheartedly even when everything seems to be going wrong or contrary to what we would like in the natural. We must hold to a firm faith in God and a realization of His love for us that will cause us to do what He asks. It is in the time of difficulty that Satan will come to us and say, "See, you really can't trust in God. He doesn't really want the best for you or He would have given you what you wanted." We must reject that word from the enemy and realize instead that God loves us dearly and has promised never to leave us or forsake us (Heb. 13:5). Obedience to God will in the long run bring the greatest blessing to us. God spoke the following words to the Israelites in a difficult time of their existence when they had been taken captive into Babylon. They are words which I believe apply to all of us...

> "'For I know the plans I have for you,' declares the LORD, 'plans to prosper you and not to harm you, plans to give you hope and a future'" (Jer. 29:11).

We must remain steadfast in our faith and obedience to the Lord and continue to follow Him wholeheartedly. Consider Joseph who was thrown in prison though he was innocent. He remained faithful to God, and God exalted him to the right hand of Pharaoh. In the middle of his difficulties, Joseph may not have had a clue as to why he was in prison, but he did not turn away from the Lord, but continued his obedience.

Job also couldn't see behind the scenes to understand that the difficulties he faced were a test designed by Satan to get him to curse God. Even Job's wife encouraged him to curse God and die. However, Job did not turn against God because he believed in God's love and faithfulness even though he did not understand what was going on.

We see that the prophet Jonah rebelled against God's Word to him and tried to run away. When he found himself in the belly of the whale, he came back to the realization that God was his true hope...

> [7]"When my soul fainted within me I remembered the LORD: and my prayer came in unto thee, into thine holy

temple. ⁸They that observe lying vanities forsake their own mercy. ⁹But I will sacrifice unto thee with the voice of thanksgiving; I will pay that that I have vowed. Salvation is of the LORD.

¹⁰And the LORD spake unto the fish, and it vomited out Jonah upon the dry land" (Jonah 2:7-10 KJV).

If we are not steadfast in our faith and understanding of God's love and are not convinced that absolute obedience to God will bring His greatest blessings, we will have a tendency to turn away from God. It will be easier for us to lose faith when we are faced with trials and tests which we don't understand. Instead of trusting and being obedient to God we will find it easy to compromise, justifying our disobedience by saying, "I'm sure God understands that I had to compromise for good reason." It is in this way that we allow sins of disobedience to creep into our lives.

We must have a commitment to trust God no matter what comes into our lives, to realize His goodness, His love for us, and to know that to trust and obey Him will bring us the absolute best.

The Levitical laws given to the Israelites laid out the requirements for the priests in Israel. These requirements provide a spiritual picture of how we as priests in the Kingdom of God (1 Pet. 2:9-10; Rev. 1:6) are to live and walk. During their ordination they were bathed and clothed in special garments made out of linen which represents holiness and righteousness (Rev. 19:8). They were anointed with oil, symbolic of the Holy Spirit. They were sanctified (set apart to God) as priests that they might represent the people before God. Daily, as they came to minister before God and to the people, they had to come to the altar to present an offering for their own sins and to wash their hands and feet in the laver. In all that they did as priests, they were to maintain a holy walk before the Lord.

So it must be for us. We cannot take lightly our calling to holiness. As priests, we are to be His representatives in a sinful world. We must order and examine our lives daily in accordance with His Word, seeking His forgiveness and cleansing from any sin that we might maintain a holy walk before Him and before the world. Our greatest desire must be to subject ourselves to His will in all things.

The Israelites had entered into a covenant with the Lord. If they would walk in accordance with the covenant they had now agreed to, they would be the recipients of all the blessings of the covenant. If not, they would be subject to its curses (see Deut. 28). God had called them to a walk of faith and obedience. We shall soon see how well they did.

After the covenant had been confirmed with the people, the Lord again spoke to Moses...

> [12]"The LORD said to Moses, 'Come up to me on the mountain and stay here, and I will give you the tablets of stone, with the law and commands I have written for their instruction.'
>
> [13]Then Moses set out with Joshua his aide, and Moses went up on the mountain of God. [14]He said to the elders, 'Wait here for us until we come back to you. Aaron and Hur are with you, and anyone involved in a dispute can go to them.'
>
> [15]When Moses went up on the mountain, the cloud covered it, [16]and the glory of the LORD settled on Mount Sinai. For six days the cloud covered the mountain, and on the seventh day the LORD called to Moses from within the cloud. [17]To the Israelites the glory of the LORD looked like a consuming fire on top of the mountain. [18]Then Moses entered the cloud as he went on up the mountain. And he stayed on the mountain forty days and forty nights" (Exod 24:12-18).

Moses ascended the mountain to now receive the tablets of stone. During his forty day absence, the Israelites became restless...

[1]*"When the people saw that Moses was so long in coming down from the mountain, they gathered around Aaron and said, 'Come, make us gods who will go before us. As for this fellow Moses who brought us up out of Egypt, we don't know what has happened to him.'*

[2]*Aaron answered them, 'Take off the gold earrings that your wives, your sons and your daughters are wearing, and bring them to me.'* [3]*So all the people took off their earrings and brought them to Aaron.* [4]*He took what they handed him and made it into an idol cast in the shape of a calf, fashioning it with a tool. Then they said, 'These are your gods,[c] O Israel, who brought you up out of Egypt.'*

[5]*When Aaron saw this, he built an altar in front of the calf and announced, 'Tomorrow there will be a festival to the LORD.'* [6]*So the next day the people rose early and sacrificed burnt offerings and presented fellowship offerings. Afterward they sat down to eat and drink and got up to indulge in revelry.*

[7]*Then the LORD said to Moses, 'Go down, because your people, whom you brought up out of Egypt, have become corrupt.* [8]*They have been quick to turn away from what I commanded them and have made themselves an idol cast in the shape of a calf. They have bowed down to it and sacrificed to it and have said, 'These are your gods[c], O Israel, who brought you up out of Egypt.'*

[9]*'I have seen these people,' the LORD said to Moses, 'and they are a stiff-necked people.* [10]*Now leave me alone so that my anger may burn against them and that I may destroy them. Then I will make you into a great nation.'*

[11]*But Moses sought the favor of the LORD his God. 'O LORD,' he said, 'why should your anger burn against your people, whom you brought out of Egypt with great power and a mighty hand?* [12]*Why should the Egyptians say, 'It was with evil intent that he brought them out, to kill them in the mountains and to wipe them off the face of the earth'? Turn from your fierce anger; relent and do not bring disaster on your people.* [13]*Remember your servants Abraham, Isaac and Israel, to whom you swore by your own self: I will make your descendants*

---

[c]Or *This is your god;* also in verse 8

174

as numerous as the stars in the sky and I will give your descendants all this land I promised them, and it will be their inheritance forever.'" [14]Then the LORD relented and did not bring on his people the disaster he had threatened.

[15]Moses turned and went down the mountain with the two tablets of the Testimony in his hands. They were inscribed on both sides, front and back. [16]The tablets were the work of God; the writing was the writing of God, engraved on the tablets.

[17]When Joshua heard the noise of the people shouting, he said to Moses, 'There is the sound of war in the camp.' [18]Moses replied: 'It is not the sound of victory, it is not the sound of defeat; it is the sound of singing that I hear.'

[19]When Moses approached the camp and saw the calf and the dancing, his anger burned and he threw the tablets out of his hands, breaking them to pieces at the foot of the mountain. [20]And he took the calf they had made and burned it in the fire; then he ground it to powder, scattered it on the water and made the Israelites drink it.

[21]He said to Aaron, 'What did these people do to you, that you led them into such great sin?'

[22]'Do not be angry, my lord,' Aaron answered. 'You know how prone these people are to evil. [23]They said to me, `Make us gods who will go before us. As for this fellow Moses who brought us up out of Egypt, we don't know what has happened to him.' [24]So I told them, `Whoever has any gold jewelry, take it off.' Then they gave me the gold, and I threw it into the fire, and out came this calf!'

[25]Moses saw that the people were running wild and that Aaron had let them get out of control and so become a laughingstock to their enemies. [26]So he stood at the entrance to the camp and said, 'Whoever is for the LORD, come to me.' And all the Levites rallied to him.

[27]Then he said to them, 'This is what the LORD, the God of Israel, says: 'Each man strap a sword to his side. Go back and forth through the camp from one end to the other, each killing his brother and friend and neighbor.' [28]The Levites did as Moses commanded, and that day about three thousand of the people died. [29]Then Moses said, 'You have been set apart to the LORD today, for you were against your own sons and brothers, and he has blessed you this day.'

30The next day Moses said to the people, 'You have committed a great sin. But now I will go up to the LORD; perhaps I can make atonement for your sin.'

31So Moses went back to the LORD and said, 'Oh, what a great sin these people have committed! They have made themselves gods of gold. 32But now, please forgive their sin—but if not, then blot me out of the book you have written.'

33The LORD replied to Moses, 'Whoever has sinned against me I will blot out of my book. 34Now go, lead the people to the place I spoke of, and my angel will go before you. However, when the time comes for me to punish, I will punish them for their sin.'

35And the LORD struck the people with a plague because of what they did with the calf Aaron had made" (Exod. 32:1-35).

The whole situation that we see here was a test of Israel's commitment and their faith and trust in God. Moses, their visual link with God was no longer with them. They had been given God's covenant promises, and in the awesome display of God's presence they had made a commitment to the Lord to live according to that covenant. Now they were left alone and their commitment would be tested.

The Israelites couldn't see God and now they couldn't see Moses. They didn't want to worship and place their trust in an unseen God but in something they could see. What foolishness to consider that an idol fashioned by themselves with a tool should be an object of worship and trust. *"These are your gods, O Israel, which brought you up out of the land of Egypt!"*

Aaron built an altar before it and made a proclamation, saying, *"Tomorrow shall be a feast to the Lord."* They rose up early the next day and offered burnt offerings and brought peace offering; and the people sat down to eat and drink, and rose up to play.

Within man there is the knowledge that there is a God. Many seek after the supernatural to grant them a greater feeling of security and to fill that void which is within them. They seek after a "god" who will make minimal demands upon them thereby allowing them to continue to do as they please. Even some who believe that the God of the Bible exists do not want to come to Him on His terms, but desire to make Him into a God of no demands, who does not require them to repent of their sin and surrender their lives to Him. And so they erect a golden calf, a god of their own design to worship. This god does not speak of sin and hell as Jesus did. He does not demand repentance from sin and a whole-hearted turning to God. He is mute about such things and allows them to "feel good" and get their "religious obligations" out of the way so that they get on with doing their own thing. Some turn to a watered-down version of Christianity, or to a generic god, or astrology, witchcraft, and other assorted "new age" (really old age) teachings which make no demands on them for holiness as God's Word does. In fact, the longer they remain in these beliefs, the more chance there is that they will become subject to greater and greater evil. They want to pursue the things of the supernatural, but certainly not the demands that God makes for holy living and obedience.

Aaron said, *"Tomorrow shall be a feast unto the Lord."* Yet, the golden calf had nothing to do with the Lord, and was in fact an abomination to Him. The calf was just a hunk of metal. If there was any power associated with it at all, it would have been demonic power. The Apostle Paul spoke in the New Testament about the significance of offering sacrifices to idols ...

> [19]*"Do I mean then that a sacrifice offered to an idol is anything, or that an idol is anything?* [20]*No, but the sacrifices of pagans are offered to demons, not to God, and I do not want you to be participants with demons.* [21]*You cannot drink the cup of the Lord and the cup of demons too; you cannot have a part in both the Lord's table and the table of demons"* (1 Cor. 10:19-21).

What Paul is saying is that demons, not gods, stand behind and are the object of idol worship. Therefore it can be easily understood why such worship is an abomination to God. The demons of hell are behind every form of false worship. There are many today who can, and do, testify to being slowly brought under demonic power and oppression as they became increasingly involved in "new age" philosophies and activities which in the beginning seemed so innocent.

Aaron invoked the name "the Lord" when he said, *"Tomorrow there will be a festival to the Lord."* I believe that he was referring to the true God when he made this announcement, but he had been intimidated into compromise with the golden calf. What was happening was a terrible mixture of religion and the Lord wasn't in it. It is similar to today where "religion" has been mixed with true biblical Christianity creating a man-made abomination which does not reflect the power of God. It makes no demands on people at all and the Lord is not in it.

It reminds me of an individual who writes regularly on religion in the newspaper. This man has the title "Reverend." He is believed by many to be a man of God and has preached in churches for years. He is venerated by the politicians and media elite for his wonderful liberal Christian views. He talks about God, he talks about the Bible, but only as it suits him. He picks and chooses what he wants from the Bible believing it to be just some kind of good book (perhaps even inspired by God) but which gives only "guidelines" for living. To him there is no hell and there is no real sin in individual lives which must be cleansed by the blood of Jesus Christ, even though the Bible clearly talks about these things. There is lots of talk about good works, positive thinking, the golden rule etc. No mention is made that men are sinners alienated from God and in need of a Savior, and certainly not that they need to be born again lest they face God's wrath and judgement. He soothes those who want to be comforted in their sin and gives them

178

wonderful assurances that if they just do good things every-thing will be all right. He erects a golden calf, fashioned by man, that people can turn to every so often when they are in need of a little religion to comfort them before they go back to their own form of revelry. The blind who follow him and others like him say, "O, isn't he such a wonderful man. I just love his preaching!" Even though such preachers have a form of godliness, it is doubtful that they have ever met Jesus personally and been born again.

There is no difference between those who use the Bible to preach a watered down powerless gospel and those who erected the golden calf. God had given the Israelites His Word and had told them what He expected of them. He said, *"I am the Lord your God, who brought you out of Egypt, out of the land of slavery."* Yet here we see rabble rousers saying after they had erected the golden calf, *"These are your gods (or this is your god), O Israel, who brought you up out of Egypt."*

God had commanded them, *"You shall have no other gods before me,"* and *"You shall not make for yourself an idol in the form of anything in heaven above or on earth beneath or in the waters below. You shall not bow down to them or worship them; for I, the Lord your God, am a jealous God, punishing the children for the sin of the fathers to the third and fourth generation of those who hate me, but showing love to a thousand generations of those who love me and keep my commandments."* They were also commanded, *"You shall not misuse the name of the Lord your God, for the Lord will not hold anyone guiltless who misuses his name."*

The Israelites had received these very specific commands from God regarding false worship and false gods. They had received these words and trembled as God displayed His awesomeness before them to keep them from sinning. Yet, in the span of a very short time (a couple of months maybe), the Israelites turned from these very specific and very clear commands from the Lord, to set up their own brand of gospel. In so doing, they had treated God with contempt.

Those who today stand as preachers or teachers of the gospel but deny in their preaching the basic doctrines of the Bible will someday face an angry God unless they repent of the error of their ways. God will not hold anyone guiltless who misuses His name.

It is also tragic to realize that there are undoubtedly many who sit in churches today who believe that they are Christians but have never truly met Jesus. They may think that they know God but they have never been born again (regenerated) by the power of the Holy Spirit and their lives reflect this lack. They are unable to understand the Bible even though they may have been in church for years, there is no real zeal for God or for holy living, there is no joy and rejoicing in the Lord and no desire to speak about Him or His Word. In reality, they do not have a vital, living relationship with the Lord Jesus Christ and lack the power to live the Christian life as Jesus requires. If they have had the gospel preached to them, they have either not understood the truth or have continually rejected it. Though they may not realize it, they are merely going through the motions.

Today it is quite possible that even the pastor who these people look to as their guide, may not know Him either. Some individuals enter and graduate from seminary without ever coming to know Jesus Christ as their Lord and Savior. Their preaching and teaching betrays them because there is no real power in their preaching and they water down and/or pervert the gospel of Jesus Christ as revealed in His Word. They do not declare to individuals that they are sinners who must repent and be born again by the power of God if they are to avoid the future wrath and judgement of God, even though the Bible clearly declares this. Instead they preach a "do good, power of positive thinking" kind of gospel which ignores sin and makes Christ's sacrificial death on the cross of no essential value.

If there is no such thing as sin then Jesus did not need to die on the cross. The Bible says that Christ died to take the penalty of our sin upon Himself. The Bible says ...

"For all have sinned..." (Rom. 3:23).

"...without the shedding of blood there is no forgiveness" (Heb. 9:22).

"For Christ died for sins once for all, the righteous for the unrighteous, to bring you to God..." (1 Pet. 3:18).

It is necessary for each individual to be "born again."

3 "...Jesus declared, 'I tell you the truth, no one can see the kingdom of God unless he is born again.'
5 '...I tell you the truth, no one can enter the kingdom of God unless he is born of water and the Spirit. 6 Flesh gives birth to flesh, but the Spirit gives birth to spirit. 7 You should not be surprised at my saying, 'You must be born again'" (John 3:3,5-7).

These words from our Savior are very clear, "you must be born again."

When we are born again we are transformed by the power of the Holy Spirit, and the Holy Spirit comes to dwell in us. As Peter said ...

"...Repent and be baptized, every one of you, in the name of Jesus Christ for the forgiveness of your sins. And you will receive the gift of the Holy Spirit" (Acts 2:38).

Jesus earlier spoke of the fact that those who would come to believe in Him would receive the Holy Spirit ...

38 "Whoever believes in me, as the Scripture has said, streams of living water will flow from within him.' 39 By this he meant the Spirit, whom those who believed in him were later to receive. Up to that time the Spirit had not been given, since Jesus had not yet been glorified'" (John 7:38-39).

It is essential to understand that if we are not born again and do not have the Holy Spirit dwelling within us, we do not belong to Christ and cannot please God ...

[8]*"Those controlled by the sinful nature cannot please God.* [9]*You, however, are controlled not by the sinful nature but by the Spirit, if the Spirit of God lives in you. And **if anyone does not have the Spirit of Christ, he does not belong to Christ"**[d](Rom. 8:8-9).*

Many have been taught in times past that they should not try and read the Bible because they cannot understand it. It is true, that much of what God's Word has to say will not be understandable to any individual who has not been born again (received salvation) and received the Spirit of God. It was by the inspiration of the Holy Spirit that the Bible was written ...

[20]*'Above all, you must understand that no prophecy of Scripture came about by the prophet's own interpretation.* [21]*For prophecy never had its origin in the will of man, but men spoke from God as they were carried along by the Holy Spirit"* (2 Pet. 1:20-21).

It is through the Holy Spirit of God that we are enabled to understand the scriptures. The things of God will appear as so much foolishness if we do not have the Holy Spirit of God living within us ...

[11]*"For who among men knows the thoughts of a man except the man's spirit within him? In the same way no one knows the thoughts of God except the Spirit of God.* [12]**We have not received the spirit of the world but the Spirit who is from**

---

[d] Emphasis added

182

God, that we may understand what God has freely given us.[e] [13]*This is what we speak, not in words taught us by human wisdom but in words taught by the Spirit, expressing spiritual truths in spiritual words.* [14]**The man without the Spirit does not accept the things that come from the Spirit of God, for they are foolishness to him, and he cannot understand them, because they are spiritually discerned"**[f] (1 Cor. 2:11-14).

So it is clear that unless a person comes to truly know God (repents of his sin, turns to God with his whole heart and is born again by the Spirit of God), he will fail to properly understand God's Word and will be unable to teach it to others. It will be the blind leading the blind. As we have seen, there will be individuals who are forever learning but are never able to come to a knowledge of the truth (2 Tim. 2:7). It is declared that God wants all men to be saved for it is then that they will be enabled to come to a Holy Spirit inspired knowledge of the truth (1 Tim. 2:3-4).

In considering this story of the rebellion of the Israelites, we see that Moses removed himself from the Israelites as he went up to meet with God. In like manner, even when we truly know God, there are times when He seems to remove Himself from us so that we are unable to sense His presence as we have at other times. It is then that we need to be careful. Our faith in Jesus must be rooted in the Word of God and not in our feelings. Even when the Lord seems distant, we must continue to read the Word, to pray and to remain steadfast in our commitment, devotion and obedience to Him.

God has given us the ability to think and make decisions apart from feelings. We certainly have much to be emotional about when we consider all that God has done for us and we have ample reason to let our emotions show as we rejoice in Him. However, those who profess Christ must not base their

---

[e] Emphasis added
[f] Emphasis added

faith on their feelings. Otherwise, when a severe disappointment or a trial comes their faith will fall apart. It is when God seems far away and trials come to test us, that we must remind ourselves of our commitment to the Lord, of His faithfulness and goodness and of His promises to us in His word. We must decide that we will not be moved from our confidence in Christ. We must continue to pray and read the word, seeking His strength to help us stand fast. We must not let our emotions rule us such that we would turn away in unbelief.

At times when God seems withdrawn from us, we too may be vulnerable to those who would scoff at our commitment to Jesus Christ. We note that the scoffers gathered around Aaron and said, *"Come, make us gods who will go before us. As for this fellow Moses who brought us up out of Egypt, we don't know what has happened to him."* In the same way, in our times of difficulty when God seems distant, we may hear Satan say to us, *"Where is this God you say you trust? He's let you down hasn't he? He's nowhere around because He's a figment of your imagination. If He were real He wouldn't have let you go through this!"*

We can wonder just who the individuals were who came and said to Aaron...*"Come, make us gods who will go before us."* Perhaps some were leaders of the people. They were certainly individuals with little or no faith and scoffers—doubting ring leaders who were able to sway others away from a position of faith during this time of Moses' absence.

I don't believe that all of the doubting Israelites turned away from the Lord of their own doing. Many were swayed into disobedience by the unbelieving ones. Those who gathered around Aaron to get him to make a golden calf and institute false worship were rabble rousers who, in spite of what they had seen, did not want to submit themselves to God. They applied pressure to Aaron and to others to turn them away from the Lord's command.

I believe that Moses' departure from the Israelites and ascension up the mountain to meet with God may be likened to Jesus' ascension into heaven after He was resurrected to life. Many now doubt He ever lived, and certainly many scoff at any thought that one day He is going to return to this earth.

> [3]"First of all, you must understand that in the last days scoffers will come, scoffing and following their own evil desires. [4]They will say, 'Where is this 'coming' he promised? Ever since our fathers died, everything goes on as it has since the beginning of creation'" (2 Pet. 3:3-4).

Such scoffers find no need to get their heart right before God and so have given themselves over to the revelries of this world without regard for the fact that a certain judgement awaits them unless they turn by faith to the Lord Jesus Christ (2 Pet. 3:5-7; Rev. 20:11-15). Their scoffing can have its effect on us if we are not firmly rooted in the faith.

Scripture tells us how we should respond to such individuals ...

> [1]"Blessed is the man who does not walk in the counsel of the wicked or stand in the way of sinners or sit in the seat of mockers. [2]But his delight is in the law of the LORD, and on his law he meditates day and night. [3]He is like a tree planted by streams of water, which yields its fruit in season and whose leaf does not wither. Whatever he does prospers.
> [4]Not so the wicked! They are like chaff that the wind blows away. [5]Therefore the wicked will not stand in the judgment, nor sinners in the assembly of the righteous. [6]For the LORD watches over the way of the righteous, but the way of the wicked will perish" (Ps. 1:1-6).

We will most surely be affected by those who mock the Lord and His Word if we make it a practice to spend time soaking up their words. We must rather let our delight be in the law of the Lord. We must let God's Word abide in our hearts. We must keep it before us always so that scoffers will not be able to steal our faith in the Lord. This becomes even more vital as we approach the "last days."

What the Israelites experienced was a type of **APOSTASY**. Webster's Dictionary defines apostasy as "the abandonment of what one has voluntarily professed; total desertion of principles or faith." Nelson's Illustrated Bible Dictionary says, *"Apostasy is generally defined as the determined, willful rejection of Christ and His teachings by a Christian believer (Heb. 10:26-29; John 15:22). This is different from false belief, or error, which is the result of ignorance. Some Christian groups teach that apostasy is impossible for those persons who have truly accepted Jesus as Savior and Lord."*

As indicated in Nelson's definition, there are differing views as to whether a believer can enter into apostasy. This will be discussed in more detail in a later chapter. Certainly, Christians have experienced temptations to doubt God, or His Word, and to turn away from Him, and some have.

Jesus Christ has made available to us the New Covenant, purchased and sealed by His shed blood. As we have seen, one of the key elements of this New Covenant is that when an individual comes to Jesus Christ by faith, he is born again by the Spirit of God. The individual's spirit is renewed and is linked with the Holy Spirit of God and the law of God is written on that person's heart. God's power is provided to help the individual live for God. The Old Covenant did not provide this indwelling power of the Holy Spirit. Yet, even though God understood this lack and their personal weaknesses, He expected them to trust and obey Him. As a just God, He could not overlook their failure to keep the covenant which He had made with them and which they had agreed to keep.

We hear much about a loving God ... and He is. He is also a God of mercy. But, HE IS GOD!! He cannot overlook the rebellion of His children any more than a father can overlook a child's rebellion against him and still be in authority.

Joshua, who brought the Israelites into the promised land after the death of Moses, later spoke to that generation of Israelites about the seriousness of serving God ...

[14]*"Now fear the LORD and serve him with all faithfulness. Throw away the gods your forefathers worshiped beyond the River and in Egypt, and serve the LORD. [15]But if serving the LORD seems undesirable to you, then choose for yourselves this day whom you will serve, whether the gods your forefathers served beyond the River, or the gods of the Amorites, in whose land you are living. But as for me and my household, we will serve the LORD."*

[16]*Then the people answered, 'Far be it from us to forsake the LORD to serve other gods! [17]It was the LORD our God himself who brought us and our fathers up out of Egypt, from that land of slavery, and performed those great signs before our eyes. He protected us on our entire journey and among all the nations through which we traveled. [18]And the LORD drove out before us all the nations, including the Amorites, who lived in the land. We too will serve the LORD, because he is our God.'*

[19]*Joshua said to the people, 'You are not able to serve the LORD. He is a holy God; he is a jealous God. He will not forgive your rebellion and your sins. [20]If you forsake the LORD and serve foreign gods, he will turn and bring disaster on you and make an end of you, after he has been good to you.'*

[21]*But the people said to Joshua, 'No! We will serve the LORD.'*

[22]*Then Joshua said, 'You are witnesses against yourselves that you have chosen to serve the LORD.'*

'Yes, we are witnesses,' they replied.

[23]*'Now then,' said Joshua, 'throw away the foreign gods that are among you and yield your hearts to the LORD, the God of Israel.'*

[24]*And the people said to Joshua, 'We will serve the LORD our God and obey him.'*

[25]*On that day Joshua made a covenant for the people, and there at Shechem he drew up for them decrees and laws. [26]And Joshua recorded these things in the Book of the Law of*

God. Then he took a large stone and set it up there under the oak near the holy place of the LORD.

[27]'See!' he said to all the people. 'This stone will be a witness against us. It has heard all the words the LORD has said to us. It will be a witness against you if you are untrue to your God'" (Josh. 24:14-27).

Joshua was speaking to Israelites who were descendants of those who had entered into the covenant at Mt. Sinai, and Joshua renewed that covenant with them. The way that Joshua approached the Israelites in this matter of who they would serve indicated the seriousness of this matter. They knew how faithful the Lord had been to them, and they knew that it would be far better for them to serve the Lord. Their commitment to serve the Lord could not be treated casually and their rebellion would have serious consequences. God would expect them to keep their word.

Joshua recorded their response in the book of the law and at that place he set a stone to be a witness of their commitment to serve the Lord. Joshua had said to them, *"You are not able to serve the LORD. He is a holy God; He is a jealous God. He will not forgive your rebellion and your sins. If you forsake the LORD and serve foreign gods, He will turn and bring disaster on you and make an end of you, after he has been good to you."*

They could not treat this matter casually, because God would take their oath seriously. We know that Israel ultimately turned away from their covenant with God and terrible, terrible consequences came upon them.

When Moses came down from the mountain and saw the Israelites in rebellion, he threw down the tablets of stone and broke them into pieces signifying that the Israelites had broken their covenant with God. Sin had come into the camp and had to be dealt with. Moses said, *"Whoever is for the Lord, come to me."* And all the Levites rallied to Him. Then he said to them, *"This is what the Lord, the God of Israel, says: 'Each man strap a sword to his side. Go back and forth through the camp from one end to the other, each killing his brother and friend and neighbor.'" The Levites did as Moses commanded, and that day about three thousand of the people died* (Exod. 32:26-29).

This was an act of God's judgement against those who had totally disregarded the covenant they had made with God. It may be difficult for us to accept that the Levites killed three thousand (probably the ring leaders of the rebellion) who disobeyed God's command. However, the Israelites had earlier voiced their agreement to the basic provisions of the covenant which Moses had spoken to the people (Exod. 24:3) and then Moses later read to them (Exod. 24:7). These basic provisions, which they agreed to, included the stipulation that ...

"Whoever sacrifices to any god other than the LORD must be destroyed" (Exod. 22:20).

They had been forewarned. We must also recognize that Satan was standing behind those who were leading the rebellion against God. Satan's purposes are not to bring man good, but evil, and to turn him away from God's path.

The judgement against the Israelites rebellion is a picture of how we must deal with sin in our own lives. We must not take rebellion against God lightly. We must repent of it, and set our hearts right before God. We must have the fear of God in our hearts, *"because our God is a consuming fire."* He longs to bless us abundantly, but He also expects us to trust and obey Him.

As the rebellion of the Israelites shows, the Lord must be first in our lives, ahead of our family members, our companions, our neighbors and our co-workers. Does this show a lack of love for those closest to us? Of course not. When we live wholeheartedly for the Lord, we will also live right and do what is right where our family members are concerned. We will truly love our wives or husbands, our children, our mothers and fathers and will seek the best for them for this

189

is what God desires of us. However, we cannot allow family members who are not Christians to turn us away from our allegiance to the Lord Jesus Christ. Certainly this may cause difficulties in our family relationships.

In the Old Testament we find God working to bring a whole nation unto Himself and His plan could have been thwarted had He allowed Israel's rebellion to stand. Today, He is calling individuals unto Himself. Each individual will be judged based on their own personal decisions regarding Jesus Christ. The New Covenant does not call for violent action to be taken to-day against those who would come to draw us away from Christ, but it is a picture of a parallel teaching which Jesus has spoken to us...

> [34]"*Do not suppose that I have come to bring peace to the earth. I did not come to bring peace, but a sword.* [35]*For I have come to turn a man against his father, a daughter against her mother, a daughter-in-law against her mother-in-law—*
> [36]*a man's enemies will be the members of his own household.'*
> [37]*"Anyone who loves his father or mother more than me is not worthy of me; anyone who loves his son or daughter more than me is not worthy of me;* [38]*and anyone who does not take his cross and follow me is not worthy of me.* [39]*Whoever finds his life will lose it, and whoever loses his life for my sake will find it"* (Matt. 10:34-39).

In this passage, We see unbelieving family members turning against those who have given their lives to Jesus Christ. In some lands, Christians have been martyred as a consequence of their betrayal by family members. This was also foretold by Jesus who said, *"Brother will betray brother to death, and a father his child; children will rebel against their parents and have them put to death. All men will hate you because of me, but he who stands firm to the end will be saved."* (Matt. 10:21-22).

Amazingly, Jesus came to bring peace between God and man and between man and his fellow man, but there is no contradiction here. His message of salvation also brings conflict between light and dark, righteousness and sin, the power of God and the power of Satan. Jesus does not ask us to take a sword against those who would come against us but rather He tells us to "...*Love your enemies, do good to those who hate you, bless those who curse you, pray for those who mistreat you*" (Luke 6:27-28).

However, God is also telling us that we must stand fast in Him in spite of family pressures and every other kind of pressure that would come against us to turn us away from Himself. Our eternal destiny, heaven or hell, is at stake. JESUS MUST HOLD THE MOST IMPORTANT AND HIGHEST PLACE IN OUR LIVES OR WE ARE NOT WORTHY OF HIM. He gave His all for us, His life, and He expects no less of us. He gave Himself that He might give us eternal life and blessings abundant, but we must stand fast in Him. This is not just a conflict between the believer and his family members and friends. It is identifying who we will serve, whether God or Satan. It is a spiritual battle and we are called to make a decision. No half-hearted decision will do. We must pray for that individual who comes to turn us away from Christ, because he needs to be delivered from Satan also.

By their obedience to God's command, the Levites (the tribe of Israelites who were the descendants of Jacob's son Levi) were consecrated (were set apart) to the Lord. They became Israel's priests and were identified as Israelites who belonged wholly to the Lord. It is said of Levi (by implication also his descendants) who took this stand for the Lord ...

"He said of his father and mother, 'I have no regard for them.' He did not recognize his brothers or acknowledge his own children, but he watched over your word and guarded your covenant" (Deut. 33:9).

191

We who come to Christ are to be consecrated (set apart) wholly to the Lord as His priests, taking our stand to serve Him in spite of every opposition that might come against us from family members or others.

Aaron was also involved in this rebellion against God. God's anger against Aaron is not specifically spelled out in the Exodus account, but is spoken of elsewhere. Moses feared God's anger, and came before God as an intercessor on behalf of those who had sinned, including Aaron. He pleaded for forty days and forty nights for God's mercy. This is spoken of in the book of Deuteronomy where Moses recounts the experiences of the Israelites in the wilderness ...

[18]"*Then once again I fell prostrate before the LORD for forty days and forty nights; I ate no bread and drank no water, because of all the sin you had committed, doing what was evil in the LORD's sight and so provoking him to anger.* [19]*I feared the anger and wrath of the LORD, for he was angry enough with you to destroy you. But again the LORD listened to me.* [20]*And the LORD was angry enough with Aaron to destroy him, but at that time I prayed for Aaron too*" (Deut. 9:18-20).

Moses came before the Lord to make an appeal for the lives of the Israelites that God would not destroy them, and God heard him. Moses' tremendous burden for the people can be seen in that he laid his own life on the altar on their behalf when he said, "*... please forgive their sin—but if not, then blot me out of the book you have written.*" Moses was not guilty, yet he was willing to lay down his life (even eternal life) for his people.

In this, Moses reveals to us the work of an intercessor— one who, because of a tremendous love for those who are badly in need of God's mercy and grace, selflessly stands before the Lord to plead on their behalf. About three thousand of the Israelites died by the sword and the Lord struck the people with a plague because of what they did with the calf Aaron had made. However, because of Moses' prayers to God it says,

"Then the Lord relented and did not bring on his people the disaster he had threatened" (Exod. 32:14). While consequences for sin came to the Israelites, it was nothing like what would have happened had Moses not appealed to the Lord for mercy.

When the Israelites had sinned in this way, the Lord said to Moses, *"Go down, because YOUR people whom you brought up out of Egypt, have become corrupt."* God addressed the Israelites as Moses' people showing that He was disowning them for breaking the covenant He had made with them. In his prayer to God (Exod. 32:7-14) Moses reverses God's statement by referring to them as God's people.

The Israelites had agreed to keep the covenant, and their action with the golden calf was in direct violation of this agreement with the Lord. They were guilty and were certainly not of a like mind with Moses. Yet Moses was willing to give his life for them. This is a picture of what Jesus did for us ...

> [6]*"You see, at just the right time, when we were still powerless, Christ died for the ungodly.* [7]*Very rarely will anyone die for a righteous man, though for a good man someone might possibly dare to die.* [8]*But God demonstrates his own love for us in this: While we were still sinners, Christ died for us"* (Rom. 5:6-8).

In the face of these examples, it is easy for us to feel very inadequate in regard to our love and intercession for others. Regardless, we are called to intercede. We are challenged to take our place in the battle for individual souls, for the nation and the world. We are called to plead for God's mercy, but also to stand against Satan's forces, the forces of darkness that come to kill and destroy. Our Lord has given us *"authority to trample on snakes and scorpions and to overcome all the power of the enemy..."* (Luke 10:19).

The spiritual walls of our nation have been broken down and the enemy is seemingly coming in like a flood. The evil has been allowed in because the people of this nation have turned away from God's ways and His commandments. His laws were provided to keep us strong and to protect us. Now, because we have forsaken Him in so many ways, the powers of darkness have been able to come in and raise havoc. The walls have been breached and we are paying the consequences.

Ezekiel chapter 22 talks about the corruption and evil that had come to exist in Israel just prior to the day that her people were taken captive and were led away from the land of Israel. This scripture identifies many evils which parallel what is happening in our land today. In speaking of these things through Ezekiel the prophet, God said,

> [30]"*I looked for a man among them who would build up the wall and stand before me in the gap on behalf of the land so I would not have to destroy it, but I found none.* [31]*So I will pour out my wrath on them and consume them with my fiery anger, bringing down on their own heads all they have done, declares the Sovereign LORD*" (Ezek. 22:30-31).

The work of an intercessor is to seek God's mercy and aid on behalf of the land that the tide of evil which has been coming through the wall may be held back, that the walls may again be built up. It is awesome to consider the power of prayer that is indicated here... "I looked for *a man*" (singular). I believe God was indicating that even one man could have made a tremendous difference if He could have found one to intercede. Jesus became the true Intercessor and Mediator between God and man so that God would not have to destroy all flesh.

Intercessory prayer is going up in our land today. While evil is still very much in evidence, there are hopeful signs appearing. God is able to bring victory out of seeming defeat when we seek God with all of our hearts. We have turned away from God's laws and so are reaping the consequences, but battles are being fought to build the wall back up. Young people are fighting to be allowed to pray and hold Bible studies in the schools. Christian lawyers are fighting to prevent our religious freedoms from being eroded any further. Certain governors and other leaders are taking stands against abortion. Christian young people are signing pledges of sexual abstinence before marriage. More and more Christians, who have taken their religious freedoms for granted are becoming alarmed and are getting involved.

The battle has not been won, but it is being waged, and we must neither get discouraged or complacent but must be resolved that we will fight on. We must take a stand as intercessors against the tide of darkness that is coming against our families, friends, co-workers and others, that they might be saved and that our nation might be delivered. *"For our struggle is not against flesh and blood, but against the rulers, against the authorities, against the powers of this dark world and against the spiritual forces of evil in the heavenly realms"* (Eph. 6:12).

CHAPTER 7

His Presence—The Only Way to Rest

As we continue in our story, we see that God instructs Moses that the Israelites are to leave Mt. Sinai.

¹*"Then the LORD said to Moses, 'Leave this place, you and the people you brought up out of Egypt, and go up to the land I promised on oath to Abraham, Isaac and Jacob, saying, `I will give it to your descendants.' ²I will send an angel before you and drive out the Canaanites, Amorites, Hittites, Perizzites, Hivites and Jebusites. ³Go up to the land flowing with milk and honey. But I will not go with you, because you are a stiff-necked people and I might destroy you on the way.'*

⁴*When the people heard these distressing words, they began to mourn and no one put on any ornaments. ⁵For the LORD had said to Moses, 'Tell the Israelites, `You are a stiff-necked people. If I were to go with you even for a moment, I might destroy you. Now take off your ornaments and I will decide what to do with you.' ⁶So the Israelites stripped off their ornaments at Mount Horeb.*

⁷*Now Moses used to take a tent and pitch it outside the camp some distance away, calling it the "tent of meeting." Anyone inquiring of the LORD would go to the tent of meeting outside the*

camp. *8And whenever Moses went out to the tent, all the people rose and stood at the entrances to their tents, watching Moses until he entered the tent. 9As Moses went into the tent, the pillar of cloud would come down and stay at the entrance, while the LORD spoke with Moses. 10Whenever the people saw the pillar of cloud standing at the entrance to the tent, they all stood and worshiped, each at the entrance to his tent. 11The LORD would speak to Moses face to face, as a man speaks with his friend. Then Moses would return to the camp, but his young aide Joshua son of Nun did not leave the tent.*

12Moses said to the LORD, 'You have been telling me., 'Lead these people.,' but you have not let me know whom you will send with me. You have said, 'I know you by name and you have found favor with me.' 13If you are pleased with me, teach me your ways so I may know you and continue to find favor with you. Remember that this nation is your people.'

14The LORD replied, 'My Presence will go with you, and I will give you rest.'

15Then Moses said to him, 'If your Presence does not go with us, do not send us up from here. 16How will anyone know that you are pleased with me and with your people unless you go with us? What else will distinguish me and your people from all the other people on the face of the earth?'

17And the LORD said to Moses, 'I will do the very thing you have asked, because I am pleased with you and I know you by name" (Exod. 33:1-17).

The Israelites had so grieved the Lord that He said He would not go with them. This pronouncement gave the Israelites no cause for jubilation. As we have already seen, God cannot coexist with sin and with evil. Because of the rebellious nature of the Israelites, God might destroy them on the way. What a tragedy it would be for God's presence to be removed from them. So, Moses pleaded with the Lord regarding this matter, and because God was pleased with Moses, He declared that His Presence would go with them and He would give them rest.

Up to this time, God's Presence had been with the Israelites. He had brought them out of Egypt with a mighty hand and out-stretched arm. He had destroyed the Egyptian army while bringing the Israelites through the Red Sea on dry ground. He had guided the Israelites in the wilderness like a flock, showing them the way to go. The Lord went ahead of them in a pillar of cloud by day and a pillar of fire by night to give them light so that they could travel by day or by night. He had performed mighty wonders in providing them with food to eat and water to drink. Though they doubted and feared, He had not failed to do all that He had promised. The wilderness was not a wonderful place, but they had been sheltered by God's Presence. The Lord (HE IS) had met every need. By trusting and obeying Him, they could enter into His rest.

When an individual comes to Jesus Christ by faith and is born again, the presence of the Almighty God indwells that individual by means of the Holy Spirit. It is that presence which distinguishes the true believers (God's people) from all other people on the face of the earth. What a wonderful thing this is. However, we must maintain a walk with Jesus which is vital and alive. This will only be the case as we nurture that One-on-one relationship with Him through prayer and meditation on the Word, and by living out our faith and obedience on a daily basis. Through faith in the finished work of Jesus Christ we are enabled to die daily to our own selfish ways and to walk in newness of life, motivated and empowered by the same power which raised Christ Jesus from the dead. It is then that His presence and His working in our lives will be most evident to us and to others. Christ will be seen in our lives.

As we remain in that vital living relationship with Him (in His presence), we are enabled to be at rest in Him. Though we may face many difficulties, we can be at rest because we have perfect confidence that His presence is with us and goes before us. This is confirmed experientially as we see His hand at work in our daily affairs.

It is God's plan that we enter into His rest, a shelter from all the turmoil of this life. However, we are enabled to be at rest only so long as we walk in trust and obedience to Christ. It is when we walk in disobedience and unbelief that our lives are subject to fear that would rob us of the rest that He wants us to have. This life is like the desert, a dry, barren place where snakes and scorpions (demonic powers) dwell and where the necessities of life may not always seem certain. Sickness, and difficulties of all kinds come to us. Yet, we must firmly believe and rely on the One who has said, *"Never will I leave you; never will I forsake you"* (Heb. 13:5), and also has said, *"... do not fear, for I am with you; do not be dismayed, for I am your God. I will strengthen you and help you; I will uphold you with my righteous right hand"* (Isa. 41:10). As we commit ourselves to wholeheartedly lay hold of this truth, we will be enabled to remain in His rest, facing our trials without fear.

Someone might say, "You certainly haven't experienced all the trials that come to try mens' souls, so how can you be so sure of your position?" This is the crux of the problem. Our decision to follow Christ must not rest on our experiences or whether we receive good or bad in our lives, but must be based on an unswerving trust and commitment to the Lord, a confidence in His Word and a conviction of His love for us. We must be as committed as Job was to serve the Lord through good times and bad times. When he had lost his sons and daughters, his servants and his livelihood, we can see how Job responded...

[20]*"At this, Job got up and tore his robe and shaved his head. Then he fell to the ground in worship* [21]*and said: "Naked I came from my mother's womb, and naked I will depart. The LORD gave and the LORD has taken away; may the name of the LORD be praised"* (Job 1:20-21).

The book of Job tells us that God knew what was happening to Job. It was not hidden from His sight. God also knew every difficulty which came to test the Israelites. He had ordained them and had a purpose for each one even though the Israel-ites were not quick to recognize it. God knows every detail of our lives and every trial and test that comes to us. We too may not understand what comes our way, but we are not to depend on our own understanding of our circumstances.

> [5]*"Trust in the LORD with all your heart and lean not on your own understanding;* [6]*in all your ways acknowledge him, and he will make your paths straight"* (Prov. 3:5-6).

We are to acknowledge that He is in control. We must com-mit ourselves to trust and hold fast to Him even when we don't understand what is happening or why.

A trust in God that is dependent on circumstances is shaky, and will not stand when the tests come.

The Israelites had been taken out of Egypt, yet they contin-ued to have a heart attachment to the securities and gods of Egypt. They were continuing to want to place their trust in the things of this world instead of in God. They failed to see that everything that God asked of them was intended to lead them to an abundant blessing which would far outweigh all of the trea-sures and securities which Egypt could offer.

In many ways we respond just like the Israelites. We have such an attachment to this world, to its securities and its trea-sures, that our hearts are not fully given over to God. We are not willing to surrender all that we are and have to Jesus Christ that His presence may be seen in us. We are afraid that He may ask more of us than we are willing to give. We fail to see the love of God which stands behind everything that He asks of us, and fail to see the blessings that He longs to bestow upon us in this life and in the life to come. So we do not surrender our lives completely to Him. We hold back, and as a consequence His presence is not revealed in our lives as we would desire it to be.

The New Testament church, as it first appeared and was written about in the book of Acts, demonstrated something different. Individuals faced the liklihood of severe persecution when they chose to follow Christ. The decision to make Him their Lord and Savior had serious implications and was not made lightly. They knew it might cost them their freedom or their lives. They came with the understanding that they stood to lose all things for Christ's sake. Speaking of these early believers it says ...

> [42]*"And they steadfastly persevered, devoting themselves constantly to the instruction and fellowship of the apostles, to the breaking of bread [including the Lord's Supper] and prayers.*
> [43]*And a sense of awe (reverential fear) came upon every soul, and many wonders and signs were performed through the apostles—the special messengers.*
> [44]*And all who believed—that is, who adhered to and trusted in and relied on Jesus Christ—were united, and together they had everything in common;*
> [45]*And they sold their possessions [both their landed property and their movable goods] and distributed the price among all, according as any had need.*
> [46]*And day after day they regularly assembled in the temple with united purpose, and in their homes they broke bread [including the Lord's Supper]. They partook of their food with gladness and simplicity and generous hearts.*
> [47]*Constantly praising God and being in favor and goodwill with all the people, and the Lord kept adding [to their number] daily those who were being saved (from spiritual death)"*
> (Acts 2:42-47 AMP).

This group of believers steadfastly persevered, were devoted to the things of God, considered the things of this world as expendable for the Kingdom, were united in purpose and constantly praised God. Without question, they were seeking first the Kingdom of God and were willing to give up all that they had if necessary to follow Jesus. Perhaps the most important attitude demonstrated was a sense of awe (reverential fear) of the Lord. If all who profess the name of Christ were to demonstrate these characteristics and attitudes today, I am convinced we would see the presence of God manifest in our churches in a wonderful way.

The presence of God was mighty on this church of Acts and was demonstrated with many signs and wonders. Under these conditions it is not surprising that a sense of awe (reverential fear) came upon every soul. How could half-hearted commitments, sin and rebellion coexist with such a manifestation of God's presence without being dealt with? We see that it was into this kind of environment, that Ananias and Saphira, a husband and wife, came in before the apostles (Acts 5). They lied about the proceeds that they had received from the sale of a property. It was their property, and they could have done with it whatever they wanted. Instead they chose to bring deception. As they individually came in and told their lie before the Apostles, and more importantly the Holy Spirit, each was struck dead. Open sin could not stand in the face of God's holy presence as it existed in that early church.

It says that after Ananias fell dead, *"... great dread and terror took possession of all who heard it"* (Acts 5:5b AMP). After his wife died, *"the whole church was appalled—great awe and strange terror and dread seized them—and all others who heard of these things"* (vs. 11 AMP). *"And none of those who were not of their number dared to join and associate with them, but the people held them in high regard and praised and made much of them"* (vs. 13 AMP). What an awesome presence of the Lord.

Has this presence of the Lord been purposely held back from the church because it is not God's will for it to be seen at this time? I do not believe so. Marvelous revivals have given testimony to this. The fault is ours. The cares of this life and the deceitfulness of wealth and prosperity have dulled our commitment to the Lord. God's presence will not come in power until those in the church are willing to give their all to the Lord and I do not believe this can come about except through our earnest prayers and the convicting work of the Holy Spirit.

Moses knew how important the presence of the Lord was. The Israelites were going through perilous territory and would be required to drive out all the inhabitants residing in the promised land before they could take possession of it. No wonder Moses said, *"If your Presence does not go with us, do not send us up from here."*

Moses did not falsely elevate or assert himself before the people, but he walked in dependence upon God knowing that as he did so God's power would be present to meet all needs, overcome all difficulties and bring to completion all that God had promised. God's presence was essential. Moses knew that his own strength and wisdom were insufficient to carry these people through to the promised land. He could do all things through God who strengthened him, and without Him he could do nothing. In this, Moses was identified as a "meek" man ...

"Now the man Moses was very meek, above all the men which were upon the face of the earth" (Num. 12:3 KJV).

Our understanding of the word meekness might lead us to believe that Moses was weak. However, the Hebrew word which is translated as meekness ("humble" in the NIV translation) has a different meaning. He was considered humble because he recognized that his authority and power flowed out from the Lord and not from himself. He was subject to God in all things. Therefore when others rose up against him, it was not Moses they were contending with but God. Moses did not have to defend himself against others. God vindicated him. In this "meekness" was great strength and power—a power which flowed out from the Lord.

So it must be with us ...

"I am the vine; you are the branches. If a man remains in me and I in him, he will bear much fruit; apart from me you can do nothing" (John 15:5).

Apart from Him I can do nothing...BUT...

"I can do everything through him who gives me strength" (Phil. 4:13).

Jesus, the Almighty Son of God, the Creator of the universe demonstrated this characteristic of meekness ...

"Jesus gave them this answer: 'I tell you the truth, the Son can do nothing by himself; he can do only what he sees his Father doing, because whatever the Father does the Son also does" (John 5:19).

"By myself I can do nothing; I judge only as I hear, and my judgment is just, for I seek not to please myself but him who sent me" (John 5:30).

What spiritual good can we do apart from God? Can we minister effectively without His presence? Can we save anyone? Can we heal anyone? Can we work any miracles? No, the true works of God are dependent on His presence and His power which will be evident in us only as we abide in Christ, remain dependent upon Him and seek to please Him and not ourselves. Everything must flow out of this relationship if it is to be of God. If we know that what we have done is of God, then we do not need to defend ourselves, because it was not of us to begin with.

4"Dwell in Me and I will dwell in you.—Live in Me and I will live in you. Just as no branch can bear fruit of itself without abiding in (vitally united to) the vine, neither can you bear fruit unless you abide in Me.'
5'I am the Vine, you are the branches. Whoever lives in Me and I in him bears much (abundant) fruit. However, apart from Me—cut off from vital union with Me—you can do nothing'" (John 15:4-5 AMP).

To abide in Christ is to first of all recognize our own insufficiency. It is then that we will seek to live in full sub-

205

mission and dependence upon the Lord. We will call upon Him for that which is needed in any given situation (i.e. His anointing, wisdom, etc.), and trust that He will provide. The Apostle Paul said,

> *"Not that we are sufficient of ourselves to think any thing as of ourselves; but our sufficiency is of God;"* (2 Cor. 3:5 KJV).

The degree to which we are able to abide in Christ will govern the measure of our fruitfulness (Matt. 13:23).

The Lord hears Moses' prayer and replies, *"My Presence will go with you, and I will give you rest."* Fear can be driven away in the knowledge of His Presence and the cares of this life can be placed into proper perspective as we enter into the sheltered place of His rest. His rest is entered into by faith. We take the initial steps to enter into His rest when we first come to Jesus Christ by faith and receive Him as our Savior ...

> [28]*"Come to me, all you who are weary and burdened, and I will give you rest.* [29]*Take my yoke upon you and learn from me, for I am gentle and humble in heart, and you will find rest for your souls.* [30]*For my yoke is easy and my burden is light"* (Matt. 11:28-30).

It must be a continual act on our part. We must daily enter into what scripture variously speaks of as His refuge, shelter, fortress, high tower, shadow of His wings, etc., by an act of our faith. Are we going to be stressed out, or are we going to enter His rest by believing in His promises and casting all of our care upon Him? ...

> [6]*"Therefore humble yourselves (demote, lower yourselves in your own estimation) under the mighty hand of God, that in due time He may exalt you.*
> [7]*Casting the whole of your care—all your anxieties, all your worries, all your concerns, once and for all—on Him; for He cares for you affectionately, and cares about you watchfully"* (1 Pet. 5:6-7 AMP).

The first responsibility is ours. By an act of our will, we are to continually cast our burdens upon Him ... then He will sustain us and give us rest ...

> "Cast your burden upon the Lord [releasing the weight of it] and He will sustain you; He will never allow the [consistently] righteous to be moved—made to slip, fall or fail" (Ps 55:22 AMP).

God has given us other excellent promises in this regard ...

> [1]"But now, this is what the LORD says—'He who created you, O Jacob, he who formed you, O Israel: 'Fear not, for I have redeemed you; I have summoned you by name; you are mine. [2]When you pass through the waters, I will be with you; and when you pass through the rivers, they will not sweep over you. When you walk through the fire, you will not be burned; the flames will not set you ablaze'" (Isa. 43:1-2).

We must say, "Yes Lord, I believe. I will this moment enter into Your rest and cast My cares upon You. I will trust you. I will not fear. I will leave all in your hands and trust You for the results."

The Israelites had difficulty walking by faith in God's promises just as we do. They would forsake God's resting place, turning instead to their own devices to save themselves from some perceived disaster. In so doing they would forsake God's resting place and enter into fear and turmoil. A scripture we have looked at before from the book of Isaiah is worth repeating ...

> [15]"This is what the Sovereign LORD, the Holy One of Israel, says:
> 'In repentance and rest is your salvation, in quietness and trust is your strength, but you would have none of it. [16]You said, 'No, we will flee on horses.' Therefore you will flee! You said, 'We will ride off on swift horses.' Therefore your pursuers will be swift! [17] A thousand will flee at the threat of one; at the threat of five you will all flee away, till you are

left like a flagstaff on a mountaintop, like a banner on a hill.' [18]Yet the LORD longs to be gracious to you; he rises to show you compassion. For the LORD is a God of justice. Blessed are all who wait for him!'" (Isa. 30:15-18).

The Amplified translation has verse 18 as follows ...

"And therefore the Lord [earnestly] waits—expectant, looking and longing—to be gracious to you, and therefore He lifts Himself up that He may have mercy on you and show loving-kindness to you; for the Lord is a God of justice. Blessed—happy, fortunate [to be envied] are all those who [earnestly] wait for Him, who expect and look and long for Him [for His victory, His favor, His love, His peace, His joy and His matchless, unbroken companionship]" (Isa. 30:18 AMP).

These scriptures show that God did not remove His resting place, but rather the Israelites ran from it as they turned to fear and unbelief and took matters into their own hands. They responded to their own fears and forsook God's mercy and in this way opened themselves up to further difficulties.

Our resting in Him by faith does not mean that we will never have difficulties, but it means that no matter what our difficulties are, and even though at times we may see no way out, we can cast these cares upon Him, and **HE WILL** sustain us.

After the Lord indicated that His Presence would go with the Israelites as Moses requested, Moses then made another request of the Lord ...

[18]"Then Moses said, 'Now show me your glory.'
[19]And the LORD said, 'I will cause all my goodness to pass in front of you, and I will proclaim my name, the LORD, in your presence. I will have mercy on whom I will have mercy, and I will have compassion on whom I will have compassion.'
[20]But, he said, 'you cannot see my face, for no one may see me and live.'
[21]Then the LORD said, 'There is a place near me where you may stand on a rock. [22]When my glory passes by, I will put you

in a cleft in the rock and cover you with my hand until I have passed by. [23]Then I will remove my hand and you will see my back; but my face must not be seen'" (Exod. 33:18-23).

The Lord instructs Moses to chisel out two more stone tablets to replace the ones which had been broken, so that the Lord might again write His laws upon them. Moses did what the Lord commanded and again went up the mountain into the presence of the Lord. Then the Lord came down in the cloud and stood there with him and proclaimed His name, the Lord. He passed in front of Moses, proclaiming...

[6]*"'...The LORD, the LORD, the compassionate and gracious God, slow to anger, abounding in love and faithfulness, [7]maintaining love to thousands, and forgiving wickedness, rebellion and sin. Yet he does not leave the guilty unpunished; he punishes the children and their children for the sin of the fathers to the third and fourth generation'"* (Exod. 34:6-7).

This event, when God caused His goodness to pass in front of Moses is spoken of in a wonderful hymn ...

A wonderful Savior is Jesus my Lord,
A wonderful Savior to me;
He hideth my soul in the cleft of the rock,
Where rivers of pleasure I see.

He hideth my soul in the cleft of the rock
that shadows a dry, thirsty land;
He hideth my life in the depths of His love,
and covers me there with His hand,
and covers me there with His hand.[a]

---

[a]Hymn- He Hideth My Soul by Fanny J. Crosby, 1820-1915 and William J. Kirkpatrick, 1838-1921

We live in a world that is harsh—where many of the consequences of mans' fall (sin, sickness and diseases, wars, famines, murders, etc.) plague mankind. Yet, as we trust and take refuge in the Lord, He hides our soul in the depth of His love and covers us there with His hand. In the middle of our difficulties we are enabled to enter and abide in His rest.

The Lord has provided us instruction and given us the responsibility to make the right choices. We can turn to His way, or we can reject Him through the exercise of our own free will. This is the way He has created us. We are not robots. The choices we make can bring blessings or they can bring evil upon us and our offspring.

Moses' conversation with the Lord continues ...

> [9]*"'O Lord, if I have found favor in your eyes,' he said, 'then let the Lord go with us. Although this is a stiff-necked people, forgive our wickedness and our sin, and take us as your inheritance.'*
>
> [10]*Then the LORD said: 'I am making a covenant with you. Before all your people I will do wonders never before done in any nation in all the world. The people you live among will see how awesome is the work that I, the LORD, will do for you. [11]Obey what I command you today. I will drive out before you the Amorites, Canaanites, Hittites, Perizzites, Hivites and Jebusites. [12]Be careful not to make a treaty with those who live in the land where you are going, or they will be a snare among you. [13]Break down their altars, smash their sacred stones and cut down their Asherah poles. [14]Do not worship any other god, for the LORD, whose name is Jealous, is a jealous God.'*
>
> [15]*'Be careful not to make a treaty with those who live in the land; for when they prostitute themselves to their gods and sacrifice to them, they will invite you and you will eat their sacrifices. [16]And when you choose some of their daughters as wives for your sons and those daughters prostitute themselves to their gods, they will lead your sons to do the same'"*
> (Exod. 34:9-16).

Israel was called to be a nation set apart unto the Lord— a nation that would show forth the glory of God. However, throughout the Old Testament we see many examples where Israel failed to live up to this calling. They became friends with, and participated in the sins of the heathen peoples around them and would fall away from the Lord. In their backslidden condition, the heathen nations would gain mastery over them and would make them their slaves. Because of their waywardness, God finally turned away from them. They were taken from their land and ultimately were scattered over the whole earth.

Without a doubt, it is because of Christianity, brought here by the pilgrims, that God has been enabled to bless the United States of America. Regardless of what the secular media would have us believe, many of our founding fathers had a faith in the Lord Jesus Christ and our nation was founded upon the principles contained in the Bible. It is because of this Christian heritage and the laws and freedoms that emanated from that heritage that our nation has been enabled to become the greatest nation on the face of the earth.

We have truly seen the awesome work that the Lord has done in and through this nation making it the head and not the tail of all nations on the face of the earth. No one was able to stand before the armies of this nation as we fought in the world wars and in Korea. We were wealthy enough to be able to lend to many nations without having to borrow from any. Our businesses have excelled and been a model for the world.

However, in our wealth and prosperity, we have been abandoning our Godly heritage and have failed to consider the Word which the Lord spoke to Moses. We have been seeking after the so-called "ancient wisdom" of the pagan religions of the world and are being taken captive by religious philosophies and the gods of those nations which have experienced poverty and deprivation for many, many years because of their false religious worship. Hinduistic practices including transcendental meditation and yoga, as well as satan worship, witchcraft, "new age" philosophies and assorted other religious practices have moved in to supplant the knowledge of the one true God and the Lord Jesus Christ. We have been allowing those who do not know God to take away the very foundation principles which have made this country great.

As a consequence of all this, we find that this nation, which at one time did not have to borrow from any, is now deeply in debt to other nations. In a sense we are being subjugated to heathen philosophies, religions, economies and the political rule of others (e.g. the increasing involvement of the United Nations in our affairs and the continuing movement toward a "one-world government"). There is no question that we are in a state of decline.

Israel ultimately forgot all that the Lord had done for them, prostituted themselves to the gods of the nations living around them in the promised land and forsook the God who had been so faithful to them. This abandonment of God for the false worship of these other nations is spoken of in Jeremiah. The words of this scripture have application to us as well, as we find ourselves increasingly abandoning the God which has so blessed us ...

1"The word of the LORD came to me: 2'Go and proclaim in the hearing of Jerusalem:'

'I remember the devotion of your youth, how as a bride you loved me and followed me through the desert, through a land not sown. 3Israel was holy to the LORD, the firstfruits of his harvest; all who devoured her were held guilty, and disaster overtook them,'" declares the LORD.

4Hear the word of the LORD, O house of Jacob, all you clans of the house of Israel.' 5This is what the LORD says: 'What fault did your fathers find in me, that they strayed so far from me? They followed worthless idols and became worthless themselves. 6They did not ask...Where is the LORD, who brought us up out of Egypt and led us through the barren wilderness, through a land of deserts and rifts, a land of drought and darkness, a land where no one travels and no one lives?... 7I brought you into a fertile land to eat its fruit and rich produce. But you came and defiled my land and made my inheritance detestable. ⁸The priests did not ask, 'Where is the LORD?' Those who deal with the law did not know me; the leaders rebelled against me. The prophets prophesied by Baal, following worthless idols.

⁹*"Therefore I bring charges against you again,' declares the LORD. 'And I will bring charges against your children's children. ¹⁰Cross over to the coasts of Kittim and look, send to Kedar and observe closely; see if there has ever been anything like this: ¹¹Has a nation ever changed its gods? (Yet they are not gods at all.) But my people have exchanged their Glory for worthless idols. ¹²Be appalled at this, O heavens, and shudder with great horror,' declares the LORD. ¹³'My people have committed two sins: They have forsaken me, the spring of living water, and have dug their own cisterns, broken cisterns that cannot hold water'"* (Jer. 2:1-13).

How important it is in this day to 1) believe that the Bible is God's Word to us, and 2) to understand what that Word says. There are many so-called ministers of the Gospel and churches that are co-mingling the philosophies of this world with Biblical Christianity and basically creating false religions which have no power. Unless those who profess the name of Christ are alert and diligent in their study and knowledge of God's Word and unless their faith is based on that Word, they stand to be taken captive and led away by these deceptive philosophies. These philosophies would attempt to make Jesus Christ just another way to God instead of the only way to God. Such beliefs make Jesus Christ out to be a liar, for He said...

"...I am the way and the truth and the life. No one comes to the Father except through me" (John 14:6).
The Apostle Peter said...

"Salvation is found in no one else, for there is no other name under heaven given to men by which we must be saved" (Acts 4:12).

Many are, and will be taken captive by these false teachings. We must take heed to the Word of God and be alert to the leading of the Holy Spirit. We do this so that we might be able to recognize and run from anything which would turn us away from the Truth, the Life and the Way which is embodied in Jesus Christ alone.

CHAPTER 8

Flunking the Exams

[11]"On the twentieth day of the second month of the second year, the cloud lifted from above the tabernacle of the Testimony. [12]Then the Israelites set out from the Desert of Sinai and traveled from place to place until the cloud came to rest in the Desert of Paran. [13]They set out, this first time, at the LORD's command through Moses" (Num. 10:11-13).

[33]"So they set out from the mountain of the LORD and traveled for three days. The ark of the covenant of the LORD went before them during those three days to find them a place to rest. [34]The cloud of the LORD was over them by day when they set out from the camp.

[35]Whenever the ark set out, Moses said, "Rise up, O LORD! May your enemies be scattered; may your foes flee before you." [36]Whenever it came to rest, he said, "Return, O LORD, to the countless thousands of Israel" (Num. 10:33-36).

The Israelites had been "on the road" now for two years and almost two months from the time they left Egypt. They had spent eleven months of this time in the region of Mt. Sinai. In spite of the commitments they made to the Lord at Mt. Sinai, and all the things which God had shown them and spoken to them during that time, they were quick to return to their old ways of complaining.

215

[1]"Now the people complained about their hardships in the hearing of the LORD, and when he heard them his anger was aroused. Then fire from the LORD burned among them and consumed some of the outskirts of the camp. [2]When the people cried out to Moses, he prayed to the LORD and the fire died down. [3]So that place was called Taberah, because fire from the LORD had burned among them" (Num. 11:1-3).

Before they had reached Mt. Sinai, the Israelites had grumbled and complained against the Lord and against Moses, but God was gracious and long-suffering toward them. He patiently tried to show by the things He did for them that His presence was with them and that He would meet their needs. So now, after all He had taught and shown them, and after establishing His covenant with them, He expected them to mature in their relationship with Him.

The Israelites could not see God, and may have considered that their complaining was just something that they did between themselves. They were tramping through a vast and dreadful desert, a thirsty and waterless land, with its venomous snakes and scorpions (Deut. 8:15). They undoubtedly became tired of the desert and their steady diet of manna. Their complaints were not too hard to understand and yet we see that it caused God to become angry.

Scripture says that the Lord is the same yesterday, today and forever (Heb. 13:8). Therefore we know that God also takes displeasure in our murmuring and complaining. Also, we know that the history we have been reviewing was written down as a warning, and to provide examples for us (1 Cor. 10:11). Paul also says in 1 Cor. 10:10, *"And do not grumble as some of them did ..."*

God was not pleased with the Israelites in this matter of complaining because they were really taking issue with Him. In spite of what they were facing, God had not left them alone. He will not forsake and abandon us either as we trust in Him. The difficult things we experience may have come upon us as a consequence of our own faithlessness and rebellion against God—or perhaps God has allowed tests to come that we might mature in our faith and obedience to Him. Whatever the reason for our trials, God expects us to walk through them without murmuring and complaining because He has promised to be our help and strength, and promised not to forsake us.

As we saw earlier, God had declared that if He went with them, He might destroy them on the way because of their rebelliousness. It is not clear what the fire was that burned among them and that consumed the edges of the camp. Perhaps it was lightning that brought fire upon the Israelites. Whatever it was, it was a sign of God's displeasure.

Now as the Israelites continued on their journey, God would become less tolerant of their failure to trust and rely upon Him and the consequences of their rebellion would become greater. Can we say that God was unjust in this anger against the Israelites? No! His purpose was to cause them to grow in their knowledge of Him and to cause them to become a people who would follow the Lord wholeheartedly and be able to defeat the enemies they would face as they approached the promised land.

We who have come to Jesus Christ have entered into a covenant with Him, and certainly we are the sheep of His pasture. What He requires of us is not burdensome and is meant for our own good that we might be brought to maturity in Him. He loves us and longs to bless us in many wonderful ways. We must realize that we now belong to Him, we are no longer our own, and therefore must respond to Him with wholehearted faith and obedience...

[19]*"Do you not know that your body is a temple of the Holy Spirit, who is in you, whom you have received from God?* **You are not your own;** [20]**you were bought at a price.**[a] *Therefore honor God with your body"* (1 Cor. 6:19-20).

---

[a]Emphasis added

Our God is longsuffering and patient towards us, but we must not treat His mercy and grace with contempt...

[11]"Serve the LORD with fear and rejoice with trembling. [12]Kiss the Son, lest he be angry and you be destroyed in your way, for his wrath can flare up in a moment. Blessed are all who take refuge in him" (Ps. 2:11-12).

We serve a loving God, but One who expects us to trust and obey. This is a truth that some would rather ignore today. The Israelites continue on their journey, but again they act in such a way as to make the Lord angry ...

[4]"The rabble with them began to crave other food, and again the Israelites started wailing and said, 'If only we had meat to eat! [5]We remember the fish we ate in Egypt at no cost—also the cucumbers, melons, leeks, onions and garlic. [6]But now we have lost our appetite; we never see anything but this manna!'

[7]The manna was like coriander seed and looked like resin. [8]The people went around gathering it, and then ground it in a handmill or crushed it in a mortar. They cooked it in a pot or made it into cakes. And it tasted like something made with olive oil. [9]When the dew settled on the camp at night, the manna also came down.

[10]Moses heard the people of every family wailing, each at the entrance to his tent. The LORD became exceedingly angry, and Moses was troubled. [11]He asked the LORD, 'Why have you brought this trouble on your servant? What have I done to displease you that you put the burden of all these people on me? [12]Did I conceive all these people? Did I give them birth? Why do you tell me to carry them in my arms, as a nurse carries an infant, to the land you promised on oath to their forefathers? [13]Where can I get meat for all these people? They keep wailing to me, 'Give us meat to eat!' [14]I cannot carry all these people by myself; the burden is too heavy for me. [15]If this is how you are going to treat me, put me to death right now—if I have found favor in your eyes—and do not let me face my own ruin'" (Num. 11:4-15).

Verse 10 says, *"The LORD became exceedingly angry."* Can anyone still believe that the Lord is not effected by our rebellion and sinfulness? In verse 4 we again see that group of individuals spoken of as "the rabble" (a promiscuous assemblage of people or riff-raff). This mixed group of people, many of whom were not true Israelites, continually incited the Israelites to rebellion. A study note in the NIV Study Bible for verse 4 says that "Those who did not know the Lord and his mercies incited those who did know him to rebel against him." The "rabble" had undoubtedly come along with the Israelites to gain part of the blessings promised to the Israelites, and yet their hearts were not truly turned to God.

The "rabble" have their counterpart in churches today. I believe that they represent individuals who have become regulars in the church, but who for some reason have never come to a personal saving knowledge of Jesus Christ. Although they may think that they are right with God, they are not, and may not even realize their lost condition. They continue to maintain a rather worldly outlook and their lives are not truly founded on the Word of God. They may be regular attenders and may in many ways be sincere, but are not true "Israelites" in the spiritual sense. They may exhibit a form of godliness but their lives do not show that they have been transformed by the redeeming power of the Lord. Since the Holy Spirit of God does not dwell within them, they often are at odds with what God is doing and seek rather to apply the world's wisdom within the church. They resent preaching that brings conviction of the sin in their lives and would prefer to hear soothing words.

> *"The man without the Spirit does not accept the things that come from the Spirit of God, for they are foolishness to him, and he cannot understand them, because they are spiritually discerned"* (1 Cor. 2:14).

> [19]*"For it is written: 'I will destroy the wisdom of the wise; the intelligence of the intelligent I will frustrate.'* [20]*Where is*

the wise man? Where is the scholar? Where is the philoso-
pher of this age? Has not God made foolish the wisdom of
the world?'" (1 Cor. 1:19-20).

I believe that it is because of this carnal influence and the "wisdom of the world" within the church that many churches have been led astray from the pure gospel of Jesus Christ. The philosophies of men are preached from the pulpits instead of the unadulterated Word of God. The rabble have infiltrated the leadership of entire denominations where they are working to get the church to conform to liberal views which are in direct conflict with the Word of God.

As just one example of this, the world now says that we must embrace homosexuality, and if we do not, we are hateful bigots. There are those—the carnal rabble—who have brought this so-called wisdom into the church and pushed it until homosexuals have even been brought in as ministers. The churches who have done this have placed man's thinking ahead of the teachings of the Bible. The Bible clearly says ...

"If a man lies with a man as one lies with a woman, both of
them have done what is detestable..." (Lev. 20:13).

Scripture also addresses this issue where women are con-cerned. The Apostle Paul, spoke about the consequences that come to those who do not know God and give themselves over to various kinds of lusts ...

[24]"Therefore God gave them over in the sinful desires of their
hearts to sexual impurity for the degrading of their bodies with
one another. [25]They exchanged the truth of God for a lie, and
worshiped and served created things rather than the Cre-
ator—who is forever praised. Amen.
[26]Because of this, God gave them over to shameful lusts.
Even their women exchanged natural relations for unnatu-
*ral ones. [27]**In the same way the men also**[b] abandoned natu-*

---

[b]Emphasis added

220

ral relations with women and were inflamed with lust for one another. Men committed indecent acts with other men, and received in themselves the due penalty for their perversion" (Rom. 1:24-27).

There is no question that these verses speak of homosexuality on the part of both men and women and refers to such acts as shameful, indecent and perverted. The words "in the same way" in verse 27 make it clear that each of the sexes were caught up in this condemned behavior.

This and other scriptures clearly indicate that the practice of homosexuality is sin. When men have a desire to engage in things which are contrary to God's ways, then many arguments, based in human (not Godly) wisdom, will be found to justify their actions. These arguments will be brought into the church in opposition to the Word of God by those who either do not truly know Jesus Christ and may not be interested in doing His will, or by those who are not willing to take a stand based on the scriptures. If one does not have the view that the Bible is the inspired Word of God and is the standard by which we are to judge matters in the church, then they will be swayed to and fro by every kind of argument.

The arguments that are made to legitimize homosexuality may appear to many as plausible, particularly the argument that those who engage in these things were born that way and therefore had no choice in the matter. However, this argument flies right in the face of the Word of God. We cannot have it both ways. Either the Word of God is our standard, and we believe and live by it and it alone, or we compromise it into nothingness by accepting all the "plausible" arguments the world will bring up.

It is true that many who engage in homosexuality find themselves in a bondage from which they cannot quickly escape. The Bible gives evidence that they are under a spiritual bondage, which is nonetheless very real. We saw in Romans 1:26 (above) that as men and women pursue ungodly and lustful ways, *God gives them over to the things they seek after, surrendering them to it so that they in essence become slaves to their own lusts and sins.*

This may even mean that they become demonically enslaved which is consistent with other passages of scripture which speak of individuals who had become demonically oppressed or possessed and could not in their own strength break away from the hold of these powers. Scripture even sites examples of children being afflicted by demonic powers from which they could not escape (Matt. 15:22-28; Mark 7:24-30[c]). We cannot see into the spirit world to understand how all of this comes about, but scripture is very clear about the reality of demonic powers and their ability to place people in bondage, and we see evidences of these forces at work in many ways.

The world is not discerning about spiritual matters, and are quick to conclude that a bent toward homosexuality is due to heredity or some other "scientifically" explainable cause. Since the religious rabble is not committed to the Word of God, they are swayed by all kinds of fine sounding arguments and push these worldly viewpoints on the church. They turn many of the weak and uncommitted to their point of view.

We who believe the inerrancy of the Word of God have a firm anchor that will not allow us to drift with every wind of doctrine. We have placed our faith in God's Word and must examine all other doctrines in that light. Based upon what the Bible has to say, we cannot concede that homosexual behavior is just another normal and acceptable lifestyle worthy of receiving special protections and rights and deserving to be encouraged and taught.

It is true that all of us have sinned and were at one time alienated from God, so none of us can take a self-righteous

---

[c]Note: The latter passage identifies the one who was demon possessed as the "little daughter" of the woman who came to Jesus. It does not explain how this little girl could have become demon possessed. It only says that she was.

position which is somehow based on our own goodness. What God provided through His Son was a way for us to be forgiven for our sinful acts and *to be delivered from the power that sin has held over us.* We are not to live in sin any longer, nor are we to establish teachings to accept and condone acts which God condemns. This is spoken of clearly in the book of 1 Corinthians...

> [9]*"Do you not know that the wicked will not inherit the kingdom of God? Do not be deceived: Neither the sexually immoral nor idolaters nor adulterers nor male prostitutes nor homosexual offenders* [10]*nor thieves nor the greedy nor drunkards nor slanderers nor swindlers will inherit the kingdom of God.* [11]*And that is what some of you were. But you were washed, you were sanctified, you were justified in the name of the Lord Jesus Christ and by the Spirit of our God"* (1 Cor. 6:9-11).

Should homosexuals be allowed to come into the church? Yes, of course, the church is to be open to any and all sinners that they might come and repent for their sins and receive Jesus Christ as their Lord and Savior. Then when they are born again, they will have the power through the Holy Spirit to be delivered from sin, including the sin of homosexuality. Those who come to Jesus with their whole heart can be set free from such bondages. God's deliverance is available to the homosexual in the same way that it is available to anyone else.

When the church accepts that practice of homosexuality as acceptable behavior on the part of those who identify themselves as Christians, they are making a mockery of God's Word. They are denying the power of God to deliver them from their sins. It is even worse when they place practicing, unrepentant homosexuals in positions of ministry. Is the church to allow *those who have clearly refused to repent of their sins* (certainly not restricted to the sins of homosexuality) to be our ministers? Are positions of ministry to be reserved for those who have repented of their sins, been cleansed of them by the blood of Jesus Christ and who have demonstrated by holy living that their lives have been transformed such that they no longer engage in any of these practices?

The unrepentant homosexual is a servant to his sin as are all individuals who have not been set free from their sins (no matter what they are) through the salvation offered in Jesus Christ. Jesus came to deliver those who have been made the captives of sin. As Jesus Himself proclaimed...

> *"The Spirit of the Lord is upon me, because he hath anointed me to preach the gospel to the poor; he hath sent me to heal the brokenhearted, **to preach deliverance to the captives**[d], and recovering of sight to the blind, to set at liberty them that are bruised..."* (Luke 4:18 KJV)

Also ...

> [34]*"Jesus replied, 'I tell you the truth, everyone who sins is a slave to sin.* [35]*Now a slave has no permanent place in the family, but a son belongs to it forever.* [36]*So if the Son sets you free, you will be free indeed'"* (John 8:34-36).

The Bible declares acts of homosexuality to be a sin and everyone who sins as a slave to sin. **AS THE ABOVE SCRIPTURE SAYS, THOSE WHO ARE SLAVES TO SIN CAN HAVE NO PERMANENT PLACE IN THE FAMILY OF GOD. THEY ARE NOT PART OF THE FAMILY OF GOD AND THEREFORE HAVE NO RIGHTFUL PLACE OF MINISTRY TO THE FAMILY.** Jesus came to set the sinner free from his slavery. He whom the Son sets free will be free indeed.

The Word of God declares that the homosexual and all other sinners can be set free from their sin through Jesus Christ. The world would rather have us accept sin into the church. Satan wants us to compromise our stand which must be based on

---

[d]Emphasis added

the Word of God. Once we have started down that slippery slope, there will be no end to our compromises.

The "rabble" would come to shake us from our faith and obedience to God and His Word. They would try to convince us that our understanding is faulty, or that our faith or our obedience is misdirected. They will try and convince us that God's love and mercy toward us makes Him tolerant of sin, and that we are just bigoted if we hold to a need for holiness. When we listen to and follow the lead of the "rabble", we will be going away from God and we will not please Him. Until we go to be with the Lord, we will always have the wayward influences of the mixed multitude around us, but we must do our best to walk in true faith and obedience to the Word of God.

The influence of the "rabble" can be very subtle. We know that church pastors, board members and others in authority within the church need to seek the Lord for His direction. However, when individuals who do not know Jesus intimately or who are not living for Him as they ought are given positions of authority, then ungodly wisdom and unbelief will gain entrance into the decision making of the church and the church will be compromised. The more this happens, the further the church will be led away from God's path, and the demonstration of God's power in the church will be diminished.

These battles can be difficult for a pastor if he is standing alone, particularly if those who are supposed to stand with him are caught up in compromise in their own lives. We see that the weight on Moses' shoulders had become very heavy. He began to wonder what he had done to displease the Lord that he should have been given the job of leading such a rebellious people. Certainly pastors and other church leaders have faced difficulties of this type where they have become weighed down and discouraged. How important it is that they should have godly people to uplift them and to share the load.

God responded with mercy to Moses' concern regarding the difficulty of leading the rebellious Israelites ...

[16]"The LORD said to Moses: 'Bring me seventy of Israel's elders who are known to you as leaders and officials among the people. Have them come to the Tent of Meeting, that they may stand there with you. [17]I will come down and speak with you there, and I will take of the Spirit that is on you and put the Spirit on them. They will help you carry the burden of the people so that you will not have to carry it alone.'"

Note that God anointed these seventy so that the same Spirit that was on Moses would be on them. They were to carry out their positions of responsibility through the wisdom and power of the Holy Spirit. This is the same Spirit that must be in evidence in the leadership of our churches if God's ways are to be exalted and if His power is to be evident to heal and deliver and if the church is not to be swallowed up by the world.

Just as Moses needed help to carry out his responsibilities, so did the early church apostles. They did not have the time to preach, teach, and manage all the daily affairs of the early church. Therefore, the disciples appointed seven others who were designated to deal with daily administrative matters. The apostles instructed that these seven were to be men who were known to be full of the Spirit and wisdom (Acts 6:3). The men selected were appointed to positions of authority within the church and were its first deacons. It was essential that these be godly men filled with the Holy Spirit, and this need has not changed today.

As we continue with our story, we see that God responds to the people's demands as well...

[18]"Tell the people: 'Consecrate yourselves in preparation for tomorrow, when you will eat meat. The LORD heard you when you wailed, 'If only we had meat to eat! We were better off in Egypt!' Now the LORD will give you meat, and you will eat it. [19]You will not eat it for just one day, or two days, or five, ten or twenty days, [20]but for a whole month—until it comes out of your nostrils and you loathe it—because you have rejected

the LORD, who is among you, and have wailed before him, saying, 'Why did we ever leave Egypt?'
²¹But Moses said, 'Here I am among six hundred thousand men on foot, and you say...I will give them meat to eat for a whole month!' ²²Would they have enough if flocks and herds were slaughtered for them? Would they have enough if all the fish in the sea were caught for them?'
²³The LORD answered Moses, 'Is the LORD's arm too short? You will now see whether or not what I say will come true for you.'
²⁴So Moses went out and told the people what the LORD had said...'" (Num. 11:16-24).

³¹Now a wind went out from the LORD and drove quail in from the sea. It brought them down all around the camp to about three feet above the ground, as far as a day's walk in any direction. ³²All that day and night and all the next day the people went out and gathered quail. No one gathered less than ten homers. Then they spread them out all around the camp. ³³But while the meat was still between their teeth and before it could be consumed, the anger of the LORD burned against the people, and he struck them with a severe plague. ³⁴Therefore the place was named Kibroth Hattaavah, because there they buried the people who had craved other food" (Num. 11:31-34).

God's reaction to the Israelites craving for other food gives us a look at an angry God—"Now the LORD will give you meat, and you will eat it."

¹⁹"You will not eat it for just one day, or two days, or five, ten or twenty days, ²⁰but for a whole month—until it comes out of your nostrils and you loathe it—because you have rejected the LORD, who is among you, and have wailed before him, saying, 'Why did we ever leave Egypt?'

The Israelite complaining and their desire to return to Egypt would now take its toll on the people. It does not say that there were any lives taken when God caused the fire to burn earlier in the outskirts of the camp, but now we see that a plague came on the people and many died. The people were being judged severely for their waywardness and this would not be the first time.

We may feel that God doesn't respond to sin in believers today as He did during the time of the Israelite wanderings. However, New Testament scriptures indicate that when individuals today treat the things of God in an unworthy manner, they can suffer sickness and even death. This was noted in regard to communion where some in the Corinthian church were partaking of communion in a way which was not pleasing to the Lord. As a consequence some were getting sick and even dying...

> [28]"A man ought to examine himself before he eats of the bread and drinks of the cup. [29]For anyone who eats and drinks without recognizing the body of the Lord eats and drinks judgment on himself. [30]That is why many among you are weak and sick, and a number of you have fallen asleep. [31]But if we judged ourselves, we would not come under judgment" (1 Cor. 11:28-31).

The term "fallen asleep" is a reference to death. Can it be that some short and longer term illnesses and perhaps even some deaths experienced among church people today is a consequence of irreverence for the things of God? Perhaps to some this may sound far fetched and yet we see that God would not be mocked by the Israelites who had claimed His name and so death came to them. The passage above also clearly indicates that we can bring judgement on ourselves by our irreverent actions.

There have been those who regularly pray for the sick who have noted linkages between specific sins and peoples' illnesses. In instances when the failure to forgive others, bitterness, complaining, self-pity, etc., are confessed and repented of, healing has come from a variety of illnesses or maladies. If we want to walk in health, we need to walk in holiness and reverence before our God and do not treat lightly this salvation He purchased for us at the cost of His Son. We need to repent of those things in our lives which are not pleasing to God.

Truly, the fear of the Lord is the beginning of wisdom. Because we cannot truly comprehend a God who could create this universe and all that is in it, it is easy for us to try and bring Him down to our level of understanding thereby making Him something less than He is. We tend to consider Him too lightly. Moses, who had seen many miraculous wonders already, was incredulous that God could somehow provide enough meat for the Israelites for a whole month. Yet God was able to command so many quail to fly into their camp that they could feed 600,000 men plus women and children for a whole month. What an awesome thing, but an easy task for the creator or the universe.

It was not just the Israelites' desire for other food which caused them difficulty, but their hearts were becoming harder and harder toward God. They had begun to rebel against the Almighty God and were rejecting Him in their hearts. As a consequence they were ready to turn around and go back to their old way of life and bondage in Egypt. They were saying they preferred that way of life to following God through the hard places. The life they were leading in the wilderness was meant to wean them away from their trust and dependence on Egypt that they might learn to trust and obey God and be the heirs of God's richest blessings, but unfortunately, they did not desire to learn God's ways. They had not determined to follow God wholeheartedly.

It is important that those of us who have come to Jesus Christ by faith relinquish all claims to our lives. There is only one thing that must have first priority, and that is to reach the goal and the prize to which we have been called in Jesus Christ (Phil. 3:4-17). If we have any lesser quest than this, we will not be diligent in following Jesus and we will not please Him.

If you have never said to Him, "Jesus, I am going to seek You as my first and foremost necessity, and will follow you wherever you lead, no matter what the cost, and am never going to go away from you," then you need to do that now. If we are not willing to do that, and yet want to be Christians, we are going to have difficulty because that which remains of "Egypt" in our hearts will be a trap and snare to us. When we have made it our total commitment to go God's way only, trusting in Him, then we will walk through difficulties without complaining because we have reserved no other agenda but His. We will seek our relief in Him alone. In so doing, His best will be worked out in our lives, and He will cause us to inherit all that He has promised us.

The Apostle Paul was able to say ...

11"...for I have learned to be content whatever the circumstances. 12I know what it is to be in need, and I know what it is to have plenty. I have learned the secret of being content in any and every situation, whether well fed or hungry, whether living in plenty or in want. 13I can do everything through him who gives me strength" (Phil. 4:11-13).

Also...

6"But godliness with contentment is great gain. 7For we brought nothing into the world, and we can take nothing out of it. 8But if we have food and clothing, we will be content with that. 9People who want to get rich fall into temptation and a trap and into many foolish and harmful desires that plunge men into ruin and destruction. 10For the love of money is a root of all kinds of evil. Some people, eager for money, have wandered from the faith and pierced themselves with many griefs.
11But you, man of God, flee from all this, and pursue righteousness, godliness, faith, love, endurance and gentleness. 12Fight the good fight of the faith. Take hold of the eternal life to which you were called when you made your good confession in the presence of many witnesses. 13In the sight of

God, who gives life to everything, and of Christ Jesus, who while testifying before Pontius Pilate made the good confession, I charge you [14]to keep this command without spot or blame until the appearing of our Lord Jesus Christ, [15]which God will bring about in his own time—God, the blessed and only Ruler, the King of kings and Lord of lords, [16]who alone is immortal and who lives in unapproachable light, whom no one has seen or can see. To him be honor and might forever. Amen.

[17]Command those who are rich in this present world not to be arrogant nor to put their hope in wealth, which is so uncertain, but to put their hope in God, who richly provides us with everything for our enjoyment. [18]Command them to do good, to be rich in good deeds, and to be generous and willing to share. [19]In this way they will lay up treasure for themselves as a firm foundation for the coming age, so that they may take hold of the life that is truly life" (1 Tim. 6:6-19).

A short time after God caused the quail to come into the camp, the Israelites neared the promised land and the Lord gave directions to Moses...

[1]"The LORD said to Moses, [2]'Send some men to explore the land of Canaan, which I am giving to the Israelites. From each ancestral tribe send one of its leaders.'

[3]So at the LORD's command Moses sent them out from the Desert of Paran. All of them were leaders of the Israelites" (Num. 13:1-3).

Twelve spies, all leaders of tribes within Israel, were chosen to go in and spy out the land of Canaan. Two spies, of particular note, were Joshua (name changed from Hoshea by Moses) and Caleb.

[17]"When Moses sent them to explore Canaan, he said, 'Go up through the Negev and on into the hill country. [18]See what the land is like and whether the people who live there are strong or weak, few or many. [19]What kind of land do

they live in? Is it good or bad? What kind of towns do they live in? Are they unwalled or fortified? ²⁰How is the soil? Is it fertile or poor? Are there trees on it or not? Do your best to bring back some of the fruit of the land.' (It was the season for the first ripe grapes.)

²¹So they went up and explored the land from the Desert of Zin as far as Rehob, toward Lebo Hamath. ²²They went up through the Negev and came to Hebron, where Ahiman, Sheshai and Talmai, the descendants of Anak, lived. (Hebron had been built seven years before Zoan in Egypt.) ²³When they reached the Valley of Eshcol, they cut off a branch bearing a single cluster of grapes. Two of them carried it on a pole between them, along with some pomegranates and figs. ²⁴That place was called the Valley of Eshcol because of the cluster of grapes the Israelites cut off there. ²⁵At the end of forty days they returned from exploring the land.

²⁶They came back to Moses and Aaron and the whole Israelite community at Kadesh in the Desert of Paran. There they reported to them and to the whole assembly and showed them the fruit of the land. ²⁷They gave Moses this account: 'We went into the land to which you sent us, and it does flow with milk and honey! Here is its fruit. ²⁸But the people who live there are powerful, and the cities are fortified and very large. We even saw descendants of Anak there. ²⁹The Amalekites live in the Negev; the Hittites, Jebusites and Amorites live in the hill country; and the Canaanites live near the sea and along the Jordan'" (Num. 13:17-29).

I believe that the report the spies brought back regarding the land of Canaan was a factual account of what they found. It was a land that did flow with milk and honey, as the Lord had promised, but they identified that there were obstacles to overcome. They had taken note of these obstacles, and now the mettle of the Israelites would be tested. How they reacted to the news brought back by the spies would be very important.

It is not inappropriate for individuals to anticipate situations which lie ahead and to determine a plan of action. Our assessment may tell us that there are problems ahead of a serious nature. How we respond to these concerns is important to us. We can look at these problems as opportunities for us to trust and depend on God, or we can worry, become fearful, and doubt our ability to make it through.

It is very clear from scripture, that Christians are not to live in fear. We are called to fear the Lord, but if we are living obediently before Him, there is nothing else that we need fear. In fact, the Lord gives a tremendous promise to us...

> [9]*"I took you from the ends of the earth, from its farthest corners I called you. I said, 'You are my servant'; I have chosen you and have not rejected you.* [10]*So do not fear, for I am with you; do not be dismayed, for I am your God. I will strengthen you and help you; I will uphold you with my righteous right hand'"*(Isa. 41:9-10).

Do we look at our future through eyes of faith, or through eyes of fear? Have we been reading the scriptures on a regular basis so that our faith in God is strong? Are we sufficiently acquainted with the promises which God has given us in His Word to know what we can expect from Him?

The Anakites were some of the people living in the land of Canaan. They were a tall and strong people and to some were looked upon as giants. Giants in scripture are a picture of obstacles that loom larger than life in our own eyes. They may be things that will never come to pass but also may be things that we see no solution for and may not know how to handle in our own strength. They can give us a great deal of dismay, and might even cause us to fear and quake.

So we think to ourselves, "I know that I cannot defeat these giants in my own strength, I've tried and I've always failed. Maybe if I get some help from individuals trained to deal with these giants, then maybe I will be able to overcome them. I also know that God tells us to call on Him when we need help and deliverance. Would He really come through if I depended solely on Him?

While we think on these things, the powers of darkness in the spirit realm try also to convince us that there is no use, that we can't possibly win against the giants that we face. They come to bring fear and doubt into our hearts.

Now the arguments of this kind that we have with ourselves may vary dependent on the situation we are in as well as our knowledge of, and our faith in, God and His Word. But certainly they are similar to the thought processes we go through as we face difficulties in our lives.

As an example, let's say you have asked Jesus into your heart. You have put your faith in Him and you trust in Him, but an old habit has come along with you into the Christian life. You smoke cigarettes and cannot seem to break the habit. You know that this cigarette habit has not kept Jesus from saving you, but you also know that it is harmful to you and may not be a good witness to others. As a result, you desire to quit. You have tried to quit before, but haven't been able to do it. This habit has become like a monstrous giant in your life that has resisted your every effort to defeat it. Now once more, you enter a stop smoking program offered by some company, and you give it one more try, but to no avail.

Then, as you are reading the Bible one day, you notice a scripture which says ...

> "Now thanks be unto God, which always causeth us to triumph in Christ..." (2 Cor. 2:14 KJV).

This passage speaks to your heart and makes you to realize by faith that Christ can set you free from your habit. So you go to God in prayer, asking Him to take away your smoking habit from you. You ask Him to cause you to triumph over it. You thank Him in advance, and daily thereafter trust Him that He will bring about the opportunity for you to lay the habit aside.

Then one day, you realize that the time has come to put your cigarettes aside. The Lord has somehow quickened it to your heart. As a consequence, you smoke your last cigarette (you consider this to be kind of a "burnt offering" to the Lord) and you throw the rest of your cigarettes away. Amazingly enough, as you proceed through your day, you find that the Lord is giving you victory without the struggle that you have sensed in the past. God has broken the power of that habit and defeated the giant which has ruled over you for so long. When others you work with realize that you are no longer smoking, they ask you if you took hypnotism, or went to some other stop smoking program ... "JUST HOW DID YOU DO IT???" Then you tell them the Lord gave you the victory, and they can't quite believe it.

We must again consider that ...

"...if the Son sets you free, you will be free indeed" (John 8:36).

The story told above is not a far-fetched one. It happened to both my wife and I at different times and in slightly different ways. God delivered us. We not only stopped smoking, but the desire was taken away too!

There are those who have gone to Alcoholics Anonymous for years to "control" an alcoholic addiction, while others have taken this giant to the Lord to have it slain and God has completely freed them from the addiction so that there was no longer any need to even continue in Alcoholic Anonymous.

We know that there are other giants around that would cause us to lose heart. Loss of income, sickness, etc., which would leave us wondering what we will do,—how will we cope,—how will our needs will be met. These giants would come to debilitate us and leave us walking in fear and despair. But our God is a giant killer if we can but lay hold of His promises by faith.

Often these giants strike without advance warning and suddenly we are face to face with a crisis. Suddenly we may be faced with a very difficult situation demanding decisions on our part. What should we do?... What is going to happen to us?...How are we going to make it?...What about this?...What about that? At that moment, we will probably not have the time to sit down with the Bible to gain a more intimate knowledge of Him and to find the promises that we will need to sustain our faith and bring us the victory in the middle of our difficulties. It may be too late to gain knowledge of the Lord through experience. Even though we may have professed Jesus as our Savior and have believed in Him for salvation and eternal life, yet we may find in that time of trial that we do not have a knowledge of how to stand fast in His promises because we have been careless and foolish in our searching after Him.

As a consequence, our peace may be lost. Have we committed ourselves to trust in the Lord no matter what comes? Have we prepared ourselves by studying God's Word and learning His promises to us, or have we instead been using our spare time to read novels, watch television or do other things? Have we been walking in obedience to the Lord and are our hearts fully committed to Him? Or have our lives been taken up with the affairs, the comforts and the pleasures of this life that we have neglected to seek after the Lord? To be a half-hearted Christian is pure foolishness! It is also very dangerous. Our folly may not become clear to us until it is too late.

To the righteous ones, who fear the Lord and delight greatly in His commandments, it is said ...

"He shall not be afraid of evil tidings: his heart is fixed, trusting in the LORD" (Ps. 112:7 KJV).

Again ...

[39]*"The salvation of the righteous comes from the LORD; he is their stronghold in time of trouble.* [40]*The LORD helps them and delivers them; he delivers them from the wicked and saves them, because they take refuge in him"* (Ps. 37:39-40).

The wording of this last verse has intrigued me. Do we forsake our own deliverance when we turn to doubt and fear? The last verse says, *"he delivers them ... and saves them, **because they take refuge in Him**ᵉ."* This deliverance is not automatic and separate from the application of our faith but is because we take refuge in Him.

The crisis comes to test our commitment to God's way. Will we stand fast in our faith and commitment to Him, or will we turn to doubt and fear?

A story in the life of king Asa illustrates the point. King Asa lived a number of years after the Israelites had finally entered into the promised land. The nation of Israel was split into two kingdoms, Israel and Judah. King Asa ruled over Judah. The account and the events of his reign is recorded in the books of 1 Kings chapters 15-16 and 2 Chronicles chapters 14-16.

It says in 2 Chronicles 14:2-7, that Asa did what was good and right in the eyes of the Lord his God. He removed places of pagan worship which had started to spring up in the land in violation of God's laws, he commanded Judah to seek the Lord the God of their fathers and to obey His laws and commands, he built cities, and it says that the Lord gave them rest and peace in the land on every side. They built and prospered. Asa also maintained an army ...

⁸"Asa had an army of three hundred thousand men from Judah, equipped with large shields and with spears, and two hundred and eighty thousand from Benjamin, armed with small shields and with bows. All these were brave fighting men" (2 Chr. 14:8).

Things looked rosy with no sign of trouble in sight, but then...

⁹"Zerah, the Cushite, marched out against them with a vast army and three hundred chariots, and came as far as Mareshah. ¹⁰Asa went out to meet him, and they took up

---

ᵉEmphasis added

battle positions in the Valley of Zephathah near Mareshah" (2 Chr. 14:9-10).

Suddenly trouble appears in the form of a "vast" army which I believe was much larger than that fielded by Asa. What to do?... what to do?? Asa had to determine how he would react and he made his choice ...

> [11]*"Then Asa called to the LORD his God and said, 'LORD, there is no one like you to help the powerless against the mighty. Help us, O LORD our God, for we rely on you, and in your name we have come against this vast army. O LORD, you are our God; do not let man prevail against you.'*
> [12]*The LORD struck down the Cushites before Asa and Judah. The Cushites fled,* [13]*and Asa and his army pursued them as far as Gerar. Such a great number of Cushites fell that they could not recover; they were crushed before the LORD and his forces. The men of Judah carried off a large amount of plunder.* [14]*They destroyed all the villages around Gerar, for the terror of the LORD had fallen upon them. They plundered all these villages, since there was much booty there.* [15]*They also attacked the camps of the herdsmen and carried off droves of sheep and goats and camels. Then they returned to Jerusalem"* (2 Chr. 14:11-15).

Asa made His choice to place his trust in the Lord, and a powerful enemy was defeated. A prophet of the Lord came to Asa and gave him a wonderful Word from the Lord ...

> [2]*"...Listen to me, Asa and all Judah and Benjamin. The LORD is with you when you are with him. If you seek him, he will be found by you, but if you forsake him, he will forsake you.* [3]*For a long time Israel was without the true God, without a priest to teach and without the law.* [4]*But in their distress they turned to the LORD, the God of Israel, and sought him, and he was found by them.* [5]*In those days it was not safe to travel about, for all the inhabitants of the lands were in great turmoil.* [6]*One nation was being crushed by another*

and one city by another, because God was troubling them with every kind of distress. ⁷But as for you, be strong and do not give up, for your work will be rewarded" (2 Chr. 15:2-7).

We each must make the choice. Are we going to trust and rely on the Lord, or are we going to forsake Him and try and go it alone without Him? The words spoken to Asa are spoken to us as well ... *"The Lord is with you when you are with him. If you seek him, he will be found by you, but if you forsake him, he will forsake you... be strong and do not give up, for your work will be rewarded."*

So how did Asa do after that? Let's continue with the story ...

¹*"In the thirty-sixth year of Asa's reign Baasha king of Israel went up against Judah and fortified Ramah to prevent anyone from leaving or entering the territory of Asa king of Judah.*

²*Asa then took the silver and gold out of the treasuries of the LORD's temple and of his own palace and sent it to Ben-Hadad king of Aram, who was ruling in Damascus. ³'Let there be a treaty between me and you,' he said, "as there was between my father and your father. See, I am sending you silver and gold. Now break your treaty with Baasha king of Israel so he will withdraw from me.'*

⁴*Ben-Hadad agreed with King Asa and sent the commanders of his forces against the towns of Israel. They conquered Ijon, Dan, Abel Maim and all the store cities of Naphtali. ⁵When Baasha heard this, he stopped building Ramah and abandoned his work. ⁶Then King Asa brought all the men of Judah, and they carried away from Ramah the stones and timber Baasha had been using. With them he built up Geba and Mizpah"* (2 Chr 16:1-6).

As we can see, Judah was attacked again, only this time by Israel. Asa sought and paid to obtain help from Ben-Hadad king of Aram who successfully attacked cities in Israel. Israel was forced to back off.

Asa had been successful in both wars. In one, he sought and obtained the help of the Lord and in the other he sought and paid for the help of the king of Aram. Well, whatever brings success is OK, right?

WRONG! After the second conflict was settled, Asa again heard from the Lord through another prophet ...

> [7]*"At that time Hanani the seer came to Asa king of Judah and said to him: 'Because you relied on the king of Aram and not on the LORD your God, the army of the king of Aram has escaped from your hand.* [8]*Were not the Cushites and Libyans a mighty army with great numbers of chariots and horsemen? Yet when you relied on the LORD, he delivered them into your hand.* [9]***For the eyes of the LORD range throughout the earth to strengthen those whose hearts are fully committed to him.**[f] *You have done a foolish thing, and from now on you will be at war.'*
>
> [10]*Asa was angry with the seer because of this; he was so enraged that he put him in prison. At the same time Asa brutally oppressed some of the people"* (2 Chr. 16:7-10).

In seeking after help from another nation and not the Lord as he had done the first time, Asa demonstrated that his heart was not fully committed to the Lord. He had relied on the Lord in the first war but in the second he relied on a worldly king and his armies. Even though this tactic took care of the problem at that time, it clearly was not pleasing to the Lord. The scripture says that the eyes of the Lord range throughout the earth to strengthen those (and that surely must include us) whose hearts are fully committed to Him. As this story shows, being committed to Him means that we are to rely on the Lord in all the difficulties we face and to trust that He can bring us through.

Another event occurred in Asa's life which illustrates this again ...

---

[f]Emphasis added

[12]"In the thirty-ninth year of his reign Asa was afflicted with a disease in his feet. Though his disease was severe, even in his illness he did not seek help from the LORD, but only from the physicians. [13]Then in the forty-first year of his reign Asa died and rested with his fathers" (2 Chr. 16:12-13).

Asa had at least three opportunities in his life to demonstrate his faith in God. The first time, he marched into the face of the giant with no visible evidence that Judah had sufficient strength to defeat the march larger army which came against them, but he went by faith, the victory was won and God commended him. In the natural, he was walking into the jaws of defeat, but he committed everything into God's hands and went on. That may be the way it is when we are walking by faith. We have no advance assurances that the victory is ours. We may just have to step out in bare faith and trust in the Lord laying everything on the line.

Illnesses such as cancer bring a person face to face with this kind of tough decision. The sickness or disease becomes a debilitating giant which puts fear into the heart of the inflicted individual as well as their loved ones. Quickly we seek help from doctors, most likely praying as we go. We have a faith that the doctor will have some kind of answer that will deliver us from what we fear. Then the doctor issues his report and says, "Yes, this really is a giant, and it will require some serious treatment." He proceeds to identify the alternatives from his point of view which generally would not include laying it all before the Lord and trusting in Him alone.

In the eyes of many, and perhaps the closest loved ones, if the patient were to just go home to wait on the Lord for healing without subjecting himself to chemotherapy, radiation or some equally serious cure, he would be stepping out in foolishness. Recognizing that not all the individuals involved may be people of faith, there would undoubtedly be more bad reports of fear and doubt spoken to dissuade the inflicted one from making any such decision. It is true, that the afflicted one as well as his closest loved ones would be laying everything on the line though medical solutions certainly offer no guarantees.

How do we compare the crisis an individual faces who is told he has cancer, with the decision which Asa or the Israelites faced? All are life and death situations appearing as 'giants' to those involved. We find that when Asa took the expedient path by hiring Ben-Hadad and his armies to fight for him, he displeased the Lord. We will soon see that the Israelites also displeased the Lord when they put greater faith in the giants, than they did in God. Might it not be good to commit ones' self totally to the Lord and pray a prayer similar to the one Asa prayed prior to his first conflict? *"LORD, there is no one like you to help the powerless against the mighty. Help [me], O LORD our God, for [I] rely on you, and in your name [I] come against this [giant of cancer]. O LORD, you are [my] God; do not let [this cancer] prevail against you."*

We live in an affluent society where there are so many Ben-Hadad's to help us that perhaps we have lost our faith to stand without such help. I desire to be one who is willing to commit myself fully to the Lord and upon His promises to sustain me.

The Israelites were undoubtedly anxious to hear the report of the spies that returned from the land of Canaan, but were their hearts ready to hear it? How would they react to the news of ... "THE GIANTS?"

It should be noted that in a Deuteronomy account of these events, Moses said that he had made the following declaration to the Israelites ...

[20]*"...'You have reached the hill country of the Amorites, which the LORD our God is giving us. [21]See, the LORD your God has given you the land. Go up and take possession of it as the LORD, the God of your fathers, told you. Do not be afraid; do not be discouraged.'*

[22]Then all of you came to me and said, "Let us send men ahead to spy out the land for us and bring back a re-

port about the route we are to take and the towns we will come to."

²³The idea seemed good to me; so I selected twelve of you, one man from each tribe'" (Deut. 1:20-23).

Moses told them that the Lord their God had given them the land and that they were to go up and take possession of it as the Lord had told them. They were not to be afraid or discouraged.

One of the men who had spied out Canaan was a man of faith who knew and trusted God. He spoke first ...

"Then Caleb silenced the people before Moses and said, 'We should go up and take possession of the land, for we can certainly do it" (Num. 13:30).

Only two of the twelve spies who went into the land of Canaan held this kind of faith—Joshua and Caleb. The others did not.

³¹"But the men who had gone up with him said, 'We can't attack those people; they are stronger than we are.' ³²And they spread among the Israelites a bad report about the land they had explored. They said, 'The land we explored devours those living in it. All the people we saw there are of great size. ³³We saw the Nephilim there (the descendants of Anak come from the Nephilim). We seemed like grasshoppers in our own eyes, and we looked the same to them' (Num. 13:31-33).

The spies who gave this frightful report were of little faith, and they spread a bad report about the land. Had they brought a good report, the Israelites would have been encouraged, but as it was, the spies destroyed what little faith the Israelites still had.

In a land abounding in experts, we have come to believe in bad reports more than we believe in God. We go to these experts who give us bad reports and we return home discouraged. Our faith is shattered. We know we won't see victory because the experts have said so. Have we not placed our faith too many times in the word of people who do not even believe in God? We probably would have been better off not to have gone to them in the first place than to let them build upon our fears and doubts.

The Israelites had not been observant to recognize how faithful God had been to them. Every time they had faced a crises, from the time of their departure from Egypt to that present moment, God had come through for them in every difficult situation. Unfortunately the Israelites gave no thought to His miracles, they did not remember His many kindnesses and soon forgot what He had done for them (Ps. 106:7,13).

God had said to the Israelites that He would lead them into the promised land. He did not say things like "...I will bring you to that land if the enemy is not too strong or if there are no giants there," etc. God did not hedge His promises in any way.

So how did the Israelites respond to the report of the spies...

> [1]"*That night all the people of the community raised their voices and wept aloud.* [2]*All the Israelites grumbled against Moses and Aaron, and the whole assembly said to them, "If only we had died in Egypt! Or in this desert!* [3]*Why is the LORD bringing us to this land only to let us fall by the sword? Our wives and children will be taken as plunder. Wouldn't it be better for us to go back to Egypt?"* [4]*And they said to each other, "We should choose a leader and go back to Egypt"* (Num. 14:1-4).

The unbelief of the Israelites led them to believe the bad report and as a consequence they began to confess despair, fear and defeat. When it comes to believing in Jesus it is said, "For it is with your heart that you believe and are justified, and it is with your mouth that you confess and are saved" (Rom. 10:10).

The reverse was happening here, however, in that the Israelites did not believe in their hearts and so with their mouths they confessed fear and defeat. They now believed that the Lord brought them into the land to let them die by the sword, that their children would be taken as plunder and it would be better for them to go back to Egypt. They were denying everything that God had said to them. What had surely been possible if they had stood fast in their faith in God, had become impossible through unbelief. The giants had stared them down and the Israelites were going off without a fight.

Bad reports are founded in unbelief and I believe they find their origin in Satan. We gain victory over Satan through faith in God. Satan arrays his forces against us, working on our minds and through others to discourage us and to cause us to turn away from trust in God. Then we begin to confess our unbelief and our doubts and we truly do go down in defeat. The victory that could have been ours is gone.

How important it is to have a daily confession of faith in God in our every circumstance. That kind of confession is in fact high praise to God. Just for a moment let us imagine that the Israelites did not turn to unbelief but instead confessed their faith in God. What would it be like?

Well, we have already seen it. Remember the song the Israelites sang to the Lord after they crossed the Red Sea? That was the song that they should have been singing now ...

> [11]*"Who among the gods is like you, O Lord? Who is like you—majestic in holiness, awesome in glory, working wonders?* [12]*You stretched out your right hand and the earth swallowed them.* [13]*In your unfailing love you will lead the people you have redeemed. In your strength you will guide them to your holy dwelling.* [14]*The nations will hear and tremble; anguish will grip the people of Philistia.* [15]*The chiefs of Edom will be terrified, the leaders of Moab will be seized with trembling, the people of Canaan will melt away;* [16]*terror and dread will fall upon them. By the power of your arm they will be as still as a stone—until your people pass by, O Lord, until the people you bought pass by.* [17]*You will bring them in and plant them on the mountain of your inheritance—the place, O Lord, you made for your dwelling, the sanctuary O Lord, your hands established.* [18]*The Lord will reign for ever and ever"* (Exod. 15:11-18).

As we stated earlier, the Israelites song beside the Red Sea reminds me of church worship services. We sing of how great our God is. We believe that He will see us through every difficulty. But then we find ourselves facing a crisis of some kind (e.g., loss of a job, lack of finances, sickness or other things which might be equally as debilitating), Satan comes to bring words of despair or discouragement to us. Would that not be a good time to confess openly and out loud our faith and trust in God? Should we not praise Him, even when things in the natural would seem to be at their worst? Should we not believe that He will bring us through and give us the victory, for He has promised that He will meet our need and will not forsake us as we are diligent to trust and obey Him? Surely it would have greatly pleased God if the Israelites had confessed the words of the song they sang at the Red Sea instead of what they did say? *Had they done so, they would have gone on to see God's hand extended to defeat the giants that stood in their path!*

Moses, Aaron, Joshua and Caleb understood the seriousness of the Israelites lack of trust in God. They had seen the same things as the rest of the spies and yet they continued to have a confession rooted in a firm faith in God...

5"Then Moses and Aaron fell facedown in front of the whole Israelite assembly gathered there. 6Joshua son of Nun and Caleb son of Jephunneh, who were among those who had explored the land, tore their clothes 7and said to the entire Israelite assembly, "The land we passed through and explored is exceedingly good. 8If the LORD is pleased with us, he will lead us into that land, a land flowing with milk and honey, and will give it to us. 9Only do not rebel against the LORD. And do not be afraid of the people of the land, because we will swallow them up. Their protection is gone, but the LORD is with us. Do not be afraid of them."

10But the whole assembly talked about stoning them..."
(Num. 14:5-10).

"... do not rebel against the Lord ... do not be afraid of the people of the land ... do not be afraid of them." However, it was too late, for the faith of the Israelites had gone. It was then that God appeared and spoke ...

[10]*"...Then the glory of the LORD appeared at the Tent of Meeting to all the Israelites.* [11]*The LORD said to Moses, 'How long will these people treat me with contempt? How long will they refuse to believe in me, in spite of all the miraculous signs I have performed among them?* [12]*I will strike them down with a plague and destroy them, but I will make you into a nation greater and stronger than they.'*

[13]*Moses said to the LORD, 'Then the Egyptians will hear about it! By your power you brought these people up from among them.* [14]*And they will tell the inhabitants of this land about it. They have already heard that you, O LORD, are with these people and that you, O LORD, have been seen face to face, that your cloud stays over them, and that you go before them in a pillar of cloud by day and a pillar of fire by night.* [15]*If you put these people to death all at one time, the nations who have heard this report about you will say,* [16]*'The LORD was not able to bring these people into the land he promised them on oath; so he slaughtered them in the desert.'*

[17]*'Now may the Lord's strength be displayed, just as you have declared:* [18]*'The LORD is slow to anger, abounding in love and forgiving sin and rebellion. Yet he does not leave the guilty unpunished; he punishes the children for the sin of the fathers to the third and fourth generation.'* [19]*In accordance with your great love, forgive the sin of these people, just as you have pardoned them from the time they left Egypt until now.'*

[20]*The LORD replied, 'I have forgiven them, as you asked.* [21]*Nevertheless, as surely as I live and as surely as the glory of the LORD fills the whole earth,* [22]*not one of the men who saw my glory and the miraculous signs I performed in Egypt and in the desert but who disobeyed me and tested me ten times—* [23]*not one of them will ever see the land I promised on oath to their forefathers. No one who has treated me with contempt will ever see it.* [24]*But because my servant Caleb has a different spirit and follows me wholeheartedly, I will bring him*

into the land he went to, and his descendants will inherit it. [25]Since the Amalekites and Canaanites are living in the valleys, turn back tomorrow and set out toward the desert along the route to the Red Sea.'

[26]The LORD said to Moses and Aaron: [27]'How long will this wicked community grumble against me? I have heard the complaints of these grumbling Israelites. [28]So tell them, 'As surely as I live, declares the LORD, I will do to you the very things I heard you say: [29]In this desert your bodies will fall—every one of you twenty years old or more who was counted in the census and who has grumbled against me. [30]Not one of you will enter the land I swore with uplifted hand to make your home, except Caleb son of Jephunneh and Joshua son of Nun. [31]As for your children that you said would be taken as plunder, I will bring them in to enjoy the land you have rejected. [32]But you—your bodies will fall in this desert. [33]Your children will be shepherds here for forty years, suffering for your unfaithfulness, until the last of your bodies lies in the desert. [34]For forty years—one year for each of the forty days you explored the land—you will suffer for your sins and know what it is like to have me against you.' [35]I, the LORD, have spoken, and I will surely do these things to this whole wicked community, which has banded together against me. They will meet their end in this desert; here they will die.'

[36]So the men Moses had sent to explore the land, who returned and made the whole community grumble against him by spreading a bad report about it —[37]these men responsible for spreading the bad report about the land were struck down and died of a plague before the LORD. [38]Of the men who went to explore the land, only Joshua son of Nun and Caleb son of Jephunneh survived.

[39]When Moses reported this to all the Israelites, they mourned bitterly. [40]Early the next morning they went up toward the high hill country. 'We have sinned,' they said. 'We will go up to the place the LORD promised.'

[41]But Moses said, 'Why are you disobeying the LORD's command? This will not succeed! [42]Do not go up, because the LORD is not with you. You will be defeated by your enemies, [43]for the Amalekites and Canaanites will face you

there. Because you have turned away from the LORD, he will not be with you and you will fall by the sword.'

⁴⁴Nevertheless, in their presumption they went up toward the high hill country, though neither Moses nor the ark of the LORD's covenant moved from the camp. ⁴⁵Then the Amalekites and Canaanites who lived in that hill country came down and attacked them and beat them down all the way to Hormah" (Num. 14:10-45).

What a tremendous loss their unbelief had brought them. The Israelites could have gone in to possess the land of Canaan in their second year after leaving Egypt, but now their time of wandering in the wilderness would be extended to forty years. Except for Joshua and Caleb, those individuals twenty years old or older would not see that promised land at all. What a terrible tragedy. God forgave the sins of the Israelites at Moses request, but the people still had to face severe consequences for their unbelief and disobedience.

The Israelites had seen the mighty hand of the Lord on many occasions. They had many opportunities to learn the ways of God and to make the decision to follow the Lord with all their heart, soul, mind and strength. Instead, they kept looking back to Egypt. Many were perhaps in it for what they could get out of it and not because of a deep and abiding love and commitment to the Lord and to His way. The Israelites reached a crisis point—the spies report. It revealed once and for all what was in their hearts.

We must certainly evaluate our own hearts in light of this history. We have perhaps come to Christ, but is the Lord the first and foremost necessity of our lives, or are our hearts still rooted in this world? Will it take a crisis or test of some kind to reveal what is truly in our hearts?

The Israelites murmuring and complaining as well as their disobedience and unbelief shut out many from the promised land but also cost many lives. As we saw at Mount Sinai, when the Israelites chose to worship the golden calf, 3,000 were slain by the Levites (Exod. 32:25-29,35). Then when they complained about their hardships in the hearing of the Lord, fire struck the outskirts of the camp although no loss of life was mentioned (Num. 11:1-3). Their numbers were reduced when they began to crave other food and a severe plague fell upon them (Num. 11:4-34). Now we see that the spies who were responsible for spreading a false report about the land were also struck down by a plague.

As they continued to wander in the wilderness after being shut out from the promised land, many more would die unnatural deaths because of their unbelief and rebellion against the Lord...

> **Numbers 16** - Korah, Dathan and Abiram rose up against Moses to challenge Moses, the one God had chosen to lead the Israelites. Korah and all who followed him as well as their wives and children were swallowed up by the earth. Then fire came from the Lord and consumed 250 men who were also involved. Later a plague struck the people who complained against Moses and Aaron because of what had happened.
>
> **Numbers 21** - Again the Israelite numbers were reduced when the people spoke against God and against Moses, complaining about their conditions and their food. God sent snakes against them and many Israelites died.
>
> **Numbers 25** - The Israelites engaged in sexual immorality with Moabite women and they began to bow down before Moabite gods. A plague consumed 24,000 Israelites.

The unbelief of the Israelites had shut them out of the promised land and their rebellion and unbelief brought about many premature deaths.

Moses and Aaron were also prevented from entering into the promised land because of a failure to do exactly as the Lord commanded when they sought water for the Israelites at the waters of Meribah (Num. 20; Deut. 3:23-29). Aaron's death is recorded in Num. 20:22-29 and he died on *"the first day of the fifth month of the fortieth year after the Israelites came out of Egypt. Aaron was a hundred and twenty-three years old when he died on Mount Hor"* (Num. 33:38-39).

Moses was buried by the Lord after he had seen the promised land from a distance. He was a hundred and twenty years old when he died. Moses was not shut out because he was a rebellious individual or did not believe in God, but because in a single moment *"the accumulated anger, exasperation and frustration of forty years came to expression"*[g] in Moses, and in his rage against the rebellious Israelites he acted in a way displeasing to the Lord. Because of the position Moses held, God judged him by a higher standard. Moses was a godly man who knew the ways of God and served Him with faithfulness and devotion. The end of Moses' life came at the end of the forty years of wilderness wandering just before the Israelites finally entered the promised land under Joshua's leadership.

[1]*"Then Moses climbed Mount Nebo from the plains of Moab to the top of Pisgah, across from Jericho. There the LORD showed him the whole land—from Gilead to Dan,* [2]*all of Naphtali, the territory of Ephraim and Manasseh, all the land of Judah as far as the western sea,* [3]*the Negev and the whole region from the Valley of Jericho, the City of Palms, as far as Zoar.* [4]*Then the LORD said to him, 'This is the land I promised on oath to Abraham, Isaac and Jacob when I said, 'I will give it to your descendants.' I have let you see it with your eyes, but you will not cross over into it.'*

[5]*And Moses the servant of the LORD died there in Moab, as the LORD had said.* [6]*He buried him in Moab, in the valley opposite Beth Peor, but to this day no one knows where his grave is.* [7]*Moses was a hundred and twenty years old when he died, yet his eyes were not weak nor his strength gone.* [8]*The Israelites grieved for Moses in the plains of Moab thirty days, until the time of weeping and mourning was over.*

[10]*Since then, no prophet has risen in Israel like Moses, whom the LORD knew face to face,* [11]*who did all those miraculous signs and wonders the LORD sent him to do in*

---

[9]NIV Study Note for Num. 20:10

*Egypt—to Pharaoh and to all his officials and to his whole
land. ¹²For no one has ever shown the mighty power or performed the awesome deeds that Moses did in the sight of all
Israel"* (Deut. 34:1-8,10-12).

Only Joshua and Caleb of all Israelites twenty years and
older at the time of the rebellion were allowed to enter the
promised land. It is said of them that they followed the Lord
"wholeheartedly" (Num. 14:24; 32:11-12; Deut. 1:35-36).
Joshua succeeded Moses as leader.

CHAPTER 9

If You Want to Win, You Must Finish the Race

We have followed the Israelites through their exodus and wilderness wanderings and have seen many wonderful teachings revealed and illustrated in this history. However, there is more to be said, in consideration of this history, on this very important subject of our faith and specifically the question of the "eternal security" of the believer. That is, can a person who has been truly saved (born again) lose their salvation by some means, or are they eternally secure in their relationship with the Lord Jesus Christ regardless of their actions? This has been a controversial subject and one which has staunch supporters on both sides. Yet I believe that it is vital for us to understand what scripture has to say regarding the eternal security of the believer. Initially we will look at this subject in light of the wilderness experiences of the people of Israel, but we will also explore many other passages of scripture. But first, a little background.

We have seen how the nation of Israel had its beginnings in Abraham. When Abram (later renamed Abraham) was told by God that he would have a son and would have a great multitude of offspring even though he was old and had been unable to have children by his wife Sarah, it says that he believed the Lord, and God credited it to him as righteousness (Gen. 15:6). Abraham placed his faith in God and the promise he had been given and as a consequence, he was declared to be righteous. This means God cleansed him of whatever sins he had committed and he was placed in a position of right standing with God. This purification was something that Abraham could not have attained by any works he might have been able to do. Rather it was a gift which God granted to Abraham as a consequence of his faith (his belief, trust, reliance and adherence to God) ...

[1]*"What then shall we say that Abraham, our forefather, discovered in this matter?* [2]*If, in fact, Abraham was justified by works, he had something to boast about—but not before God.* [3]*What does the Scripture say? 'Abraham believed God, and it was credited to him as righteousness.'* [4]*Now when a man works, his wages are not credited to him as a gift, but as an obligation.* [5]*However, to the man who does not work but trusts God who justifies the wicked, his faith is credited as righteousness"* (Rom. 4:1-5).

These same truths apply to us also ...

[23]*"The words 'it was credited to him' were written not for him alone,* [24]*but also for us, to whom God will credit righteousness—for us who believe in him who raised Jesus our Lord from the dead'"* (Rom. 4:23-24).

We have seen that there is no way we can be cleansed of our sinfulness except through Jesus Christ. Apart from Him, we are all subject to the judgements of God for our sins. Jesus, by His death on the cross, took the penalty for our sins upon Himself. However, His sacrifice is of no value to us unless we receive its benefits by faith. When we come to God and place our faith in Him, our record is cleared before God, we are declared to be no longer guilty, and righteousness is credited to our account. We are justified (made to be "just-as-if-we'd-never-sinned") before God. Our sins are buried in the sea of God's forgetfulness.

So, Abraham, as a consequence of his faith, was declared to be righteous before God and became one of God's very own children. This fact was written down hundreds of years before Jesus came to this earth and affirms that faith in God (trust, reliance and adherence to Him) has always been, from the time of Adam onward, the only way to attain right standing (salvation) with God.

Some may believe that the Israelites who lived before Jesus Christ were made right with God by keeping the law. God gave the law to Moses and all Israel. This law was good and it was God's intention that the Israelites should keep the law. Yet, the Bible clearly teaches, that the law in and of itself could not make anyone righteous in God's sight. Rather the law provided the standard whereby sin could be identified.

> [20]*"Therefore no one will be declared righteous in his sight by observing the law; rather, through the law we become conscious of sin.* [21]*But now a righteousness from God, apart from law, has been made known, to which the Law and the Prophets testify.* [22]*This righteousness from God comes through faith in Jesus Christ to all who believe..."* (Rom. 3:20-22).

The Bible teaches that good works, the keeping of the law, etc., has never, and will never change a sinner into a saint. Salvation has been by faith (trust, reliance and adherence to God) and faith alone from the very beginning of man's existence on this earth.

What about the Israelites who Moses led out of Egypt? Did they, like Abraham, become "believers," and were they cleansed of their sins and placed in right standing with God because of their faith? This is an important question.

The Israelites demonstrated a faith in God at a number of points during their exodus from Egypt. When the Lord went throughout the land of Egypt to slay the firstborn, the Israelites were protected from God's judgements because they kept that Passover by faith, partaking of the lamb (a type of Christ) and by placing the blood of the lamb on the doorpost of their houses. These very actions saved them from the judgements of God which fell on the firstborn of Egypt. As noted earlier, these things are a picture of the salvation which we have received through Jesus Christ. They believed and acted on God's instructions to them through Moses and their actions confirmed their faith. It is also clearly stated that after they saw God's hand extended in great power to bring them out of Egypt and had arrived on the other side of the Red Sea, they put their trust in God...

> [30]*"That day the LORD saved Israel from the hands of the Egyptians, and Israel saw the Egyptians lying dead on the shore.* [31]*And when the Israelites saw the great power the LORD displayed against the Egyptians,* **the people feared the LORD and put their trust in Him**[a] *and in Moses his servant"* (Exod. 14:30-31).

If we can say that Abraham became an heir of God because he believed (trusted in and relied on) God, then it follows that the same would be true of the Israelites when they believed what God had said and put their trust in Him. Fear of the Lord is the beginning of wisdom, and trust (or believing) in the Lord is the prerequisite for salvation.

The fact that they had come to a place of faith in God is confirmed in the book of Hebrews ...

> **"By faith**[b] *the people passed through the Red Sea as on dry land; but when the Egyptians tried to do so, they were drowned"* (Heb. 11:29).

---

[a]Emphasis added
[b]Emphasis added

The Israelites put their trust in God and in Moses His servant and responded to God's Word by faith on more than one occasion. Therefore it must be that they became God's children and were declared righteous before God. They were believers just as Abraham was, who, in a moment of time, was declared righteous as he believed God. However, the scriptures we have been reviewing (as well as others we will look at) reveal that many of those Israelites, if not the vast majority, lost that right standing with God when they reverted back to unbelief. They lost the position which they had originally attained by faith.

Let's look at what the writer of Hebrews had to say about all of this...

5"Moses was faithful as a servant in all God's house, testifying to what would be said in the future. 6But Christ is faithful as a son over God's house. And we are his house, if we hold on to our courage and the hope of which we boast."
7So, as the Holy Spirit says:

"Today, if you hear his voice, 8do not harden your hearts as you did in the rebellion, during the time of testing in the desert, 9where your fathers tested and tried me and for forty years saw what I did. 10That is why I was angry with that generation, and I said, 'Their hearts are always going astray, and they have not known my ways.' 11So I declared on oath in my anger, 'They shall never enter my rest.'"

12See to it, brothers, that none of you has a sinful, unbelieving heart that turns away from the living God. 13But encourage one another daily, as long as it is called Today, so that none of you may be hardened by sin's deceitfulness. 14We have come to share in Christ if we hold firmly till the end the confidence we had at first. 15As has just been said:

"Today, if you hear his voice, do not harden your hearts as you did in the rebellion."

16Who were they who heard and rebelled? Were they not all those Moses led out of Egypt? 17And with whom was he angry for forty years? Was it not with those who sinned, whose bodies fell in the desert? 18And to whom did God swear that they would never enter his rest if not to those who disobeyed[c]? [19]So we see that they were not able to enter, because of their unbelief" (Heb. 3:5-19).

[1]"Therefore, since the promise of entering his rest still stands, let us be careful that none of you be found to have fallen short of it. [2]For we also have had the gospel preached to us, just as they did; but the message they heard was of no value to them, because those who heard did not combine it with faith. [3]Now we who have believed enter that rest, just as God has said, 'So I declared on oath in my anger, 'They shall never enter my rest.'

And yet his work has been finished since the creation of the world. [4]For somewhere he has spoken about the seventh day in these words: 'And on the seventh day God rested from all his work.' [5]And again in the passage above he says, 'They shall never enter my rest.'

[6]It still remains that some will enter that rest, and those who formerly had the gospel preached to them did not go in, because of their disobedience. [7]Therefore God again set a certain day, calling it Today, when a long time later he spoke through David, as was said before:

"Today, if you hear his voice, do not harden your hearts."

[8]For if Joshua had given them rest, God would not have spoken later about another day. [9]There remains, then, a Sabbath-rest for the people of God; [10]for anyone who enters God's rest also rests from his own work, just as God did from his. [11]Let us, therefore, make every effort to enter that rest, so that no one will fall by following their example of disobedience" (Heb. 4:1-11).

The Israelites very clearly exhibited faith in God in the events surrounding their exodus from Egypt. Scripture declares that they put their trust in God. Then, in spite of all they saw God do, and the wonders He performed, their hearts became hard and went astray from the faith which they initially held. The Israelites had great confidence in God when they had crossed the Red Sea and all their enemies lay dead behind

---

[c]or *disbelieved*

them. It was by that sea that they sang their joyous song of faith before the Lord, extolling the great deliverance He had won for them. As stated previously, this is certainly a picture of the joyous songs of faith Christians sing in church extolling the deliverance which they have been provided from Satan's dominion. They are true songs of the redeemed which they have every right to sing.

It was from this position that the Israelites proceeded to fall as they faced the perils of the wilderness. The Israelites "turned away" from the living God. They did not hold on to their courage and the hope of which they boasted (Heb. 3:6) they did not hold to the end the confidence they had at first (Heb. 3:14), and so they were not able to enter because of their unbelief (Heb. 3:19). They did not enter God's rest nor did they come to share in Christ (to share in all that Jesus Christ has purchased by His death for them). This is clearly a warning for us.

The writer of Hebrews refers to his readers (which includes us) as brothers which implies he is addressing believers in Jesus Christ. He recounts the history of the Israelites to warn his brother believers that they must see to it that they do not have a sinful unbelieving heart that would **turn away** from the living God, further stating that we come to share in Christ **IF we hold firmly till the end** the confidence we had at first. Then in Hebrews 4:11 he encourages us to make every effort to enter the rest of God "so that no one will **fall** by following their example of disobedience."[d] Again he is speaking of believers. No one can fall from a position they never held. Just as the Israelites had a confidence in God, a faith at the outset, so do those who have come by faith to Jesus Christ. We are admonished to hold that confidence steadfast to the end.

In this passage, the terms "turn away" and "fall" imply a condition where we have lost our salvation. It cannot be some kind of backsliding where we are just errant children who still retain our right standing with God, because it says,

---

[d]Emphasis added

"We are his [God's] house if we hold on to our courage and the hope of which we boast." This indicates that we can lose our place in God's house (our salvation) if we do not hold on to our faith. This is not a passage written to non-believers because the writer talks about holding on to "our" courage and the hope of which "we" boast, including himself among those he warns. He speaks to those who presently have a hope (a salvation) of which they are able to boast (have in their present possession). We who are believers are to "encourage one another daily—so that none of you may be hardened by sin's deceitfulness." It is that subtle deceitfulness of sin which can slowly cause us to be drawn aside from Christ.

What is this "rest" spoken of in the above passage? I think that a study note for Heb. 4:3 and 4:9 in the Full Life Study Bible says it very well...

> "**4:3 ENTER THAT REST.** Only we who have believed the saving message of Christ enter God's spiritual rest. Christ takes our burdens and sins and gives us the "rest" of his forgiveness, salvation and Spirit (Matt. 11:28). However, in this life our rest is only partial, for we are pilgrims plodding through a harsh world. One by one, as we die in the Lord, we enter his perfect rest in heaven."

> "**4:9 REMAINS, THEN, A SABBATH-REST.** God's promised rest is not only earthly, but heavenly as well (vv. 7-8; cf. 13:14). For believers, there remains an eternal rest in heaven (Jn 14:1-3; cf. Heb 11:10,16). Entering this final rest means ceasing from the labors, sufferings and persecutions common to our lives on this earth (cf. Rev 14:13), participating in God's own rest, and experiencing unending joy, delight, love and fellowship with God and other redeemed saints. It will be a seventh day without end (Rev 21-22)."

When we come to Christ, it is God's desire that we enter into a rest of faith wherein we cease our own struggling and striving to live the Christian life and realize that it is only through the power of God's Holy Spirit that we can be victorious over sin and Satan. We surrender to God all that we are and have, and trust Christ to bring forth in us all that He desires. So the promise of entering God's rest represents a spiritual rest in this life but also looks ahead to the ultimate rest we will experience after this life is over when we go to be with the Lord (see Rev. 14:13). The promise of entering God's rest still stands, but we must be careful that we do not come short of it. We must be diligent to make every effort to enter that rest, so that we who have believed will not fall by following the Israelites' example of disobedience.

So often faith is spoken of as something that is required for us to receive salvation—to be born again—and this is true. However, genuine faith is not something which is only needed when we initially come to Jesus Christ for salvation, but it must be our way of life from that point forward. We do not enter at the door by faith only to forget about that faith once we have entered. Rather, we enter in *and remain* solely by faith and the obedience that springs from it.

This is where the Israelites failed. They entered by faith, but did not act out that faith as they continued their journey through the wilderness. They became hardened by sin's deceitfulness and in the tests that came their way, they turned away from that faith in God which they had held originally.

It must be noted that we certainly can have ups and downs in our Christian experience without losing our salvation. Through all of these things we may still have a true faith in God. However, through carelessness, lukewarmness and apathy in seeking after Christ, and with the advent of certain tests and trials in our lives the conditions can be brought about where a fatal fall can occur—a fall wherein our confidence (our faith) in Christ is shattered and lost.

A very important point must be made here, that faith is not just believing for heaven and salvation. It is believing (trusting in, relying on and adhering to) Christ in our everyday situations. We have seen that God expected the Israelites to trust Him for all things, i.e., food, clothing, shelter, health, security, victory over their enemies, etc. and not just for the promised land. It was to be a total trust in God.

Failure to trust God in each new trial and test which was presented to them ultimately hardened their hearts so that they did not even regard the miraculous way in which God had provided for them. This hardening caused them to rebel, to disobey God and to ultimately lose their confidence (their saving faith) in Him. They were prevented from experiencing God's rest in this life and were shut out of the promised land. They were also rejected and prevented from entering God's eternal rest and inheritance. They lost their salvation. We will be wise to consider again the following admonition ...

> [12]"See to it, brothers, that none of you has a sinful, unbelieving heart that turns away from the living God. [13]But encourage one another daily, as long as it is called Today, so that none of you may be hardened by sin's deceitfulness. [14]We have come to share in Christ if we hold firmly till the end the confidence we had at first" (Heb. 3:12-14).

God will bring situations into our lives to test our trust and obedience to Him in all of these areas. Just as the Israelite response to their trials and tests determined the fate of the people who had come out of Egypt with Moses, so will it be for us. Our response to the tests we face in this life will determine if our faith is "genuine" and if we will be able to inherit all that we have been promised.

The following passage is power packed with information regarding the Christian's hope and faith. In fact the central word of this passage is faith ...

> [3]"Praise be to the God and Father of our Lord Jesus Christ! In his great mercy he has given us new birth into a living hope through the resurrection of Jesus Christ from the dead, [4]and into an inheritance that can never perish, spoil or fade—

kept in heaven for you, ⁵who through faith are shielded by God's power until the coming of the salvation that is ready to be revealed in the last time. ⁶In this you greatly rejoice, though now for a little while you may have had to suffer grief in all kinds of trials. ⁷These have come so that your faith—of greater worth than gold, which perishes even though refined by fire—may be proved genuine and may result in praise, glory and honor when Jesus Christ is revealed. ⁸Though you have not seen him, you love him; and even though you do not see him now, you believe in him and are filled with an inexpressible and glorious joy, ⁹for you are receiving the goal of your faith, the salvation of your souls" (1 Pet. 1:3-9).

The first sentence is a long one, but if you look at it carefully you will note that everything the Christian receives is received by faith. We receive the new birth into the Kingdom of God by faith in Jesus Christ who died and rose from the dead. Through faith we have an eternal inheritance that can never perish, spoil or fade which is being kept (held on reserve) for us in heaven. We are shielded by God's power through faith until the time we leave this life and enter into the final salvation that will occur when we are taken to be with the Lord.

As Christians we receive and hold our salvation now by faith. It is secured in the same way that we might hold a key to a locker in a airport terminal. The contents of the locker (our eternal inheritance and salvation) are secured (cannot perish, spoil or fade). Those contents are held (reserved) for us... **IF** we do not lose the key (our faith). Everything depends upon us having (and not losing) the key. The contents of the locker are ours now, even if we have not yet actually taken hold of them. They are ours by virtue of the fact that we have the key in our possession (we are even now receiving the goal of our faith, the salvation of our souls). ***HOW VERY CRITICAL IS OUR FAITH!!!***

As a side note here, to be "shielded by God's power" through faith is a wonderful thing. However, when we suc-

263

cumb to fear and doubt and therefore step away from a position of faith, our shield (Eph. 6:16) is lowered and we become vulnerable to the attacks of the enemy.

The passage in 1 Peter 1:3-9 which we have just read, has its parallel in the Old Testament where Moses recounts to the Israelites, who are to finally go into the promised land, what their wilderness journey was all about ...

> *[2]"Remember how the LORD your God led you all the way in the desert these forty years, to humble you and to test you in order to know what was in your heart, whether or not you would keep his commands. [3]He humbled you, causing you to hunger and then feeding you with manna, which neither you nor your fathers had known, to teach you that man does not live on bread alone but on every word that comes from the mouth of the LORD"* (Deut. 8:2-3).

Here we see that God allowed these tests to come on the Israelites to determine the genuiness of their faith and their commitment to obey every Word of the Lord. It says that He humbled them and tested them to see what was in their heart. He caused them to hunger. Was their commitment to Him based only on what they could get from it, or was it based on a desire to love, trust and obey Him no matter what came their way?

It is in these test and trials that a persons' faith in God is proven or is denied. We are given the opportunity in this life up to the point of death (or the point when Jesus Christ returns to take His own) to establish that our faith is genuine. If our faith is deemed genuine, then we will go to be with the Lord. If not, we will face the eternal judgements which God will bring against all who have rejected Him.

A scripture which emphasizes our need to remain steadfast through trials and tests is James 1:12 ...

"Blessed is the man who perseveres under trial, because when he has stood the test, he will receive the crown of life that God has promised to those who love him" (James 1:12).

Our salvation will be assured dependent upon how we endure the tests. It says, *"...when he has stood the test, he will receive the crown of life..."*

When tests come, it may seem that God is not real. It is a time when you wish that He would appear and come and talk to you to help you understand why you are going through such severe difficulties. But alas, He does not appear, in fact there is very little evidence coming your way that He even exists. It is under conditions of this type that the genuiness of your faith will be determined. Perhaps you have just lost a son or daughter, a husband or wife or some other very close loved one. Or you are facing difficulties in your marriage that are leaving you feeling helpless. Or you, (or someone who is very close to you) have come down with a lingering illness or infirmity which is placing a severe burden on you. You do not understand. You have sought God for these things and yet the heavens are like brass. There is no response. What will be all important to your salvation at such a time will be the out-working of the decisions and commitment you made to the Lord, the knowledge of His Word and the relationship you cultivated with Him before the trial ever came.

Often, the tests we face come to us suddenly with no warning. There may be no time, or we may not have the heart to sit down when the trial hits to study His Word and to learn what should have been learned earlier. The trial will reveal the depth of our knowledge and understanding of God and His Word, will reveal the strength of our commitment to Him and will expose the true condition of our heart.

[24]"Therefore everyone who hears these words of mine and puts them into practice is like a wise man who built his house on the rock. [25]The rain came down, the streams rose,

and the winds blew and beat against that house; yet it did not fall, because it had its foundation on the rock. [26]But everyone who hears these words of mine and does not put them into practice is like a foolish man who built his house on sand. [27]The rain came down, the streams rose, and the winds blew and beat against that house, and it fell with a great crash" (Matt. 7:24-27).

These words serve to underline the importance of hearing and heeding everything which Jesus said to us. The two houses mentioned in this passage were obviously built during a time when there was no storm or turmoil. One man made sure that he built on rock, understanding the importance of hearing and applying the whole Word of God to his life. The other man may have considered that there would only be good times and therefore it wasn't important to build such a sturdy foundation, or he may not have understood the vital importance of taking God's Word into his heart. He undoubtedly heard the Word once in awhile and obeyed it to a degree. He had received Jesus as His Savior but there were so many other things of importance which occupied his mind and life that he didn't really spend the time to understand and apply the Word of God to the fullest.

Both men were caught in the storm and neither one could have told you when it was coming, but one man was prepared and the other wasn't. Only one of them went through the storm with his faith intact because he was confident in His God. His faith was strong because he had daily sought God and learned how to apply the Word of God in his life. He knew what to do when the storm hit. The other man had no strength to stand. He had heard Jesus' words but he had not been putting them into practice. His faith had not been rooted and grounded in the Word of God, so he did not have anything to take hold of when the storm hit. He had an unstable foundation. As a consequence, when the trials and difficulties came, he fell and lost his place with God.

When a severe trial comes it can be devastating. It may consume most if not all of your time and may be on your mind morning, noon and night. It may be difficult to think about anything else because of its overwhelming nature. **If you have not established a firm, unshakable trust in Christ and a walk of righteousness before Him, you will not obtain it at the time of your test. In fact, it will become easy to turn away from God because you are unable to understand how a loving God could cause such a thing to happen. As your faith, which was weak to begin with, begins to disappear, you will be unable to reconcile it all in your mind. You may not have the faith to even ask for God's help. Your faith may be at such a low point, because of the discouragement you are under, that you cannot even gain faith by reading the Bible, in fact you may not even have the faith to open it.**

Under such circumstances, you can become offended in the Lord, considering that He has turned away from you, or was not real to begin with. The very faith in God which saved you can at that point be irretrievably lost. As it says, ...

"The rain came down, the streams rose, and the winds blew and beat against that house, and it fell with a great crash" (Matt. 7:27).

It says of Joshua and Caleb, who went through the wilderness with Moses and the Israelites, that they followed the Lord "wholeheartedly." This is what is required if we are not to turn away from Him in the time of tests and trials. Only God knows when our trials will come and what they will entail. **It is before that trial ever comes that we must seek to build up our most holy faith and set ourselves to follow Him wholeheartedly.** The Lord has never said that He would keep us from the trials, but only that He would go through them with us and would bring us through as we continue to trust and obey Him.

I am convinced that today there are many who profess to be Christians who do not really know Jesus Christ even though they may have attended church for years. They may be sitting in dead churches where the true salvation message is not even preached and Bibles are not very much in evidence. For whatever reason, these individuals have never truly committed themselves by faith to the Lord Jesus Christ and been transformed by the renewing power of the Holy Spirit. Their faith is not genuine and they need to repent of their sins, surrender their lives to Christ and place their complete trust in God that they might receive salvation. Some might believe that the passages regarding falling away are directed to such individuals, but this is not the case. Rather, it is clear that these passages are written to those who presently have confidence in Christ—have come to a saving faith in Him. It is the true believers who are admonished to hold steadfast to the end the confidence they had at first and to be careful that they do not fall from their present secure position.

Many do not want to speak about this subject of our eternal security because it is so controversial. But again, I believe that it is such an important subject and so vital to us that it must not be ignored or brushed over lightly. In this chapter we will thoroughly investigate this doctrine from both sides based upon many more scriptures. I have identified close to seventy different passages which deal with this subject in varying degrees of depth and strength. All but two of these are found in the New Testament. We will not look at every one of these, but certainly at those passages which make the strongest case either for or against the idea of "once-saved-always-saved."

In the book of Revelation, Jesus speaks words of encouragement and warning to seven churches of Asia Minor (chapters 2-3). In these passages, Jesus indicates the blessings that will come to those who overcome in the trials and tests that face them. He uses the word "overcome" seven times in these passages. If we have believed that once a person is saved they can never lose their salvation, then what is there to overcome? Why are so many warnings given to us regarding the need to stand firm and to be careful how we believe and how we walk.

If these warnings are not meant for believers, are they for unbelievers? Unbelievers don't need to be careful that they don't fall, for they have never stood in Christ to begin with. First they need to come to Jesus Christ to be saved.

It is the Christian who is called to walk faithfully with Jesus Christ who must fight the good fight of faith to overcome sin, the world and Satan. In Rev. 2:10, Jesus speaks to the believers in the Church in Smyrna. He says ...

> *"Do not be afraid of what you are about to suffer. I tell you, the devil will put some of you in prison to test you, and you will suffer persecution for ten days. Be faithful, even to the point of death, and I will give you the crown of life"* (Rev. 2:10).

The believers in this church were to suffer persecution because of their faith. They were encouraged by the Lord Himself to *"be faithful, **even to the point of death** and I will give you the crown of life."*[e] This crown spoken of is the crown of eternal life. A footnote in the NIV Study Bible for Revelation 2:10 says, "... "Crown" does not refer to a royal crown (Rev. 12:3; 13:1; 19:12) but to the garland or wreath awarded to the winner in athletic contests (Rev. 3:11; 4:4,10; 6:2; 9:7; 12:1; 14:14)." The direct implication of this scripture (Rev. 2:10) is that though they are believers, if they do not remain faithful to the point of death, they will not receive eternal life.

The Apostle Paul made reference to this same crown in 1 Cor. 9:24-27 ...

> [24]*"Do you not know that in a race all the runners run, but only one gets the prize? Run in such a way as to get the*

---

[e]Emphasis added

prize. *[25]Everyone who competes in the games goes into strict training. They do it to get a crown that will not last; but we do it to get a crown that will last forever. [26]Therefore I do not run like a man running aimlessly; I do not fight like a man beating the air. [27]No, I beat my body and make it my slave so that after I have preached to others, I myself will not be disqualified for the prize"* (1 Cor. 9:24-27).

Paul makes reference to the crown given to the winner in an athletic race and likens it to the crown that will last forever, the crown of eternal life. Paul is certainly a Christian, yet he declares that he does not run aimlessly, but with purpose, doing everything that he can to keep himself in line so that he will not finally be disqualified to receive this crown of eternal life. He declares that many runners run, but we must run in such a way to acquire the winners crown. The crown is not awarded to all who start the race, but only to those who persevere to the end and finish the race.

Paul continues this discussion started in chapter 9 (above) with the following words which are directly related in context.

[1]"For I do not want you to be ignorant of the fact, brothers, that our forefathers were all under the cloud and that they all passed through the sea. [2]They were all baptized into Moses in the cloud and in the sea. [3]They all ate the same spiritual food [4]and drank the same spiritual drink; for they drank from the spiritual rock that accompanied them, and that rock was Christ. [5]Nevertheless, God was not pleased with most of them; their bodies were scattered over the desert.

[6]Now these things occurred as examples to keep us from setting our hearts on evil things as they did. [7]Do not be idolaters, as some of them were; as it is written: 'The people sat down to eat and drink and got up to indulge in pagan revelry.' [8]We should not commit sexual immorality, as some of them did—and in one day twenty-three thousand of them died. [9]We should not test the Lord, as some of them did—and were killed by snakes. [10]And do not grumble, as some of them did—and were killed by the destroying angel.

[11]These things happened to them as examples and were written down as warnings for us, on whom the fulfillment of the ages has come. [12]So, if you think you are standing firm, be careful that you don't fall! [13]No temptation has seized you except what is common to man. And God is faithful; he will not let you be tempted beyond what you can bear. But when you are tempted, he will also provide a way out so that you can stand up under it" (1 Cor 10:1-13).

I believe that Paul saw the Israelites as believers in God. They had experienced God's redemption and His grace, they had been brought out of bondage, had been baptized, had been sustained by God's provision in the wilderness and had experienced a fellowship with Christ. *They were believers*, but we see that they set their hearts on all kinds of evil things and so they were rejected by God. Paul addresses these concerns to those who may think they are standing firm in the Lord. We must be careful that we do not fall. Even though we may be tempted and tried, God will provide a way out if we do not give up and succumb to the pressures to turn away from Him.

Jesus made the following declaration ...

"Whoever believes in the Son has eternal life, but whoever rejects the Son will not see life, for God's wrath remains on him" (John 3:36).

Only two courses exist after this life for all who have lived upon this earth. They are either going to have eternal life, or will not see that life but will face God's wrath. When a person comes to God by faith, his name is written down in a book—the book of life, which is also referred to as the Lamb's book of life (Rev. 21:27) ...

[11]"Then I saw a great white throne and him who was seated on it. Earth and sky fled from his presence, and there was no place for them. [12]And I saw the dead, great and small, standing before the throne, and books were opened. Another

271

book was opened, which is the book of life. The dead were judged according to what they had done as recorded in the books. [13]The sea gave up the dead that were in it, and death and Hades gave up the dead that were in them, and each person was judged according to what he had done. [14]Then death and Hades were thrown into the lake of fire. The lake of fire is the second death. [15]If anyone's name was not found written in the book of life, he was thrown into the lake of fire" (Rev. 20:11-15).

The book of life identifies those who have come by the way of faith to the Lord Jesus Christ and have thereby received eternal life. Their names have been written in that book. We also see that whoever does not have their name written in the book of life will be thrown into the lake of fire.

Jesus made some interesting comments related to this when He spoke by a Word of prophecy to the church in Sardis...

[1]"To the angel of the church in Sardis write: These are the words of him who holds the seven spirits of God and the seven stars. I know your deeds; you have a reputation of being alive, but you are dead. [2]Wake up! Strengthen what remains and is about to die, for I have not found your deeds complete in the sight of my God. [3]Remember, therefore, what you have received and heard; obey it, and repent. But if you do not wake up, I will come like a thief, and you will not know at what time I will come to you.

[4]Yet you have a few people in Sardis who have not soiled their clothes. They will walk with me, dressed in white, for they are worthy. [5]He who overcomes will, like them, be dressed in white. I will never blot out his name from the book of life, but will acknowledge his name before my Father and his angels" (Rev. 3:1-5).

The people in the church at Sardis had heard and received the truth but had since become dead in their relationship with Christ. Their clothes (their robes of righteousness) were at one time spotless, having been cleansed by the shed blood of Jesus when they received Him as their Savior. Now their spiritual robes were soiled through sin and indifference. In this passage it is made clear that it is possible for an individual who has at one time had their name written in the book of life to have it blotted out. However, He encourages those in Sardis by saying that those who overcome, who remain steadfast to the end, will not have their names blotted out of the book of life. To have your name blotted out is to say that you no longer have eternal life. It is to be condemned to the lake of fire (Rev. 20:15). A PERSONS NAME COULD NOT BE BLOTTED OUT OF THE BOOK OF LIFE UNLESS IT HAD BEEN WRITTEN THERE TO BEGIN WITH. This is very clear evidence that it is possible for one who has been saved to subsequently do that which would cause them to lose their salvation.

We may remember that Moses spoke to the Lord on behalf of the Israelites who had sinned against God. He said, ...

[31]"...Oh, what a great sin these people have committed! They have made themselves gods of gold. [32]But now, please forgive their sin—but if not, then blot me out of the book you have written." [33]The LORD replied to Moses, 'Whoever has sinned against me I will blot out of my book'" (Exod. 32:31-33).

Again, only those whose names have been written in the book can have them blotted out. As was said earlier, the Israelites had put their trust in God. Their names were written in the book of life. However, through unbelief and rebellion, their hearts were turned away from God. Their hearts became hard toward the Lord and God removed their names from the book of life.

It is clear that no person or any thing can take us away from God's love and the salvation He has purchased for us...

[28]"I give them eternal life, and they shall never perish; no one can snatch them out of my hand. [29]My Father, who has

given them to me, is greater than all; no one can snatch them out of my Father's hand" (John 10:28-29).

No one can take us out of the Father's hand, BUT WE CAN DO IT OURSELVES if we are careless and allow ourselves to become lukewarm toward the Lord. Our hearts may become hardened to the extent that we return to a state of continued disobedience and unbelief as the Israelites did. As the Lord said to the church at Sardis,

> [1]*"...I know your deeds; you have a reputation of being alive, but you are dead.* [2]*Wake up! Strengthen what remains and is about to die, for I have not found your deeds complete in the sight of my God.* [3]*Remember, therefore, what you have received and heard; obey it, and repent. But if you do not wake up, I will come like a thief, and you will not know at what time I will come to you"* (Rev. 3:1-3).

Though scripture clearly states that we can turn away from the Lord, it is also clear that so long as we set our hearts to trust and rely upon Him and to walk with Him in obedience, we can never be separated from the love of Christ ...

> [28]*"And we know that in all things God works for the good of those who love him, who have been called according to his purpose.* [29]*For those God foreknew he also predestined to be conformed to the likeness of his Son, that he might be the firstborn among many brothers.* [30]*And those he predestined, he also called; those he called, he also justified; those he justified, he also glorified.*
>
> [31]*What, then, shall we say in response to this? If God is for us, who can be against us?* [32]*He who did not spare his own Son, but gave him up for us all—how will he not also, along with him, graciously give us all things?* [33]*Who will bring any charge against those whom God has chosen? It is God who justifies.* [34]*Who is he that condemns? Christ Jesus, who died—more than that, who was raised to life—is at the right hand of God and is also interceding for us.* [35]*Who shall*

separate us from the love of Christ? Shall trouble or hardship or persecution or famine or nakedness or danger or sword? ³⁶As it is written: 'For your sake we face death all day long; we are considered as sheep to be slaughtered.'

³⁷No, in all these things we are more than conquerors through him who loved us. ³⁸For I am convinced that neither death nor life, neither angels nor demons, neither the present nor the future, nor any powers, ³⁹neither height nor depth, nor anything else in all creation, will be able to separate us from the love of God that is in Christ Jesus our Lord" (Rom. 8:28-39).

As we walk with Christ, there is nothing that can separate us from the love of Christ, but we must stand fast and not turn away from Him. As we walk in faith and obedience to the Lord Jesus Christ, who can condemn us? We have been cleansed by the blood of the Lamb and our sins have been forgiven. As we walk with a firm trust in Christ, not even trouble, hardship, persecution, famine, nakedness, danger or sword can separate us from Christ for it is for His sake that we face death all the day long.

In Matthew 22:14 we find that Jesus declared, at the conclusion of telling a parable, that many are called or invited to follow Him, but only a few—those identified as the chosen—actually will. In Rev. 17:14, it is made clear that this few is narrowed down even further when it identifies those who will be with the Lamb when the powers on the earth come to make war against Him...

"They will make war against the Lamb, but the Lamb will overcome them because he is Lord of lords and King of kings—and with him will be his called, chosen and faithful followers" (Rev. 17:14).

We see that those who follow Jesus are not only those who have been *called* (invited) and *chosen*, but who are also *faithful*—those who have remained steadfast in Christ.

There are some scriptures which would seem to imply that we cannot fall away once we have received salvation...

"Who are you to judge someone else's servant? To his own master he stands or falls. And he will stand, for the Lord is able to make him stand" (Rom. 14:4).

[7]*"Therefore you do not lack any spiritual gift as you eagerly wait for our Lord Jesus Christ to be revealed.* [8]*He will keep you strong to the end, so that you will be blameless on the day of our Lord Jesus Christ.* [9]*God, who has called you into fellowship with his Son Jesus Christ our Lord, is faithful"* (1 Cor. 1:7-9).

These two passages clearly state that the Lord will cause the Christian to stand firm and be strong to the end that he will not fall. The Apostle Paul wrote both of these passages, but he also wrote the following passage which provides added insight...

[21]*"Now it is God who makes both us and you stand firm in Christ. He anointed us,* [22]*set his seal of ownership on us, and put his Spirit in our hearts as a deposit, guaranteeing what is to come.* [23]*I call God as my witness that it was in order to spare you that I did not return to Corinth.* [24]*Not that we lord it over your faith, but we work with you for your joy, because it is by faith you stand firm"* (2 Cor. 1:21-24).

Here it is declared that God makes us stand firm in Christ, but then in verse 24 Paul also notes that is by faith we stand firm. Paul did not intend for this to be contradictory. God works in us to do His will that we might stand firm in Christ, but that does not take away our responsibility to be diligent in our faith. In a letter to the Philippians he writes...

[12]*"Therefore, my dear friends, as you have always obeyed— not only in my presence, but now much more in my absence—continue to work out your salvation with fear and trembling,* [13]*for it is God who works in you to will and to act according to his good purpose"* (Phil. 2:12-13).

276

Let's look at these same verses in the Amplified Bible ...

[12] *"Therefore, my dear ones, as you have always obeyed [my suggestions], so now, not only [with the enthusiasm you would show] in my presence but much more because I am absent, work out—cultivate, carry out to the goal and fully complete—your own salvation with reverence and awe and trembling [self-distrust, that is, with serious caution, tenderness of conscience, watchfulness against temptation; timidly shrinking from whatever might offend God and discredit the name of Christ]"* (Phil. 2:12-13 AMP).

In this verse (12) we see the part that the believer must play in working out his salvation. In the next verse in this passage we see how God cooperates and works with us in this endeavor...

[13]*"[Not in your own strength] for it is God Who is all the while effectually at work in you—energizing and creating in you the power and desire—both to will and to work for His good pleasure and satisfaction and delight."*

God cooperates with our faith to cause us to stand firm in Christ. However, we can choose to be careless, not working out our salvation with the fear and trembling that is called for. Through carelessness, we can come to the place where we forfeit the salvation which God has given us. The potential loss of our salvation would be worthy of a little fear and trembling don't you think?. Again, why are there so many injunctions in scripture to be careful, to be afraid of falling and of turning away from the faith, if such a thing were impossible?

We again want to recall that it says in 1 Pet. 1:5 that it is through faith that we are shielded by God's power. A study note in the NIV Study Bible for this verse hits the mark when it says...

"Through faith ... by God's power. There are two sides to the perseverance of the Christian. He is shielded (1) by

God's power and (2) by his own faith. Thus he is never kept contrary to his will nor apart from God's activity."

As we walk by faith and obedience to our Lord, He will show Himself faithful to see us through to the end. His faithfulness has never been in question. He will complete the work He started in us. This can be likened to the promises God gave to Abraham, that He would bring the Israelites into the promised land. It was a sure promise that was fulfilled under Joshua. But it is also true that those who originally received the promise did not go in because of their unbelief and disobedience. Did God fail to keep His word? No! His promise did not fail, but some fell short of it because of their unbelief and disobedience.

God is able to keep us from falling as we are diligent to follow after Him, however, we must seek to strengthen our faith and trust in Him ...

[20]*"But you, dear friends, build yourselves up in your most holy faith and pray in the Holy Spirit.* [21]*Keep yourselves in God's love as you wait for the mercy of our Lord Jesus Christ to bring you to eternal life.* [22]*Be merciful to those who doubt;* [23]*snatch others from the fire and save them; to others show mercy, mixed with fear—hating even the clothing stained by corrupted flesh.* [24]*To him who is able to keep you from falling and to present you before his glorious presence without fault and with great joy—* [25]*to the only God our Savior be glory, majesty, power and authority, through Jesus Christ our Lord, before all ages, now and forevermore! Amen"* (Jude 20-25).

God is able to keep us from falling, but it is *"through faith that we are shielded by God's power"* (1 Pet. 1:5). So we must be diligent to build ourselves up in that most holy faith.

You may be one who has attended church on Sundays almost like a ritual. It has perhaps become something you do in order to keep your hell fire insurance policy paid up. You believe in hell, don't want to have any part of it and desire eternal life. However, you very rarely read the Word and may not understand it, you seldom pray, and other things in your life may have achieved a place of greater importance to you than the Lord. You have reasonable financial security so you find very little reason to have to look to Him for help. Jesus spoke about such conditions when He addressed the church in Laodicea in the book of Revelation ...

[14]"To the angel of the church in Laodicea write:
These are the words of the Amen, the faithful and true witness, the ruler of God's creation. [15]I know your deeds, that you are neither cold nor hot. I wish you were either one or the other! [16]So, because you are lukewarm—neither hot nor cold—I am about to spit you out of my mouth. [17]You say, 'I am rich; I have acquired wealth and do not need a thing.' But you do not realize that you are wretched, pitiful, poor, blind and naked. [18]I counsel you to buy from me gold refined in the fire, so you can become rich; and white clothes to wear, so you can cover your shameful nakedness; and salve to put on your eyes, so you can see. [19]Those whom I love I rebuke and discipline. So be earnest, and repent. [20]Here I am! I stand at the door and knock. If anyone hears my voice and opens the door, I will come in and eat with him, and he with me. [21]To him who overcomes, I will give the right to sit with me on my throne, just as I overcame and sat down with my Father on his throne. [22]He who has an ear, let him hear what the Spirit says to the churches" (Rev. 3:14-22).

This message is not just addressed to the church at Laodicea. Verse 22 makes it plain that it is addressed to us all.

A study note in the NIV Study Bible for Revelation 3:20 says ...

I stand at the door and knock. Usually taken as a picture of Christ's knocking on the door of the individual unbeliever's heart. In context, however, the self-deluded members of the congregation are being addressed.

279

A similar study note for Revelation 3:20 in the Full Life Study Bible says...

> *If anyone hears my voice.* In its self-sufficient prosperity and worldliness (vv. 15-18), the church in Laodicea had excluded the Lord Jesus Christ from its congregations. Christ's invitation, spoken from outside the door, is a request for fellowship with any individual who will repent of and overcome the spiritual lukewarmness of the church (v. 21).

It is certainly possible that we may generate fear in the hearts of some people when we say that there is a possibility that a person can lose their salvation. Some might even think it unkind to suggest such a thing. Yet we have seen that we are to work out our salvation with fear and trembling. This is a word to all of us. Some people would feel more comfortable knowing exactly how far they can drift away from the Lord without getting into trouble. They want to know exactly where the boundaries are. Then they can relax to the extent that they don't cross over the line. But that is a wrong attitude. If we truly love the Lord and want to please Him, then we will *"seek first the kingdom of God and His righteousness,"*[f] and not be looking for how much room we have to be careless.

I speak as one who is confident of my salvation. Yet I know how easy it is to let the Lord take a back seat in my life. If we are going to follow the Lord with our whole heart, it is necessary that we discipline ourselves. We must have the same mind in us, that Paul had ...

> [26] *"...I do not run like a man running aimlessly; I do not fight like a man beating the air.* [27]*No, I beat my body and make it my slave so that after I have preached to others, I myself will not be disqualified for the prize"* (1 Cor. 9:26-27).

---

[f]Emphasis added

As we diligently seek to follow the Lord we can be assured that He will complete the good work He has started in us just as the following verses make clear ...

> *"...being confident of this, that he who began a good work in you will carry it on to completion until the day of Christ Jesus"* (Phil 1:6).

> *"...I know whom I have believed, and am convinced that he is able to guard what I have entrusted to him for that day"* (2 Tim. 1:12b).

The anointing of the Holy Spirit was given in the times of the Old Testament for special purposes. The Lord's prophets spoke as the Holy Spirit gave them utterance and kings of Israel such as Saul and David were anointed by the Holy Spirit through the hand of the prophets so that they might be specially empowered to fulfill their God given responsibilities. However, it was not until the death, resurrection and ascension of the Lord Jesus Christ that the Holy Spirit was given as a promise of the Lord to all believers and is a proof that they belong to Christ.

> *"...if anyone does not have the Spirit of Christ, he does not belong to Christ"* (Rom. 8:9b).

In several places, scripture refers to the giving of the Holy Spirit as a seal or pledge of the eternal inheritance we are to receive.

> [13]*"And you also were included in Christ when you heard the word of truth, the gospel of your salvation. Having believed, you were marked in him with a seal, the promised Holy Spirit,* [14]*who is a deposit guaranteeing our inheritance until the redemption of those who are God's possession—to the praise of his glory"* (Eph. 1:13-14).

[22]*"...we ourselves, who have the firstfruits of the Spirit, groan inwardly as we wait eagerly for our adoption as sons, the redemption of our bodies. [24]For in this hope we were saved. But hope that is seen is no hope at all. Who hopes for what he already has? [25]But if we hope for what we do not yet have, we wait for it patiently"* (Rom 8:23-25).

[5]*"Now it is God who—has given us the Spirit as a deposit, guaranteeing what is to come"* (2 Cor. 5:5).

Can we lose the Holy Spirit, that pledge of our eternal inheritance, after He has once taken up residence within us?.

I have found no scriptures that would directly verify this point one way or the other. We know that when David sinned with Bathsheba and his sin was revealed, he repented. In his prayer to the Lord (Ps. 51) he said,

[11]*"Do not cast me from your presence or take your Holy Spirit from me"* (Ps. 51:11).

It may not be proper to consider this passage as an evidence that the Lord would remove His Holy Spirit because, as we have said, the Holy Spirit was given only to certain individuals and only for special purposes during the times recorded in the Old Testament. However, we are given a specific command by the Apostle Paul which says ...

"...Do not grieve the Holy Spirit of God, with whom you were sealed for the day of redemption" (Eph. 4:30).

A scripture in the Old Testament sheds some light on this by revealing what happened to the Israelites when they grieved the Holy Spirit...

[8]*"He said, 'Surely they are my people, sons who will not be false to me"; and so he became their Savior. [9]In all their distress he too was distressed, and the angel of his presence*

saved them. In his love and mercy he redeemed them; he lifted them up and carried them all the days of old. ¹⁰Yet they rebelled and grieved his Holy Spirit. So he turned and became their enemy and he himself fought against them'" (Isa. 63:8-10).

The Lord turned and became the enemy of the very people He had redeemed and saved because they rebelled and grieved His Holy Spirit.

This scripture is not a proof in and of itself that God would remove His Holy Spirit from a New Testament (New Covenant) believer. However, we have seen that a believer who has had his name written down in the Lamb's book of life, indicating he was a possessor of eternal life, can subsequently have his name blotted out if he turns away from the Lord. With his name removed from the book of life, he would be destined to be cast into the lake of fire (Rev. 20:15). Therefore, the Holy Spirit, the deposit guaranteeing eternal life and an eternal inheritance, would have to depart any individual whose name was to be removed from the Lamb's book of life.

John 15 speaks of Jesus as being the true vine and His Father is the gardener. Those who belong to Christ are identified as branches in that vine.

> ¹*"I am the true vine, and my Father is the gardener. ²He cuts off every branch in me that bears no fruit, while every branch that does bear fruit he prunes so that it will be even more fruitful. ³You are already clean because of the word I have spoken to you. ⁴Remain in me, and I will remain in you. No branch can bear fruit by itself; it must remain in the vine. Neither can you bear fruit unless you remain in me.*
>
> ⁵*"I am the vine; you are the branches. If a man remains in me and I in him, he will bear much fruit; apart from me you can do nothing. ⁶If anyone does not remain in me, he is like a branch that is thrown away and withers; such branches are picked up, thrown into the fire and burned. ⁷If you remain in me and my words remain in you, ask whatever you*

wish, and it will be given you. ⁸This is to my Father's glory, that you bear much fruit, showing yourselves to be my disciples.

⁹"As the Father has loved me, so have I loved you. Now remain in my love. ¹⁰If you obey my commands, you will remain in my love, just as I have obeyed my Father's commands and remain in his love. ¹¹I have told you this so that my joy may be in you and that your joy may be complete. ¹²My command is this: Love each other as I have loved you. ¹³Greater love has no one than this, that he lay down his life for his friends. ¹⁴You are my friends if you do what I command" (John 15:1-14).

This passage of scripture makes it clear that those who belong to Christ are those who remain in Him (the Vine). This word "remain" (or "abide" in the King James translation) is taken from a Greek word which means to stay in a given place, state, relation or expectancy. If we do not remain in Christ by maintaining a close walk with Him, surrendering ourselves to Him daily, trusting in Him and gaining nourishment from Him through the reading of the Word and through prayer, our spiritual lives will begin to dry up and wither. A continued hardening of the heart, or a wind of testing or temptation may cause us, at some point, to break off completely from Christ.

As this passage says, *⁶"If anyone does not remain in me, he is like a branch that is thrown away and withers; such branches are picked up, thrown into the fire and burned."* The rejected and burned branches are those who at one time united with Christ but who did not remain in Him. Unless they repent and return, they will be thrown away and their end is to be burned in the lake of fire. It is difficult to establish any other interpretation of this passage than the loss of salvation for those who at one time were united with Christ. The removed branches referred to here cannot be non-believers because they would never have been in the Vine to begin with and therefore could not be expected to remain.

This passage in John 15 is backed up by 1 John 2:24-25...

[24]"See that what you have heard from the beginning remains in you. If it does, you also will remain in the Son and in the Father. [25]And this is what he promised us—even eternal life" (1 John 2:24-25).

Again, if we continue to walk in the truth of the gospel which we have heard from the beginning, we will remain in Christ and have eternal life, otherwise we will not.

Some additional verses of the same kind ...

[11]"Here is a trustworthy saying: If we died with him, we will also live with him; [12]if we endure, we will also reign with him. If we disown him, he will also disown us; [13]if we are faithless, he will remain faithful, for he cannot disown himself" (2 Tim. 2:11-13).

[1]"Now, brothers, I want to remind you of the gospel I preached to you, which you received and on which you have taken your stand. [2]By this gospel you are saved, if you hold firmly to the word I preached to you. Otherwise, you have believed in vain" (1 Cor. 15:1-2).

The key words in these scriptures are "endure," and "hold firmly to the word."

Jesus, in speaking of the times of persecution to come on believers, made it very clear that we must stand firm to the end if we are to be saved. We must persevere in our faith so that we will not be drawn aside...

"All men will hate you because of me, but he who stands firm to the end will be saved" (Matt 10:22 and Mark 13:13).

[9]"Then you will be handed over to be persecuted and put to death, and you will be hated by all nations because of me. [10]At that time many will turn away from the faith and will betray and hate each other, [11]and many false prophets will

appear and deceive many people. [12]Because of the increase of wickedness, the love of most will grow cold, [13]but he who stands firm to the end will be saved" (Matt 24:9-13).

[17]*"All men will hate you because of me. [18]But not a hair of your head will perish. [19]By standing firm you will gain life"* (Luke 21:17-19).

We must stand by faith throughout our lives or face the loss of all things ...

[35]*"So do not throw away your confidence; it will be richly rewarded. [36]You need to persevere so that when you have done the will of God, you will receive what he has promised. [37]For in just a very little while...He who is coming will come and will not delay. [38]But my righteous one will live by faith. And if he shrinks back, I will not be pleased with him. [39]But we are not of those who shrink back and are destroyed, but of those who believe and are saved"* (Heb. 10:35-39).

Very clearly, God's righteous ones, those cleansed through faith in Christ, must *live by faith*. If they shrink back from that faith they will be destroyed. Another scripture speaks to this also...

[21]*"Once you were alienated from God and were enemies in your minds because of your evil behavior. [22]But now he has reconciled you by Christ's physical body through death to present you holy in his sight, without blemish and free from accusation—[23]if you continue in your faith, established and firm, not moved from the hope held out in the gospel. This is the gospel that you heard and that has been proclaimed to every creature under heaven, and of which I, Paul, have become a servant"* (Col. 1:21-23).

We receive salvation and all its benefits ... **IF we continue in our faith**, established and firm, not moved away from the hope held out in the gospel.

In Matthew 25, Jesus reveals what the kingdom of heaven will be like at the time of His return. In this context He presented the parable of the talents in Matt. 25:14-30...

> [14]"Again, it will be like a man going on a journey, who called his servants and entrusted his property to them. [15]To one he gave five talents of money, to another two talents, and to another one talent, each according to his ability..."

When he returned, the first servant who had been given five talents had gained five more. The second servant who had been given two talents had gained two more. The third servant who had been given one talent went out and buried his talent in the ground and returned only the original one to the master. He had gained nothing more than what he had originally been given...

> [26]"His master replied, 'You wicked, lazy servant! So you knew that I harvest where I have not sown and gather where I have not scattered seed? [27]Well then, you should have put my money on deposit with the bankers, so that when I returned I would have received it back with interest.
> [28]"'Take the talent from him and give it to the one who has the ten talents. [29]For everyone who has will be given more, and he will have an abundance. Whoever does not have, even what he has will be taken from him. [30]And throw that worthless servant outside, into the darkness, where there will be weeping and gnashing of teeth" (Mat. 25:26-30).

Some might believe that this parable is giving instruction on how we should invest our money in this life, but it is not. It is speaking of Jesus, our Master returning to His servants and reviewing what they have done with their lives for the kingdom of God and for the Master. It provides a warning to us that our place and rewards in heaven will be determined by the faithfulness and diligence with which the believer (the Lord's servant) applies his God given talents, abilities, resources and time in the service of the King. If we become servants of the Lord through salvation, but then demonstrate that we are lazy and unwilling to take a stand for the Lord and be participants in the work of the Kingdom, then we face the loss of all. For that unworthy servant to be cast "outside, into the darkness, where there will be weeping and gnashing of teeth," clearly implies the loss of his eternal salvation.

So long as we continue to live this life, we may have the opportunity to repent of wayward hearts and personal apostasy (abandonment of the faith), presuming that we will again desire to do so. However, it is impossible to know when our life will be over or the day or the hour of the Lord's return. Jesus warned at many times that we may be taken by surprise, and if such is the case, there would be no opportunity for us to repent and reestablish a right relationship with the Lord. This is spoken of in another parable ...

[42]"The Lord answered, 'Who then is the faithful and wise manager, whom the master puts in charge of his servants to give them their food allowance at the proper time? [43]It will be good for that servant whom the master finds doing so when he returns. [44]I tell you the truth, he will put him in charge of all his possessions. [45]But suppose the servant says to himself, 'My master is taking a long time in coming,' and he then begins to beat the menservants and maidservants and to eat and drink and get drunk. [46]The master of that servant will come on a day when he does not expect him and at an hour he is not aware of. He will cut him to pieces and assign him a place with the unbelievers.'

[47]'That servant who knows his master's will and does not get ready or does not do what his master wants will be beaten with many blows. [48]But the one who does not know and does things deserving punishment will be beaten with few blows. From everyone who has been given much, much will be demanded; and from the one who has been entrusted with much, much more will be asked.

[49]"I have come to bring fire on the earth, and how I wish it were already kindled!"' (Luke 12:42-49).

In this parable it is clear that Jesus is in fact the "master", and the "faithful and wise manager" is the believer who has been entrusted with knowledge and responsibilities within the kingdom. Over time, this manager (believer) gets careless and indifferent, and his heart becomes hardened. When the Lord's return catches him unawares, he has no time to repent. He is cast out and assigned a place with unbelievers. All who are judged by the Lord in this way will receive punishments which are directly related with the depth of their knowledge of what God required and the severity of their deviance from that revealed will.

2 Peter 2 is another scripture which speaks of individuals departing from the faith. It talks of those who have left the way of the Lord and wandered off because of desire for mans' acclaim and for greedy gain. They include those who preach false doctrines and lead many astray who come seeking the Lord. They preach doctrines that are pleasing to men and promise freedom, but which take them away from the freedom that can only be found in Christ through true repentance. Referring to such individuals it says ...

[20]"If they have escaped the corruption of the world by knowing our Lord and Savior Jesus Christ and are again entangled in it and overcome, they are worse off at the end than they were at the beginning. [21]It would have been better for them not to have known the way of righteousness, than to have known it and then to turn their backs on the sacred command that was passed on to them. [22]Of them the proverbs are true: 'A dog returns to its vomit,' and, 'A sow that is washed goes back to her wallowing in the mud'" (2 Pet 2:20-22).

There is no doubt that this passage is speaking of born again believers who lose their salvation. They were those who had "escaped the corruption of the world by knowing our Lord and Savior Jesus Christ." We can only know Jesus as Lord and Savior when we are born again. It is only then that we are enabled to escape the corruption of the world—the hold of sin upon our lives. The illustration of the sow indicates that they had been "washed," but we see that they turned to become entangled in the world and were "overcome" instead of being "overcomers." Their end is not enviable for it says that it would have been better for them never to have known of the Lord's way than to have known it and then turned away from it. Their punishment will be greater because they had previously been numbered among the redeemed.

Another scripture which I believe speaks quite clearly regarding the loss of salvation is Heb. 6:4-12 ...

> [4]"It is impossible for those who have once been enlightened, who have tasted the heavenly gift, who have shared in the Holy Spirit, [5]who have tasted the goodness of the word of God and the powers of the coming age, [6]if they fall away, to be brought back to repentance, because to their loss they are crucifying the Son of God all over again and subjecting him to public disgrace.
>
> [7]Land that drinks in the rain often falling on it and that produces a crop useful to those for whom it is farmed receives the blessing of God. [8]But land that produces thorns and thistles is worthless and is in danger of being cursed. In the end it will be burned.
>
> [9]Even though we speak like this, dear friends, we are confident of better things in your case—things that accompany salvation. [10]God is not unjust; he will not forget your work and the love you have shown him as you have helped his people and continue to help them. [11]We want each of you to show this same diligence to the very end, in order to make your hope sure. [12]We do not want you to become lazy, but to imitate those who through faith and patience inherit what has been promised" (Heb. 6:4-12).

I believe it is clear from this passage that those spoken of have been born again because how else could they have shared in (been made partakers of[g]) the Holy Spirit? Also verse 11 admonishes believers to show diligence to the very end in order to make their hope sure. The word "hope" means to anticipate (usually with pleasure); to have expectation or confidence. Believers have that kind of expectation or hope. They believe that they are going to inherit eternal life. However, this scripture says that it will require continued diligence, faith and patience up to the end for that expectation to be fulfilled.

As the passage above makes very clear, if we continually harden our hearts against God, fail to trust in Him, ignore the Spirit's voice to us and continue in willful sin, we may reach a point where we fall away and repentance is no longer possible. Scripture talks about Jacob's brother Esau who sold his birthright to Jacob for a meal of stew (Gen. 25:29-34). This is referenced in the New Testament ...

> [16]"See that no one is sexually immoral, or is godless like Esau, who for a single meal sold his inheritance rights as the oldest son. [17]Afterward, as you know, when he wanted to inherit this blessing, he was rejected. He could bring about no change of mind, though he sought the blessing with tears" (Heb. 12:16-17).

There are those who profess to be Christians and yet are living in open sin. Many of them have undoubtedly never really met Christ. They may have asked Christ into their heart at one time, and then turned away. They have believed the doctrine of "once-saved-always-saved" and have considered that they can continue to live in sin and everything will be all right. Well, it will not be OK. They must come to Christ and truly repent of their sins.

There is a lack of holiness in the lives of Christians today for the same reason. They have understood that you cannot

---

[g]King James translation

lose your salvation, so living careless, lukewarm lives has become more acceptable. A greater measure of holiness would come to the church if the doctrine of "once-saved-always-saved" were strongly refuted from the pulpits.

No room is given for lukewarmness or carelessness in any of the passages we have been reviewing, but only warnings that we must be diligent in our Christian life and in our faith, and that we must remain steadfast to the very end, whether that be by death, or by the Lord's return to take up His own.

Someone might say, "Well the fact that a person did not stand fast to the end is only an indication that they were not saved to begin with." That begs the question because it is very likely that they *thought* they were saved.

I believe, from what we have seen, that even those who have experienced a true conversion can fall away if they do not remain diligent and steadfast in Christ. This is implied again in 2 Pet. 3:16-17. In speaking about the letters (epistles) of the Apostle Paul it says ...

[16]"*...His letters contain some things that are hard to understand, which ignorant and unstable people distort, as they do the other Scriptures, to their own destruction. [17]Therefore, dear friends, since you already know this, be on your guard so that you may not be carried away by the error of lawless men and fall from your secure position*" (2 Pet. 3:16b-17).

The secure position of a believer is in Christ, the Vine. I can't think of any other secure position that could be in view here. If we allow ourselves to become taken by false teachings and are led away from the truth of the gospel (i.e., salvation only by grace and through faith in the finished work of Jesus Christ), then we can fall from our secure position.

This is the message of the book of Galatians where Paul chastises the Galatians for being led astray into believing that they could be saved by the keeping of the law (works) instead of by faith. Paul was clearly upset by this movement away from salvation by faith and there was a reason for it. If the Galatians were to continue in this error, to try to sustain their salvation through works instead of by faith as they had originally heard and received it from Paul, then they would be led away from their salvation in Christ. Why would Paul become so excited about this, as we find him in the book of Galatians, if he did not believe that this error could cause them to lose their salvation? Was it only so that they would have a correct message to unbelievers? I don't think so. I believe it was so that the Galatians who had already received Christ would not be led away from their salvation. Paul said, ...

> [6]"*I am astonished that you are so quickly deserting the one who called you by the grace of Christ and are turning to a different gospel*—[7]*which is really no gospel at all. Evidently some people are throwing you into confusion and are trying to pervert the gospel of Christ.* [8]*But even if we or an angel from heaven should preach a gospel other than the one we preached to you, let him be eternally condemned!* [9]*As we have already said, so now I say again: If anybody is preaching to you a gospel other than what you accepted, let him be eternally condemned!*" (Gal. 1:6-9).

Paul considered that anyone who would come to them and preach something that would lead them away from a faith based gospel should be eternally condemned. As Gal. 3:11 says, "The righteous will **live** by faith.[h]" It is worth repeating again that we are not only saved by faith, but we must live by faith. We must persevere in that faith to the very end of our lives. An admonition of a similar kind is found in the following passage...

> [7]"*Many deceivers, who do not acknowledge Jesus Christ as coming in the flesh, have gone out into the world. Any such person is the deceiver and the antichrist.* [8]*Watch out that you do not lose what you have worked for, but that you may be rewarded fully.* [9]*Anyone who runs ahead and does*

---

[h]Emphasis added

293

not continue in the teaching of Christ does not have God;
whoever continues in the teaching has both the Father and
the Son" (2 John 1:7-9).

If we are deceived and drawn away from the truth of the gospel, we face the loss of that which we have worked for. If we do not continue in the teachings of Christ, we will face the loss of all things.

There may be those who are reading these words who have become concerned about their own walk with the Lord. Perhaps you have been lukewarm toward the Lord, or you have been careless in seeking after Him. Perhaps you wonder if you have really been born again at all.

Now is the time for you to set your hearts right before God, to make a decision that you are going to seek first the kingdom of God and His righteousness (Matt. 6:33) follow Him with all of your heart, soul, mind and strength (Mark 12:30), place your confidence in Him in every situation, be diligent to know and respond to His Word and seek His face in prayer. We must be as Joshua and Caleb, making up our minds to follow the Lord "wholeheartedly." It is not that we are going to retain our salvation by works, but rather that we need to build ourselves up in our most holy faith that we will be enabled to stand no matter what comes our way. We must fight the good fight, holding on to faith and a good conscience so that we do not shipwreck our faith ...

[18]*"Timothy, my son, I give you this instruction in keeping with*
the prophecies once made about you, so that by following
them you may fight the good fight, [19]*holding on to faith and a*
good conscience. Some have rejected these and so have ship-
wrecked their faith. [20]*Among them are Hymenaeus and*
Alexander, whom I have handed over to Satan to be taught
not to blaspheme" (1 Tim. 1:18-20).

This is speaking of the terrible possibility of coming to a personal apostasy (a loss of our salvation). This happened in the case of Hymenaeus and Alexander who had turned away from the Lord and were undoubtedly expelled from the church. They would be exposed to Satanic attacks. It was Paul's desire that in this process they would repent and turn once again to true faith and salvation in Christ, but no word of this happening is ever given in scripture.

The message is clear. Conditions may be set up in our lives where it is possible for us to lose our salvation if we are not diligent to seek the Lord as our first and foremost priority. The decision is ours.

All of this can be summed up in a scripture which is found in the book of Isaiah. Two kings had come against Judah at Jerusalem to overtake the city. Isaiah came to Ahaz, the king of Judah, to give him a message from the Lord. Included in that message were the following words which we would do well to consider...

"If you do not stand firm in your faith, you will not stand at all..." (Isa. 7:9).

CHAPTER 10

Counting Your Chickens— A Dangerous Proposition

The Jewish people lived in the land of Israel for many years after they originally entered that land under the leadership of Joshua. God blessed them, and they reached their peak as a nation under King David. David desired to build a temple for the Lord in Jerusalem. That task was accomplished, however, under King Solomon, David's son. The Lord appeared to Solomon at that time...

[11]"When Solomon had finished the temple of the LORD and the royal palace, and had succeeded in carrying out all he had in mind to do in the temple of the LORD and in his own palace, [12]the LORD appeared to him at night and said:
'I have heard your prayer and have chosen this place for myself as a temple for sacrifices. [13]When I shut up the heavens so that there is no rain, or command locusts to devour

the land or send a plague among my people, ¹⁴if my people, who are called by my name, will humble themselves and pray and seek my face and turn from their wicked ways, then will I hear from heaven and will forgive their sin and will heal their land. ¹⁵Now my eyes will be open and my ears attentive to the prayers offered in this place. ¹⁶I have chosen and consecrated this temple so that my Name may be there forever. My eyes and my heart will always be there.'

¹⁷'As for you, if you walk before me as David your father did, and do all I command, and observe my decrees and laws, ¹⁸I will establish your royal throne, as I covenanted with David your father when I said, 'You shall never fail to have a man to rule over Israel.'

¹⁹'But if you turn away and forsake the decrees and commands I have given you and go off to serve other gods and worship them, ²⁰then I will uproot Israel from my land, which I have given them, and will reject this temple I have consecrated for my Name. I will make it a byword and an object of ridicule among all peoples. ²¹And though this temple is now so imposing, all who pass by will be appalled and say, 'Why has the LORD done such a thing to this land and to this temple?' ²²People will answer, 'Because they have forsaken the LORD, the God of their fathers, who brought them out of Egypt, and have embraced other gods, worshiping and serving them—that is why he brought all this disaster on them.''
(2 Chr. 7:11-22).

We see that clear warnings were given by God to King Solomon and the nation at the peak of their prosperity and blessings under God. If they continued in God's ways, then the nation would be blessed, but if not, then calamity would come to them. We know that Solomon started out with a heart devoted to God. God blessed him exceedingly, but as his reign continued, Solomon slowly began to turn away from the Lord. With some notable exceptions, the kings which succeeded Solomon continued to lead the nation farther from God.

Calamities plagued the nation as God's presence, blessing and protection were removed from them. God sent His prophets to speak to the nation to encourage them to repent and to turn back to Him. They warned the people of the terrible things that would befall them if they persisted in going their own way. Ultimately, the curses which were spoken as warnings by Moses to the Israelites when they were about to enter the promised land (see Deut. 28), as well as other dire predictions spoken through Israel's prophets, were visited upon the nation of Israel. In the end, they were uprooted from their homeland and were scattered to many lands around the world by the successive actions of Assyria, Babylon and Rome. Their suffering as a people has been intense.

Some might think that God was unfair to allow such terrible suffering to come upon the people of Israel. Yet God gave them a free will to choose the way that they would go. He gave them every reason to obey Him. When they obeyed Him, He showered His blessings upon them. He caused them to enjoy peace and to prosper greatly, and no other nation could touch them. But when they began to reject Him and to turn away from His ways, then the difficulties, which they had repeatedly been warned about, came upon them. God had revealed Himself to this nation like no other, so they were judged in accordance with the understanding they had received.

This history gives great insight into the nature of God. The western civilized nations have been greatly blessed of God, so long as they have regarded Him and given Him honor. Christianity has been the foundational belief of these nations. But one cannot help but wonder, when considering the history of the nation of Israel, how long God will withhold His judgement from us as we take more and more steps to expunge Him from our public consciousness and turn away from His laws. It would do well for us to consider the "blessings" and "curses" of the law (Deuteronomy 28) spoken by Moses which can be read in Deuteronomy 28. We must consider this passage in light of the blessings which the United States has experienced over its' history and the difficulties which we are now facing. If our nation continues in its' present trend to turn away from God and to reject Him, then I believe that we can fully expect the predicted curses to fall on us in increasing measure.

I believe that these considerations can be applied to any nation. Russia, Cuba, China and other nations have sought to eliminate God from their consciousness, and as a consequence, they have experienced terrible suffering. Even though the Iron Curtain has come down, yet the republics that made up the former Soviet Union are in turmoil. There is no faith and moral foundation to hold them together. *IT IS ONLY WHEN THE ALMIGHTY GOD AND THE LAWS HE HAS GIVEN US IN THE BIBLE ARE MADE THE FOUNDATION FOR A NATION'S MORALITY WILL THERE BE A FIRM FOUNDATION FOR PEACE, PROSPERITY, FREEDOM AND STABILITY.*

The founding fathers stated that the Constitution of the United States was designed for, and dependent upon a moral people for its' success. They believed that it could not function any other way. The laws of our land were based upon moral laws found in the Bible. That foundation served to make this country great. Now we are choosing to turn aside from that foundation, and if we continue along this path, we will suffer the consequences.

By what I consider to be almost treasonous actions on the part of the Supreme Court and others, we have been turned loose from the moral absolutes which have made this country great.[a] If we reject the Biblical foundation recognized by the founding fathers (and this is what is happening in our society today), there is no other valid foundation available to take its' place. Without any means to reach a consensus on basic moral issues, how can our society function? How can our lawmakers come to agreement on vital issues? We will be ruled by

---

[a]The Supreme Court in the 1960's deliberately ignored and departed from legal precedents which had been firmly established and confirmed in many preceding Supreme Court cases. By doing so, they set the nation on a new and disastrous course.

laws that come about in response to whoever yells the loudest.

It reminds me of conditions spoken about in the Biblical book of Judges, a time in the early history of Israel when they turned against God. They rejected God's laws, and as they did, their nation went through many hardships. When conditions got bad enough, they would finally cry out in their distress and God would send them someone to deliver them from their enemies and to turn them around. But as soon as things were going OK, they would again forget God's laws, and the process would repeat itself. This cycle occurred many times. A comment is made about the nation at that time that I believe relates to our society today...

"In those days Israel had no king; everyone did as he saw fit" (Judges 17:6).

A picture that continually comes to my mind is of our country as a majestic three masted sailing ship being driven along with the wind. A view under the ship shows that the anchor is down, but it is not secured to the bottom, and so the wind is driving the ship first one way and then another. Whichever way the wind goes, so the ship goes without direction and purpose. It's demise against the rocks is almost guaranteed. I believe that our country will be racked by greater and greater evil unless there is a spiritual awakening that finds its' root in Jesus Christ and a return to Biblical absolutes.

God gave His laws to prevent the breakdown of society. When His laws are violated, a spiritual wall of protection is broken down which the evil one (Satan) can exploit. Today we are seeing increasing evidence that this is the case as witnessed by the difficulties that are upon us, i.e., the murders and violence that we see around us, rampant crime, drug dependency, the AID's epidemic, high incidents of venereal disease, child abuse, etc., all of which are on the increase. Even as this is being written, the Congress of the United States is working to pass a "crime bill" in the hopes of finding some way to curb the lawlessness that is sweeping the land. Yet, at the same time as a nation we are systematically removing plaques containing The Ten Commandments from any public buildings, because of the "great harm" that the display of such things might do to our nation.

These plaques contain such admonitions as *"Honour thy father and thy mother," "Thou shalt not kill," "Thou shalt not commit adultery," "Thou shalt not steal," "Thou shalt not bear false witness against thy neighbor," Thou shalt not covet—anything that is thy neighbors,"* and yes, *"Thou shalt have no other gods before me."* And I have recently heard that someone is bringing a suit against the government to have "In God We Trust" taken from our coins.

There are those who say that it was the intent of the framers of the Constitution that there should be "separation of church and state." If this is true, then how did the statement "one nation under God" get put into our Pledge of Allegiance? How did our coins come to carry the phrase "In God We Trust?" How did daily prayer and a chaplain get put into place in the Congress of the United States?" How did so many of our greatest presidents from George Washington on make so many references to our dependence on an Almighty God?" How was it that early school books in our land contained scripture? Now, those of us who want to hold on to these values are called "radical," as though we are trying to institute something new.

From creation onward, man, who is but flesh and blood, has rebelled against the creator of the universe, the One who makes plants to grow and provides the sun and the rain and all things that are needed by mankind, and has arrogantly stated that he doesn't need God. Scripture declares that ...

"The fool says in his heart, 'There is no God...'" (Ps. 14:1).

[1]"Why do the nations conspire and the peoples plot in vain?
[2]The kings of the earth take their stand and the rulers gather

together against the LORD and against his Anointed One.
³'Let us break their chains,' they say, 'and throw off their
fetters.' ⁴The One enthroned in heaven laughs; the Lord scoffs
at them" (Ps. 2:1-4).

While the prophets of Israel were warning the nation of
Israel that they would be uprooted from their land if they persisted in their sin, they were also stating that there would
come a day when God would have mercy upon the people of
that nation and would bring them back to their land. This was
predicted about 2600 years ago by prophets such as Jeremiah
and Ezekiel. Jeremiah said ...

⁷"'So then, the days are coming,' declares the LORD,
'when people will no longer say, 'As surely as the LORD lives,
who brought the Israelites up out of Egypt,' ⁸but they will say,
'As surely as the LORD lives, who brought the descendants of
Israel up out of the land of the north and out of all the coun-
tries where he had banished them.' Then they will live in their
own land'" (Jer. 23:7-8).

On May 14, 1948, the Nation of Israel was established in
Palestine. Since that time, in fulfillment of Biblical prophecies made so many years ago, the descendants of Israel have
been participating in an exodus from all the lands in which
they have lived in order that they might return to their homeland, the nation of Israel.

Bible scholars consider the re-establishment of the nation of Israel and the return of the Jews to their homeland to
be one of the major signs indicating that we are very near to
a time variously identified in scripture as "the last days,"
"the end of the age," "the time of the end," "the day of
judgment," etc.—a time when great difficulties will come
upon the peoples of this earth. There are differing views
related to the chronological timing and nature of the "end
time" events spoken of in the Bible. It is not the purpose of
this book to discuss these things in detail since there have

been many books written which already do that. The principle concern to be addressed here is rather one of preparedness—are we spiritually ready for what lies ahead?

The disciples of Jesus questioned Him about these things...

> [3]*"As Jesus was sitting on the Mount of Olives, the disciples came to him privately. "Tell us," they said, "when will this happen, and what will be the sign of your coming and of the end of the age?"*
>
> [4]*Jesus answered: "Watch out that no one deceives you.* [5]*For many will come in my name, claiming, 'I am the Christ,' and will deceive many.* [6]*You will hear of wars and rumors of wars, but see to it that you are not alarmed. Such things must happen, but the end is still to come.* [7]*Nation will rise against nation, and kingdom against kingdom. There will be famines and earthquakes in various places.* [8]*All these are the beginning of birth pains.*
>
> [9]*"Then you will be handed over to be persecuted and put to death, and you will be hated by all nations because of me.* [10]*At that time many will turn away from the faith and will betray and hate each other,* [11]*and many false prophets will appear and deceive many people.* [12]*Because of the increase of wickedness, the love of most will grow cold,* [13]*but he who stands firm to the end will be saved.* [14]*And this gospel of the kingdom will be preached in the whole world as a testimony to all nations, and then the end will come"* (Matt. 24:3-14).

Here we see the Lord Jesus declare that "... *he who stands firm to the end will be saved*" (Matt. 24:13). Certainly for any individual, that end could be their appointed time of natural death. But I believe that in the context in which Jesus spoke, He was referring to a time identified in the Bible as the "end of the age." I believe that we are very near to that time. We see evidence of this around us...

> [1]*"But mark this: There will be terrible times in the last days.* [2]*People will be lovers of themselves, lovers of money, boastful, proud, abusive, disobedient to their parents, ungrate-*

ful, unholy, ³without love, unforgiving, slanderous, without self-control, brutal, not lovers of the good, ⁴treacherous, rash, conceited, lovers of pleasure rather than lovers of God" (2 Tim. 3:1-4).

Scripture clearly teaches that there are many evidences for God's existence, and when men choose to turn away from such evidences, they are without excuse. As they turn away, a deterioration of society begins which ultimately results in the necessity for God to bring His judgements...

¹⁸*"The wrath of God is being revealed from heaven against all the godlessness and wickedness of men who suppress the truth by their wickedness,* ¹⁹*since what may be known about God is plain to them, because God has made it plain to them.* ²⁰*For since the creation of the world God's invisible qualities—his eternal power and divine nature—have been clearly seen, being understood from what has been made, so that men are without excuse.*

²¹*For although they knew God, they neither glorified him as God nor gave thanks to him, but their thinking became futile and their foolish hearts were darkened.* ²²*Although they claimed to be wise, they became fools* ²³*and exchanged the glory of the immortal God for images made to look like mortal man and birds and animals and reptiles.*

²⁴*Therefore God gave them over in the sinful desires of their hearts to sexual impurity for the degrading of their bodies with one another.* ²⁵*They exchanged the truth of God for a lie, and worshiped and served created things rather than the Creator—who is forever praised. Amen.*

²⁶*Because of this, God gave them over to shameful lusts. Even their women exchanged natural relations for unnatural ones.* ²⁷*In the same way the men also abandoned natural relations with women and were inflamed with lust for one another. Men committed indecent acts with other men, and received in themselves the due penalty for their perversion.*

²⁸*Furthermore, since they did not think it worthwhile to retain the knowledge of God, he gave them over to a depraved*

mind, to do what ought not to be done. ²⁹They have become filled with every kind of wickedness, evil, greed and depravity. They are full of envy, murder, strife, deceit and malice. They are gossips, ³⁰slanderers, God-haters, insolent, arrogant and boastful; they invent ways of doing evil; they disobey their parents; ³¹they are senseless, faithless, heartless, ruthless. ³²Although they know God's righteous decree that those who do such things deserve death, they not only continue to do these very things but also approve of those who practice them" (Rom. 1:18-32).

Can we not see these things taking place today?

Satan has had great influence in this world from the time of Adam and Eve onward. He has worked to thwart God's purposes in the earth from the very beginning. We know that Jesus Christ came to earth to die on a cross that He might win the victory over Satan and over sin. This age of sin and the provision of God's grace to sinners through Jesus Christ, will come to a conclusion when Satan is finally seized and bound. This will occur at the time Jesus Christ comes to establish His kingdom on earth where He will rule for a thousand years (a millennium) (Rev. 20:4-6). Satan will be bound during that thousand years, thereafter to be released again only for a short time before he is finally thrown into the lake of fire (Rev. 20:1-3,7-10).

It is commonly believed among Bible scholars that a seven year period of intense trouble and tribulation will precede Christ's return to rule. This seven year period of extreme difficulty, which is split into two three and one-half year segments, is identified based upon prophecies contained within the books of Daniel and Revelation (Dan. 9:24-27; 12:1-13; Rev. 11:2-3; 12:6; 13:5-7). This seven year period is also referred to as the seventieth week of Daniel.

While there are various interpretations of biblical passages dealing with the events to occur within this seven year period, it is clear from scripture that it will include a time when God's wrath will be poured out on those remaining inhabitants of the earth who have rejected God and refused to repent of their sins (Rev. 6:15-17; 11:17-18; 14:9-11; 14:15-20; 16:1-21). It is also clear from scripture that those who know God and have been cleansed of their sins will **not** have to suffer this wrath of God.

> [8]*"But since we belong to the day, let us be self-controlled, putting on faith and love as a breastplate, and the hope of salvation as a helmet.* [9]*For God did not appoint us to suffer wrath but to receive salvation through our Lord Jesus Christ"* (1 Thes. 5:8-9).

> [8]*"But God demonstrates his own love for us in this: While we were still sinners, Christ died for us.* [9]*Since we have now been justified by his blood, how much more shall we be saved from God's wrath through him!"* (Rom. 5:8-9).

During Noah's time, the earth was deluged with a flood and all people were destroyed, but righteous Noah and his family were delivered by God. When Sodom and Gomorrah were destroyed, God brought Lot and his family out of the city of Sodom. So it will be when God's wrath is poured out. Those who are standing by faith in God will not be allowed to suffer the wrath of God but will be removed from the holocaust. It is believed by many Christians that the removal of believers still living at that time will be accomplished through what has been identified as the "rapture," the physical translation and transformation of believers spoken of in 1 Cor. 15:51-57; Phil. 3:20-21; 1 Thes. 4:13-18. Again, it is not the purpose of this book to either attempt to support or refute these beliefs.

Various views exist as to when this rapture will actually take place. The pretribulation rapture position is probably the most prevalent view which holds that Christ will rapture true believers prior to the onset of the seven year tribulation period. I imagine that some who hold this view might be taking comfort in the belief that they will not have to undergo any of the suffering which is to occur during the tribulation. However, in my view, it is foolishness for Christians to become overly confident in the absolute correctness of any interpretation of end time prophecy.

The concern is, that we must be prepared for any and all eventualities. While we can learn much from scripture about the things that will take place, much of prophecy is written in veiled language and is therefore hard to interpret. Different individuals who have done careful study of the scriptures regarding end time prophecies still arrive at conflicting conclusions. It is a subject that is filled with controversy.

Let me cite an example taken from the book, "The Pre-Wrath Rapture of the Church," by Marvin Rosenthal. Mr. Rosenthal was a ...

"convinced, sincere, unbending, and, in retrospect, to my shame, intolerant pretribulation rapturist for thirty-five years. My pretribulation rapture position was widely known. I had preached it with conviction and sincerity around the world. I had not been hiding it under a bushel. I am both on tape and in print supporting pretribulation rapturism. The Friends of Israel Gospel Ministry is a Bible-believing faith mission which I directed. Upon my recommendation, the board of trustees unanimously approved a doctrinal statement which embraced pretribulation rapturism. I have participated in many of the major prophetic conferences in North America, in churches, schools, and Bible conferences—and always as a pretribulation rapturist. I edited and published Israel My Glory, a magazine with a circulation of over three hundred thousand subscribers and a readership of almost a million people, and all articles had to be consistent with pretribulation rapturism. The schools I attended, my contemporary heroes of the faith, the overwhelming majority of churches in which I minister, and all of my beloved colleagues in the ministry are pretribulation rapturists ... I was an uncompromising pretribulationist."

Mr. Rosenthal had held to the pretribulation rapture position for thirty-five years. However, he had a friend who had been earnestly searching the scripture for many years to understand end time events. This friend was a persistent individual who continued to call Mr. Rosenthal almost daily for over three months to discuss these matters and what he was finding in his study of the Word. The end result of it all was that Mr. Rosenthal's views of end time events were changed. He subsequently wrote and published a book, "The Prewrath Rapture of the Church,"[b] which provides a considerably altered view of end time events from that which he held for so many years.

The purpose in mentioning Mr. Rosenthal's book, is not to promote his views. Instead, it is to emphasize that while we may feel that our views about such matters are firmly rooted in scripture, as he did, WE MUST PREPARE OURSELVES TO STAND FIRM IN THE LORD IN THE DAYS AHEAD EVEN THOUGH NOTHING MAY COME TO PASS AS WE HAVE THOUGHT IT WOULD. WE MUST NOT ALLOW OURSELVES TO BECOME SO COMFORTABLE IN OUR END TIME DOCTRINE THAT WE ARE THROWN OFF BALANCE SHOULD THESE END TIME EVENTS OCCUR DIFFERENTLY.

Basically, it is Mr. Rosenthal's view now, that the rapture of the church will not occur until sometime in the last three and one-half years of the seven year tribulation period. He believes that this rapture will occur just prior to a period of time identified as "The Day of the Lord," which will come on the earth in the last part of the seven year period. It is also his view that the severe difficulties on this earth which will precede the time of God's wrath, but will nonetheless occur within the seven year period, will be the consequence of man's evil and not God's wrath.

Mr. Rosenthal gives considerable scriptural evidence to substantiate his position. If his understanding of scripture is

---

[b]Published in 1990 by Thomas Nelson Publishers

correct, then believers will have to face the time of the Antichrist's (the "beast's") rule. This runs against the popularized belief that Christians would be taken out of the earth prior to the seven year period of tribulation and the Antichrist's rule, and thus would not have to face the evils of that time. However, scripture clearly shows, that there will be saints present on the earth during the time of the Antichrist (Rev. 13, esp. v. 7)

To be a Christian or not to be a Christian is based upon who, or what, we trust. If we place our trust in God, as Abraham did, then we are declared righteous and become God's children. If we continue to place our trust in this world and its' securities, or in the gods of this world, then we will ultimately face the wrath of God. If Christians will be on earth during the time of the Antichrist's rule, then there will come a time of decision—a time when all who live on the earth will have to choose who, or what, they will serve and trust in. The rule on this earth of the Antichrist, who is also identified as the first beast, is spoken of in Rev. 13.

> [5]*"The beast was given a mouth to utter proud words and blasphemies and to exercise his authority for forty-two months. [6]He opened his mouth to blaspheme God, and to slander his name and his dwelling place and those who live in heaven. [7]He was given power to make war against the saints and to conquer them. And he was given authority over every tribe, people, language and nation. [8]All inhabitants of the earth will worship the beast—all whose names have not been written in the book of life belonging to the Lamb that was slain from the creation of the world. [9]He who has an ear, let him hear. [10]If anyone is to go into captivity, into captivity he will go. If anyone is to be killed with the sword, with the sword he will be killed. This calls for patient endurance and faithfulness on the part of the saints.*
>
> [11]*Then I saw another beast, coming out of the earth. He had two horns like a lamb, but he spoke like a dragon. [12]He exercised all the authority of the first beast on his behalf, and*

made the earth and its inhabitants worship the first beast, whose fatal wound had been healed. [13]And he performed great and miraculous signs, even causing fire to come down from heaven to earth in full view of men. [14]Because of the signs he was given power to do on behalf of the first beast, he deceived the inhabitants of the earth. He ordered them to set up an image in honor of the beast who was wounded by the sword and yet lived. [15]He was given power to give breath to the image of the first beast, so that it could speak and cause all who refused to worship the image to be killed. [16]He also forced everyone, small and great, rich and poor, free and slave, to receive a mark on his right hand or on his forehead, [17]so that no one could buy or sell unless he had the mark, which is the name of the beast or the number of his name.

[18]This calls for wisdom. If anyone has insight, let him calculate the number of the beast, for it is man's number. His number is 666" (Rev. 13:5-18).

We see from this scripture that the Antichrist (the first beast) will exercise authority on the earth for forty-two months (3½ years). He is given power to make war against the saints and to conquer them. The things that will occur on the earth during that time will call for "patient endurance and faithfulness on the part of the saints." During the Antichrist's rule will come a time of final separation between those who truly believe in the Lord, and those who do not. A decision will be required. Each person on the earth will have to decide in who or what they are going to trust—in God and His Son Jesus Christ, or the world system and the Antichrist. The choice to worship or not worship the beast, and to receive or not receive his mark, will have eternal consequences.

[9]"A third angel followed them and said in a loud voice: 'If anyone worships the beast and his image and receives his mark on the forehead or on the hand, [10]he, too, will drink of the wine of God's fury, which has been poured full strength into the cup of his wrath. He will be tormented with burning sulfur in the presence of the holy angels and of the Lamb.

[11]And the smoke of their torment rises for ever and ever. There is no rest day or night for those who worship the beast and his image, or for anyone who receives the mark of his name." [12]This calls for patient endurance on the part of the saints who obey God's commandments and remain faithful to Jesus.

[13]Then I heard a voice from heaven say, 'Write: Blessed are the dead who die in the Lord from now on.'

'Yes,' says the Spirit, 'they will rest from their labor, for their deeds will follow them' (Rev. 14:9-13).

The decision that the Antichrist will bring will not be just a spiritual decision divorced from everyday realities as some choose to live it now, but will involve the necessities of life—food, clothing, shelter, etc. The reality of each persons' faith will be proven. No longer will a person be able to trust Christ for heaven while trusting in the world for the necessities of life. It will be all for Christ, or not at all, a time of separation between the sheep (those who trust in Christ) and the goats (those who do not).

We see that the antichrist was given authority over every tribe, people, language and nation. We also see that he forced everyone, small and great, rich and poor, free and slave, to receive a mark on his right hand or on his forehead, so that no one could buy or sell unless he had the mark. When such a mark is instituted it would appear that money would have to be eliminated, otherwise, how could sales be so rigidly controlled.

There are many logical reasons for eliminating money, credit cards, etc., because of the crime that exists in our society. And today we find nations such as Iran producing great quantities of counterfeit money. What a solution! Take away all cash, checks and credit cards and implant under the skin of each person a tiny microcomputer chip which could be accessed by readers such as are used today for the reading of product bar codes. Such chips could contain the identity of the person, their available funds, etc. Payments might be made electronically just as today they are made from debit cards without any cash being involved.

Today, you can even have a tiny electronic chip injected under the skin of your pet to allow easy identification should it become lost. Such chips have also been injected into tiny fish to allow marine biologists to track their return at a later date. Today, we also find the increasing proliferation of banking machines, bar code readers, credit card readers, etc., and we now have computer networks of increasing sophistication spanning the globe. People sitting at a personal computer at home, can access people and information around the planet. All of the necessary technology is being activated which could allow such a cashless society to be implemented in the immediate future.

But such a system also means control. When a person walks into a store and his I.D. is electronically read, then "the system" knows exactly where that person is. If the state decides that a person is no longer to be allowed to buy or sell, then it can be so noted in electronic files, and their ability to buy or sell can be cut off.

The only reason for discussing all of this is to note that we are fast approaching a time when all of the predictions made in the Bible could come to pass. It is just around the corner.

Those who take the mark and thereby submit to, and confirm their allegiance and trust in the antichrist and the world system, will be able to buy and sell for a time but will subsequently experience the full wrath of God. Those who do not take the mark of the beast, will not be able to buy or sell in the marketplace. They will be stepping out into a wilderness, placing their entire trust in Christ alone for all that they will need. While they will face difficulties on this earth for a time, they will not face the wrath of God and will inherit eternal life as they stand firm in Christ. It may very well be that following this time of decision and separation brought about by the mark of the beast, that the age of grace for the Gentiles will have ended in that no further decisions to come to Jesus Christ will be possible.

Again, the question is not whether Mr. Rosenthal's view or some other view of end time events is correct. The concern is that we must not go to sleep, but must be ready for whatever comes. In this light, let us consider the parable of the ten virgins ...

> [1]"At that time the kingdom of heaven will be like ten virgins who took their lamps and went out to meet the bridegroom. [2]Five of them were foolish and five were wise. [3]The foolish ones took their lamps but did not take any oil with them. [4]The wise, however, took oil in jars along with their lamps. [5]The bridegroom was a long time in coming, and they all became drowsy and fell asleep.
>
> [6]"At midnight the cry rang out: 'Here's the bridegroom! Come out to meet him!'
>
> [7]"Then all the virgins woke up and trimmed their lamps. [8]The foolish ones said to the wise, 'Give us some of your oil; our lamps are going out.'
>
> [9]"'No,' they replied, 'there may not be enough for both us and you. Instead, go to those who sell oil and buy some for yourselves.'
>
> [10]"But while they were on their way to buy the oil, the bridegroom arrived. The virgins who were ready went in with him to the wedding banquet. And the door was shut.
>
> [11]"Later the others also came. 'Sir! Sir!' they said. 'Open the door for us!'
>
> [12]"But he replied, 'I tell you the truth, I don't know you.'
>
> [13]"Therefore keep watch, because you do not know the day or the hour" (Matt. 25:1-13).

This passage demonstrates that there will be many who are looking for the appearing of the bridegroom (Jesus Christ) who will be caught unprepared as the darkness (midnight) comes, and their faith will not be sufficient to carry them through to the end. As a consequence their lamps will go out. They will be those who did not strengthen their faith and commitment to the Lord while they had the chance. They will be those who were not diligent in their pursuit of God because of lukewarmness and carelessness. Perhaps they will be those who were lulled to sleep by a "pretribulation rapture" theory or by the doctrine of "once-saved-always-saved" (eternal security).

In any event, we must not be careless. We must not place our trust in one end time scenario or another. Instead, we must be diligent to continually seek after the Lord and to love and trust Him with all of our heart, soul, mind and strength (Mark 12:30). We must "... *keep watch, because we do not know the day or the hour"* of our Lord's coming. We may face very, very difficult times before the Lord comes to take His own to be with Him. We will either have prepared ourselves to stand, or we will be like the foolish virgins and find our lamps going out as we approach the midnight hour.

When Israel marched out of Egypt, they had the promised land in view, and not the wilderness. They had become accustomed to being provided for in Egypt and were not ready for the doubts and fears that the wilderness would bring. After their songs of praise to the Lord for their deliverance through the Red Sea, they turned around to find themselves face-to-face with the new reality of the wilderness, which they were not ready to cope with. It caught them off balance and they had difficulty adjusting to it. They had grown up trusting in Egypt and had not had to trust in the Lord for their day-to-day needs. Then suddenly, all of this changed as they entered the wilderness, and they were never really able to make the transition to fully trust in the Lord. So it was that they began to whine and complain, to rebel against the Lord and finally to turn away from Him.

We who have grown up in the United States, Canada and other industrialized and prosperous nations, have become accustomed to the security of our jobs, bank accounts, insurance policies, etc., etc. We have not had to trust God, it would seem, for very much. However, as we approach the last days, all of that could change, and what we have trusted in for so long could suddenly be wiped out. Have we prepared our hearts to trust in God, whatever may come? This is a warning to all of us who are called by the name of the Lord. We must learn now how to seek first the kingdom of God and to come to know our Lord more intimately.

We have seen in our study of scripture that Egypt bears a likeness to this present evil world. There is a time of judgement coming on this world which scripture declares will be much more severe than the plagues which the Lord brought upon Egypt. Yet, even today, there are many who reject Christ and who believe that they do not need the Lord. They have a blind faith in this world system and do not see that calamity may be just around the corner. Isaiah spoke a Word from the Lord regarding Egypt, and it is also a Word for today...

> [1]*"Woe to those who go down to Egypt for help, who rely on horses, who trust in the multitude of their chariots and in the great strength of their horsemen, but do not look to the Holy One of Israel, or seek help from the LORD.* [2]*Yet he too is wise and can bring disaster; he does not take back his words. He will rise up against the house of the wicked, against those who help evildoers.* [3]*But the Egyptians are men and not God; their horses are flesh and not spirit. When the LORD stretches out his hand, he who helps will stumble, he who is helped will fall; both will perish together"* (Isa. 31:1-3).

Speaking about Babylon, which is also a picture of our end time world, Isaiah says ...

> [8]*"Now then, listen, you wanton creature, lounging in your security and saying to yourself, 'I am, and there is none besides me. I will never be a widow or suffer the loss of children.'* [9]*Both of these will overtake you in a moment, on a single day: loss of children and widowhood. They will come upon you in full measure, in spite of your many sorceries*

and all your potent spells. ¹⁰You have trusted in your wickedness and have said, 'No one sees me.' Your wisdom and knowledge mislead you when you say to yourself, 'I am, and there is none besides me.' ¹¹Disaster will come upon you, and you will not know how to conjure it away. A calamity will fall upon you that you cannot ward off with a ransom; a catastrophe you cannot foresee will suddenly come upon you. ¹²Keep on, then, with your magic spells and with your many sorceries, which you have labored at since childhood. Perhaps you will succeed, perhaps you will cause terror. ¹³All the counsel you have received has only worn you out! Let your astrologers come forward, those stargazers who make predictions month by month, let them save you from what is coming upon you. ¹⁴Surely they are like stubble; the fire will burn them up. They cannot even save themselves from the power of the flame. Here are no coals to warm anyone; here is no fire to sit by. ¹⁵That is all they can do for you—these you have labored with and trafficked with since childhood. Each of them goes on in his error; there is not one that can save you" (Isa. 47:8-15).

We remember that the firstborn sons struck down in Egypt by the hand of the Lord were representative of Egypt's present and future hope. In one stroke, God struck down that hope. It will be the same in the last days. There will be those who have lounged in their security and who have said to themselves, "I am, and there is none beside me." They have placed great pride and dependence upon their own wisdom and strength and have scoffed at God in spite of the fact that they can't stop the rain from coming, can't stop the lightning, can't stop hurricanes, can't stop tornadoes, can't stop earthquakes, can't stop meteors from coming, and are really impotent to stand in any way against the Almighty God. Suddenly, their wisdom and strength will come to nothing when God's wrath falls. Their disdain for the one true God will be shown to be utter foolishness.

When the last plague fell on Egypt it affected all, from the firstborn son of Pharaoh to the firstborn son of the slave girl and the firstborn son of the prisoner who was in the dungeon (Exod. 11:5; 12:29). It did not discriminate based on position, wealth or any other factor. So it will be in the end times...

[1]"See, the LORD is going to lay waste the earth and devastate it; he will ruin its face and scatter its inhabitants—[2]it will be the same for priest as for people, for master as for servant, for mistress as for maid, for seller as for buyer, for borrower as for lender, for debtor as for creditor. [3]The earth will be completely laid waste and totally plundered. The LORD has spoken this word. [4]The earth dries up and withers, the world languishes and withers, the exalted of the earth languish. [5]The earth is defiled by its people; they have disobeyed the laws, violated the statutes and broken the everlasting covenant. [6]Therefore a curse consumes the earth; its people must bear their guilt. Therefore earth's inhabitants are burned up, and very few are left" (Isa. 24:1-6).

There was loud wailing in Egypt when they got up during the night and discovered that there was not a house without someone dead. In the same way, there will be no rejoicing on the earth when God's judgements fall...

[7]"The new wine dries up and the vine withers; all the merrymakers groan. [8]The gaiety of the tambourines is stilled, the noise of the revelers has stopped, the joyful harp is silent. [9]No longer do they drink wine with a song; the beer is bitter to its drinkers. [10]The ruined city lies desolate; the entrance to every house is barred. [11]In the streets they cry out for wine; all joy turns to gloom, all gaiety is banished from the earth. [12]The city is left in ruins, its gate is battered to pieces. [13]So will it be on the earth and among the nations, as when an olive tree is beaten, or as when gleanings are left after the grape harvest" (Isa. 24:7-13).

[17]"Terror and pit and snare await you, O people of the earth. [18]Whoever flees at the sound of terror will fall into a pit; whoever climbs out of the pit will be caught in a snare. The floodgates of the heavens are opened, the foundations of the earth shake. [19]The earth is broken up, the earth is split asunder, the earth is thoroughly shaken. [20]The earth reels like a drunkard, it sways like a hut in the wind; so heavy upon it is the guilt of its rebellion that it falls—never to rise again. [21]In that day the LORD will punish the powers in the heavens above and the kings on the earth below. [22]They will be herded together like prisoners bound in a dungeon; they will be shut up in prison and be punished after many days. [23]The moon will be abashed, the sun ashamed..." (Isa. 24:17-23).

God will say to those who are His ...

[20]"Go, my people, enter your rooms and shut the doors behind you; hide yourselves for a little while until his wrath has passed by. [21]See, the LORD is coming out of his dwelling to punish the people of the earth for their sins. The earth will disclose the blood shed upon her; she will conceal her slain no longer" (Isa. 26:20-21).

And so today, God is calling on all to turn to Him ...

[21]"...there is no God apart from me, a righteous God and a Savior; there is none but me. [22]'Turn to me and be saved, all you ends of the earth; for I am God, and there is no other. [23]By myself I have sworn, my mouth has uttered in all integrity a word that will not be revoked: Before me every knee will bow; by me every tongue will swear. [24]They will say of me, 'In the LORD alone are righteousness and strength.' All who have raged against him will come to him and be put to shame. [25]But in the LORD all the descendants of Israel will be found righteous and will exult'" (Isa. 45:21-25).

Many, many scriptures from different books of the Bible, both in the Old and New Testaments could have been used to amplify what has been stated above. The Bible makes it very clear that the wrath of God is going to come on this earth. But as has already been stated, the Bible also makes clear that the wrath of God will not come upon those who have placed their trust in Jesus Christ.

The Apostle Paul, speaking to the church at Thessalonica, said, ...

> [6]*"God is just: He will pay back trouble to those who trouble you* [7]*and give relief to you who are troubled, and to us as well. This will happen when the Lord Jesus is revealed from heaven in blazing fire with his powerful angels.* [8]*He will punish those who do not know God and do not obey the gospel of our Lord Jesus.* [9]*They will be punished with everlasting destruction and shut out from the presence of the Lord and from the majesty of his power* [10]*on the day he comes to be glorified in his holy people and to be marveled at among all those who have believed. This includes you, because you believed our testimony to you"* (2 Thes. 1:6-10).

I believe that a word of warning from the Lord given to the Jews through Ezekiel the prophet around 585 B.C., also has application to us today ...

> [1]*"The word of the LORD came to me:* [2]*'Son of man, speak to your countrymen and say to them: 'When I bring the sword against a land, and the people of the land choose one of their men and make him their watchman,* [3]*and he sees the sword coming against the land and blows the trumpet to warn the people,* [4]*then if anyone hears the trumpet but does not take warning and the sword comes and takes his life, his blood will be on his own head.* [5]*Since he heard the sound of the trumpet but did not take warning, his blood will be on his own head. If he had taken warning, he would have saved himself.* [6]*But if the watchman sees the sword coming and does not blow the trumpet to warn the people and the sword comes and takes the life of one of them, that man will be*

taken away because of his sin, but I will hold the watchman accountable for his blood.'

[7]'Son of man, I have made you a watchman for the house of Israel; so hear the word I speak and give them warning from me. [8]When I say to the wicked, 'O wicked man, you will surely die,' and you do not speak out to dissuade him from his ways, that wicked man will die for his sin, and I will hold you accountable for his blood. [9]But if you do warn the wicked man to turn from his ways and he does not do so, he will die for his sin, but you will have saved yourself.'

[10]'Son of man, say to the house of Israel, 'This is what you are saying: 'Our offenses and sins weigh us down, and we are wasting away because of them. How then can we live?' [11]Say to them, 'As surely as I live, declares the Sovereign LORD, I take no pleasure in the death of the wicked, but rather that they turn from their ways and live. Turn! Turn from your evil ways! Why will you die, O house of Israel?'

[12]'Therefore, son of man, say to your countrymen, 'The righteousness of the righteous man will not save him when he disobeys, and the wickedness of the wicked man will not cause him to fall when he turns from it. The righteous man, if he sins, will not be allowed to live because of his former righteousness.' [13]If I tell the righteous man that he will surely live, but then he trusts in his righteousness and does evil, none of the righteous things he has done will be remembered; he will die for the evil he has done. [14]And if I say to the wicked man, 'You will surely die,' but he then turns away from his sin and does what is just and right—[15]if he gives back what he took in pledge for a loan, returns what he has stolen, follows the decrees that give life, and does no evil, he will surely live; he will not die. [16]None of the sins he has committed will be remembered against him. He has done what is just and right; he will surely live. [17]Yet your countrymen say, 'The way of the Lord is not just.' But it is their way that is not just. [18]If a righteous man turns from his righteousness and does evil, he will die for it. [19]And if a wicked man turns away from his wickedness and does what is just and right, he will live by doing so'" (Ezek. 33:1-19).

If you are reading this, and have not surrendered your heart and life to the Lord Jesus Christ, there is no time like the present. The Lord longs for you to come to Him. The following scripture is for you...

> 6*"Seek the LORD while he may be found; call on him while he is near. 7Let the wicked forsake his way and the evil man his thoughts. Let him turn to the LORD, and he will have mercy on him, and to our God, for he will freely pardon"* (Isa. 55:6-7).

For all who desire to be found in Christ when He comes for His bride, let us commit ourselves to SEEK FIRST the Kingdom of God and His righteousness. Let us commit ourselves to stand firm in faith and obedience, for surely, *"If [we] do not stand firm in our faith, [we] will not stand at all"* (Isa. 7:9b).

ADDENDUM

God's Beginnings— The Nation of Israel

In the Old Testament portion of the Bible the historical account of the rise and fall of the nation of Israel is given as it occurred prior to the advent of Jesus Christ. In the first six of these Old Testament books—Genesis, Exodus, Leviticus, Numbers, Deuteronomy and Joshua—we find:

1. a description of Israel's origins as a people;
2. the promises that God made regarding them;
3. their entry into the land of Egypt while still small in number and their rapid increase in population while in that land;
4. their slavery and oppression in Egypt under Pharaoh and his task masters;
5. the coming of the man Moses, sent by God to bring a message of hope to the Israelites informing them that the Lord was aware of their suffering, and would deliver them from Pharaoh's grasp and would take them to a land of His choosing, "a land flowing with milk and honey";

6. their subsequent exodus from Egypt brought about by God's mighty hand under the leadership of Moses;
7. their journey to the promised land through a vast wilderness where they experienced many trials and difficulties;
8. and their final entry as a nation into that promised land, the land of Canaan.

Though this story may now be considered ancient history, it teaches many lessons which are vital for us today. One of the most important of these lessons is the absolute necessity to have and maintain a deep faith and trust in God that will remain steadfast through every difficulty.

God desires us to have a trust in Him that holds no reservations. A trust that is focused on God and not in the securities of this world. A trust that believes there is no situation where He is not in control. A trust that commits itself to God when the most vital issues of life are at stake. A trust that does not turn away from God in the time of crisis.

In this story of the Israelites, the love and the trustworthiness of God is revealed. We see God reaching out time and time again to the Israelites to show them that He loved them and that they could put their trust in Him without reservation. Yet they spurned His great love and continually turned away from Him to find their own source of security. They failed to grasp and to act upon what He offered them, and so placed themselves in great grief and jeopardy.

In Jeremiah, God speaks about the Israelites in this way:

¹³*"My people have committed two sins: They have forsaken me, the spring of living water, and have dug their own cisterns, broken cisterns that cannot hold water"(Jer. 2:13).*

Their story is very important for us today. I believe that other Old and New Testament scripture dealing with this vital area of trust, will take on new depth of meaning as we begin to receive the revelation that this historical account provides.

GOD'S COVENANT WITH ABRAM

The story begins in Genesis chapter 11 with the man Abram. Abram was born to a man named Terah who lived in Ur of the Chaldeans[a]. It was while they were in that land, that Abram was married to a woman named Sarai. Sometime later, Terah took his son Abram, his daughter-in-law Sarai and his grandson Lot, and started out to go to Canaan, but when they came to a place called Haran, they settled there (see Gen. 11:27-32). It was while they were in that land that the Lord spoke to Abram...

[1]*"The LORD had said to Abram, 'Leave your country, your people and your father's household and go to the land I will show you. [2]'I will make you into a great nation and I will bless you; I will make your name great, and you will be a blessing. [3]I will bless those who bless you, and whoever curses you I will curse; and all peoples on earth will be blessed through you.'*

[4]*So Abram left, as the LORD had told him; and Lot went with him. Abram was seventy-five years old when he set out from Haran. [5]He took his wife Sarai, his nephew Lot, all the possessions they had accumulated and the people they had acquired in Haran, and they set out for the land of Canaan, and they arrived there.*

[6]*Abram traveled through the land as far as the site of the great tree of Moreh at Shechem. At that time the Canaanites were in the land. [7]The LORD appeared to Abram and said, 'To your offspring I will give this land.' So he built an altar there to the LORD, who had appeared to him'"* (Gen. 12:1-7).

---

[a] Present day Iraq

Abram went into a land which was not his own, the land of Canaan. Canaan was situated in the area which we now know as Israel. We see that God gave Abram a promise that his descendants would some day receive this land from the Lord, even though it was inhabited by another people. This promise was repeated and expanded upon later when God spoke to Abram again.

> [14]*"The LORD said to Abram after Lot had parted from him, 'Lift up your eyes from where you are and look north and south, east and west. [15]All the land that you see I will give to you and your offspring forever. [16]I will make your offspring like the dust of the earth, so that if anyone could count the dust, then your offspring could be counted. [17]Go, walk through the length and breadth of the land, for I am giving it to you'"* (Gen. 13:14-17).

This land would belong to Abram's offspring *forever.* However, Abram didn't have any children, and this was a source of concern to him.

> [1]*"After this, the word of the LORD came to Abram in a vision:*
> *'Do not be afraid, Abram.*
> *I am your shield,*
> *your very great reward.'*
>
> [2]*But Abram said, 'O Sovereign LORD, what can you give me since I remain childless and the one who will inherit my estate is Eliezer of Damascus?' [3]And Abram said, 'You have given me no children; so a servant in my household will be my heir'"* (Gen. 15:1-3).

God responded to this concern of Abram's...

> [4]*"...'This man will not be your heir, but a son coming from your own body will be your heir.' [5]He took him outside and said, 'Look up at the heavens and count the stars—if*

indeed you can count them.' Then he said to him, 'So shall your offspring be.'

⁶Abram believed the LORD, and he credited it to him as righteousness'" (Gen. 15:4-6).

Then God repeated His promise to Abram, that this land of Canaan would indeed be given to him and his descendants...

⁷"...'I am the LORD, who brought you out of Ur of the Chaldeans to give you this land to take possession of it.'

⁸But Abram said, 'O Sovereign LORD, how can I know that I will gain possession of it?'

⁹So the LORD said to him, 'Bring me a heifer, a goat and a ram, each three years old, along with a dove and a young pigeon.'

¹⁰Abram brought all these to him, cut them in two and arranged the halves opposite each other; the birds, however, he did not cut in half. ¹¹Then birds of prey came down on the carcasses, but Abram drove them away.

*¹²As the sun was setting, Abram fell into a deep sleep, and a thick and dreadful darkness came over him. ¹³Then the LORD said to him, '**Know for certain that your descendants will be strangers in a country not their own, and they will be enslaved and mistreated four hundred years. ¹⁴But I will punish the nation they serve as slaves, and afterward they will come out with great possessions. ¹⁵You, however, will go to your fathers in peace and be buried at a good old age. ¹⁶In the fourth generation your descendants will come back here, for the sin of the Amorites has not yet reached its full measure.'***

*¹⁷When the sun had set and darkness had fallen, a smoking firepot with a blazing torch appeared and passed between the pieces. ¹⁸On that day the LORD made a covenant with Abram and said, '**To your descendants I give this land, from the river of Egypt to the great river, the Euphrates—¹⁹the land of the Kenites, Kenizzites, Kad-***

monites, [20]Hittites, Perizzites, Raphaites, [21]Amorites, Canaanites, Girgashites and Jebusites"[b] (Gen. 15:7-21).

All of these things that Abram did with the animals and the birds, and the movement of a smoking firepot with a torch passing between their pieces, may seem somewhat strange to us. The purpose of it all is summed up in verse 18 where it says, *"On that day the LORD made a covenant with Abram."* God was in fact making a very solemn promise to Abram, a promise which He would surely keep.

We can read Old Testament passages which speak of the slaughter of many men, women and children. Some of these incidents were gruesome in nature. We find ourselves wondering how a God of love could allow such things to take place. Such violence took place when Abram's descendants finally entered the land of Canaan and annihilated whole cities. It makes for rather grim reading. However, it is clear that the people who occupied the land of Canaan were extremely wicked. In verse 16 in the passage we have just read, it is stated that it would not be until the fourth generation of Abram's descendants that they would be allowed to go into Canaan to take the land, *"...for the sin of the Amorites has not yet reached its full measure."* God was giving the Amorites every opportunity to turn from sin, even though He knew they would not do so. Only after every opportunity had been given them to repent did God allow the slaughter which ultimately took place.

A study note to Genesis 15:16 in the NIV Translation says:

"Just how sinful many Canaanite religious practices were is now known from archaeological artifacts and from their own epic literature, discovered at Ras Shamra (ancient Ugarit) on the north Syrian coast beginning in 1929. Their "worship" was polytheistic and included child sacrifice,

---

[b] Emphasis added

idolatry, religious prostitution and divination (cf. Dt 18:9-12). God was patient in judgement, even with the wicked Canaanites."

Today we see a world that is becoming increasingly evil, even as the Bible has predicted it will be in the last days.

1"But mark this: There will be terrible times in the last days. 2People will be lovers of themselves, lovers of money, boastful, proud, abusive, disobedient to their parents, ungrateful, unholy, 3without love, unforgiving, slanderous, without self-control, brutal, not lovers of the good, 4 treacherous, rash, conceited, lovers of pleasure rather than lovers of God—5having a form of godliness but denying its power. Have nothing to do with them" (2 Tim. 3:1-5).

Considering this increase of evil predicted in the Bible, there is surely coming a time when the sin of the peoples of this earth will have reached its full measure. At that time, there will be terrible difficulties across the earth as the wrath of God falls upon all who have rejected Jesus and have given themselves over to every kind of evil. Unrestrained sin will ultimately bring its consequences.

4"For if God did not spare angels when they sinned, but sent them to hell, putting them into gloomy dungeons to be held for judgment; 5if he did not spare the ancient world when he brought the flood on its ungodly people, but protected Noah, a preacher of righteousness, and seven others; 6if he condemned the cities of Sodom and Gomorrah by burning them to ashes, and made them an example of what is going to happen to the ungodly; 7and if he rescued Lot, a righteous man, who was distressed by the filthy lives of lawless men 8(for that righteous man, living among them day after day, was tormented in his righteous soul by the lawless deeds he saw and heard)—9if this is so, then the Lord knows how to rescue godly men from trials and to hold the unrighteous for the day of judgment, while continuing their punishment" (2 Pet. 2:4-9).

The book of Revelation, speaking of the end times, says that even after some of these judgements (plagues) begin to fall, the people will still not repent.

[20]*"The rest of mankind that were not killed by these plagues [spoken of earlier in the book of Revelation]*[c] *still did not repent of the work of their hands; they did not stop worshiping demons, and idols of gold, silver, bronze, stone and wood—idols that cannot see or hear or walk.* [21]*Nor did they repent of their murders, their magic arts, their sexual immorality or their thefts"* (Rev. 9:20-21).

These words, which speak of a time of difficulty yet to come, were written nearly 2,000 years ago.

Today we have AIDS, a disease spread first by homosexuals. While this disease is not identified in the book of Revelation, I believe that we could still ask the question: "Has this 'plague' caused many to repent of such immorality?" No, it has not. Instead it is said, "We must find better ways to protect ourselves when we engage in these acts so we don't get disease." We are also hearing it said that..."we must not condemn such acts, because those who engage in them cannot help themselves. They were born that way. We must recognize homosexuality as an alternative life style."

AIDS is also being spread to heterosexuals. Yet there is no outcry in the media telling us to stop our wrongful sexual relations to avoid the spread of this disease. In essence what is being said by those engaging in such practices is..."We don't want to stop doing what we're doing, therefore the answer is to find and use better protective devices. We don't want to take on the responsibility of children that might result as a consequence of our fun, so we must have abor-

---

[c] Bracketed insertion added

tions. Don't tell us to stop our immorality because that's old fashioned. We are more liberated now. In this day and age we can do as we please. There is no higher law that we need to respect."

The disease of AIDS points to the immorality in our land and exposes it. The 'plague' would die out if we turned away (repented) from that immorality, but such an obvious solution is not acceptable today. All we are willing to accept is a medical solution that doesn't infringe on our sexual freedom. (Wouldn't it be much more appropriate in this case to define freedom as, "Not the right to do what I want, but the power to do what I ought.") Millions have been spent to launch an all out attack on this lethal disease. It is considered that AIDS care costs will sky-rocket and that the death toll will rise dramatically unless a medical solution is found soon. We are looking at a tremendous cost in lives and money, yet no recommendation is made that hits at the heart of the problem... the immorality that is increasing and becoming more acceptable in our nation every day. If we do not repent, but continue in our evil, we will become even more calloused and experience even greater and more difficult consequences.

So it is that we have come to accept and embrace immorality and other sins that God's Word condemns. Though we receive warnings such as AIDS, we reject these warnings and refuse to repent of our sins and so our sin becomes even greater.

(I cannot speak of these things from some self-righteous position, as one who has never sinned. Only Jesus could do that. However, I can speak as one who made a decision to turn away (repent) from a life of sin, degradation and sorrow to seek God's forgiveness and to receive the power that He gives to live a life that can be pleasing to him. This way is open to all. God requires us to repent and turn to Him if we are to avoid His wrath.)

I believe it is important to look again at Revelation 9:20-21, because it is in some ways being fulfilled right now:

> [20]*"The rest of mankind that were not killed by these plagues* **still did not repent** *of the work of their hands;* **they did not stop** *worshiping demons, and idols of gold, silver, bronze, stone and wood—idols that cannot see or hear or walk.* [21]**Nor did they repent** *of their murders, their magic arts, their sexual immorality or their thefts"*[d] (Rev. 9:20-21).

This was the situation with the Amorites. The sin of the Amorites one day reached its full measure, and they were destroyed. Abram's offspring would receive the land of Canaan, but not until the Amorites had been given every opportunity to change. The sin of the Amorites had "not yet reached its full measure."

Abram reached the age of ninety-nine, and still the child which was promised to him and Sarai had not come. They had tried in their own way to have a child through Sarai's Egyptian maidservant Hagar. This was not what God wanted, even if it was acceptable according to the customs of the day. Abram slept with Hagar and the child Ishmael was born. However, Ishmael was the child of Abram and Sarai's planning and not the fulfillment of God's promise to Abram.

The Lord appeared to Abram later and again confirmed His promise, that He would give Abram a son through Sarai.

> [1]*"When Abram was ninety-nine years old, the LORD appeared to him and said, 'I am God Almighty; walk before me and be blameless.* [2]*I will confirm my covenant between me and you and will greatly increase your numbers.'*
> [3]*Abram fell facedown, and God said to him,* [4]*'As for me, this is my covenant with you: You will be the father of many nations.* [5]*No longer will you be called Abram; your name will be Abraham, for I have made you a father of many*

---

[d] Emphasis added

nations. [6]*I will make you very fruitful; I will make nations of you, and kings will come from you.* [7]*I will establish my covenant as an everlasting covenant between me and you and your descendants after you for the generations to come, to be your God and the God of your descendants after you.* [8]*The whole land of Canaan, where you are now an alien, I will give as an everlasting possession to you and your descendants after you; and I will be their God.'*

[9]*Then God said to Abraham, 'As for you, you must keep my covenant, you and your descendants after you for the generations to come.* [10]*This is my covenant with you and your descendants after you, the covenant you are to keep: Every male among you shall be circumcised.* [11]*You are to undergo circumcision, and it will be the sign of the covenant between me and you.* [12]*For the generations to come every male among you who is eight days old must be circumcised, including those born in your household or bought with money from a foreigner—those who are not your offspring.* [13]*Whether born in your household or bought with your money, they must be circumcised. My covenant in your flesh is to be an everlasting covenant.* [14]*Any uncircumcised male, who has not been circumcised in the flesh, will be cut off from his people; he has broken my covenant.'*

[15]*God also said to Abraham, 'As for Sarai your wife, you are no longer to call her Sarai; her name will be Sarah.* [16]*I will bless her and will surely give you a son by her. I will bless her so that she will be the mother of nations; kings of peoples will come from her.'* [17]*Abraham fell facedown; he laughed and said to himself, 'Will a son be born to a man a hundred years old? Will Sarah bear a child at the age of ninety?"* [18] *And Abraham said to God, "If only Ishmael might live under your blessing!'*

[19] *Then God said, 'Yes, but your wife Sarah will bear you a son, and you will call him Isaac. I will establish my covenant with him as an everlasting covenant for his descendants after him.* [20] *And as for Ishmael, I have heard you: I will surely bless him; I will make him fruitful and will greatly increase his numbers. He will be the father of twelve*

rulers, and I will make him into a great nation. ²¹But my covenant I will establish with Isaac, whom Sarah will bear to you by this time next year.' ²²When he had finished speaking with Abraham, God went up from him'" (Gen. 17:1-22).

So we see from this scripture, that Isaac was to be the son which would inherit the covenant promises given to Abraham. It would be through him and his offspring that these promises would be carried forward, and not through Ishmael. We also see that the males of these offspring would be required to be marked in a special way. Circumcision was a mandatory requirement if they were to be eligible to inherit these covenant promises. The significance of this will be discussed later in some detail.

THE COVENANT PROMISE IS PASSED ON TO ISAAC

Finally, Isaac was born to Abraham and Sarah just as God had promised. When Isaac was forty years old he married Rebekah, who was a grandniece of his father Abraham. It was not too long after that God established His covenant with Isaac as He had done previously with Abraham.

²"The LORD appeared to Isaac and said, 'Do not go down to Egypt; live in the land where I tell you to live. ³Stay in this land for a while, and I will be with you and will bless you. For to you and your descendants I will give all these lands and will confirm the oath I swore to your father Abraham^e. ⁴I will make your descendants as numerous as the stars in the sky and will give them all these lands, and through your offspring all nations on earth will be blessed, ⁵ because Abraham obeyed me and kept my requirements, my commands, my decrees and my laws'" (Gen. 26:2-5).

---

^e Emphasis added

334

THE COVENANT PROMISE IS CARRIED
FORWARD TO JACOB

Isaac and Rebekah became parents of twin boys. One was Esau, the oldest, and the other was Jacob. Quite a bit of feuding took place between these two.

In ancient times, the eldest son held the birthright which included the inheritance rights. However, we see that Jacob was a schemer, who sought to get the best from his brother. So it was that Jacob caught Esau in a weak moment and was able to outwit Esau to get the birthright away from him. How this was done can be seen in Genesis 25:19-34.

When Isaac was getting very old and was almost blind, he sought to give his final blessing to Esau his eldest son. This blessing carried considerable significance in that day. The blessing delegated and passed on the fathers' authority and special blessing to the one receiving it. Isaac was heir and steward of God's covenant originally given to Abraham. In giving his blessing, he was transmitting that heritage to the one receiving it, by a legally binding bequest. However, Jacob tricked his father (since his father was nearly blind) into believing that he was giving the blessing to Esau when in fact it was Jacob. The complete story can be read in Genesis 27.

All of this does not make Jacob sound like a very nice individual. He wasn't. However, God's ultimate plan was being worked out. Before his life would be over, the transforming power of God would leave its mark on Jacob's life. I believe that it was by God's appointment and care, not because of Jacob's scheming, that he was able to receive the birthright and the blessing.

Esau was understandably upset with all of Jacob's trickery, so much so that he began to plot the murder of his brother (Gen. 27:41). His mother heard of this plot and instructed Jacob to flee at once to her brother Laban.

[10]"Jacob left Beersheba and set out for Haran. [11]When he reached a certain place, he stopped for the night because the sun had set. Taking one of the stones there, he put it under his head and lay down to sleep. [12]He had a dream in which he saw a stairway resting on the earth, with its top reaching to heaven, and the angels of God were ascending and descending on it. [13]There above it stood the LORD, and he said: **'I am the LORD, the God of Isaac. I will give you and your descendants the land on which you are lying.'[f]** *[14]Your descendants will be like the dust of the earth, and you will spread out to the west and to the east, to the north and to the south. All peoples on earth will be blessed through you and your offspring. [15]I am with you and will watch over you wherever you go, and I will bring you back to this land'"* (Gen. 28:10-15).

The same promise the Lord had previously given to Abraham and Isaac was now given to Jacob.

Jacob continued to Haran. He lived with his uncle Laban and after a month went to work for him. Jacob was a deceiver, but Laban was no slouch in that department either, and Jacob received from Laban (more than once) a little of the same medicine he had dished out to Esau earlier.

Jacob desired to marry Rachel, the youngest of Laban's two daughters, but he ended up with Leah, the oldest daughter, as well as Rachael due to a deception perpetrated against him by Laban.

Jacob had twelve sons and one daughter through Leah and Rachael, and their two handmaidens Bilhah and Zilpah. These children, in order by their age, were: Reuben, Simeon, Levi, Judah, Dan, Naphtali, Gad, Asher, Issachar, Zebulun, Dinah, Joseph and Benjamin. All of these children were born while they were in Paddan Aram except for Benjamin, who was born later. Jacob's journey to Haran, and all he experi-

---

[f] Emphasis added

enced there, may be read about in more detail in Genesis 27:41— 31:55

> *3"Then the LORD said to Jacob, 'Go back to the land of your fathers and to your relatives, and I will be with you'"* (Gen. 31:3).

I'm sure that Jacob was not unhappy that he would be leaving Laban. However, going back to the land of his birth would mean facing his brother Esau. This prospect was of sufficient concern to Jacob that he sent messengers ahead to try and prepare Esau for his coming in the hope he might receive his brothers' favor.

> *6"When the messengers returned to Jacob, they said, 'We went to your brother Esau, and now he is coming to meet you, and four hundred men are with him.'*
> *7In great fear and distress Jacob divided the people who were with him into two groups, and the flocks and herds and camels as well. 8He thought, 'If Esau comes and attacks one group, the group that is left may escape.'*
> *9Then Jacob prayed, 'O God of my father Abraham, God of my father Isaac, O LORD who said to me, 'Go back to your country and your relatives, and I will make you prosper,' 10I am unworthy of all the kindness and faithfulness you have shown your servant. I had only my staff when I crossed this Jordan, but now I have become two groups. 11Save me, I pray from the hand of my brother Esau, for I am afraid he will come and attack me, and also the mothers with their children. 12But you have said, 'I will surely make you prosper and will make your descendants like the sand of the sea, which cannot be counted'"* (Gen. 32:6-12).

We see in Jacob's prayer, a man whose heart was beginning to turn to the Lord.

Jacob had prospered working for Laban. Now he did all he could do now to pacify Esau by sending gifts on ahead to him, hoping that by the time he arrived, Esau would be more kindly disposed toward him. It was while in this frame of mind that Jacob had a confrontation with God.

> [22]"...That night Jacob got up and took his two wives, his two maidservants and his eleven sons and crossed the ford of the Jabbok. [23]After he had sent them across the stream, he sent over all his possessions. [24]So Jacob was left alone, and a man wrestled with him till daybreak. [25]When the man saw that he could not overpower him, he touched the socket of Jacob's hip so that his hip was wrenched as he wrestled with the man. [26]Then the man said, 'Let me go, for it is daybreak.' But Jacob replied, 'I will not let you go unless you bless me.' [27]The man asked him, 'What is your name?'
>
> 'Jacob,' he answered.
>
> [28]Then the man said, 'Your name will no longer be Jacob, but Israel, because you have struggled with God and with men and have overcome.'
>
> [29]Jacob said, 'Please tell me your name.'
>
> But he replied, 'Why do you ask my name?' Then he blessed him there.
>
> [30]So Jacob called the place Peniel, saying, 'It is because I saw God face to face, and yet my life was spared'" (Gen. 32:22-32).

Jacob had been a person who sought what he wanted by his own strength and cunning, not being willing to truly submit himself to God's ways as Abraham and Isaac had done. In fact, Jacob had referred to God as the God of his father, and not as his own God, on more than one occasion (see Gen. 31:5 and 32:9). However, at Peniel, Jacob had a confrontation with God and God placed His mark upon him. Jacob was a changed man, and the Lord gave him a new name. A commentary in the NIV Study Bible says in reference to Gen. 32:28:

> "Now that Jacob had acknowledged God as the source of blessing and was about to reenter the promised land, the LORD acknowledged Jacob as his servant by changing his

name... Here in Father Jacob/Israel, the nation of Israel got her name and her characterization: the people who struggle with God (memorialized in the name Israel) and with men (memorialized in the name Jacob) and overcome..."

Could a man truly wrestle with God? Such an idea may seem rather strange and yet God somehow had appeared to Jacob in a form which allowed Jacob to wrestle with him. Jacob wrestled and refused to let go until he received the blessing from God which he sought. This was an action of faith, a faith which changed Jacob forever and brought him into right relationship with God.

After Jacob met Esau, and they parted peaceably, Jacob went to Shechem in Canaan. There he bought a plot of ground where he pitched a tent and he set up an altar to the Lord (see Gen. 33:18-20). He named the altar El Elohe Israel which can mean God, the God of Israel or mighty is the God of Israel. Now Jacob/Israel had made the God of his fathers his God as well.

JOSEPH

The story of Joseph is one of my favorites. In his life we can see many similarities to events in the life of Christ. These similarities are so pronounced as to make the account of Joseph's life a confirmation in itself that Jesus truly was (and is) Israel's promised Messiah. These parallels continue right up to the present time and beyond with prophetic significance consistent with other scripture. The story of Joseph's life may be read in its entirety in Genesis chapters 37, and 39-50.

Jacob/Israel had twelve sons and one daughter. He had two sons by way of his beloved wife, Rachel. These two, who were the last to be born to Jacob/Israel, were Joseph and Benjamin.

3"Now Israel loved Joseph more than any of his other sons, because he had been born to him in his old age; and he made a richly ornamented robe for him. 4When his brothers saw that their father loved him more than any of them, they hated him and could not speak a kind word to him.

5Joseph had a dream, and when he told it to his brothers, they hated him all the more. 6He said to them, 'Listen to this dream I had' 7We were binding sheaves of grain out in the field when suddenly my sheaf rose and stood upright, while your sheaves gathered around mine and bowed down to it.'

8His brothers said to him, 'Do you intend to reign over us? Will you actually rule us?' And they hated him all the more because of his dream and what he had said.

9Then he had another dream, and he told it to his brothers. 'Listen,' he said, 'I had another dream, and this time the sun and moon and eleven stars were bowing down to me.'

10When he told his father as well as his brothers, his father rebuked him and said, 'What is this dream you had? Will your mother and I and your brothers actually come and bow down to the ground before you?' 11His brothers were jealous of him, but his father kept the matter in mind'" (Gen. 37:3-11).

Because of his dreams, and the fact that he was obviously his father's favorite son, Joseph was hated by his brothers, and so they plotted to kill him. However, as this plan was about to be carried out, the brothers saw a caravan of Ishmaelites coming from Gilead.

26"Judah said to his brothers, 'What will we gain if we kill our brother and cover up his blood? 27Come, let's sell him to the Ishmaelites and not lay our hands on him; after all, he is our brother, and our own flesh and blood.'

28So when the Midianite merchants came by, his brothers pulled Joseph up out of the cistern [where they had tem-

porarily confined him]⁸ and sold him for twenty shekels of silver to the Ishmaelites, who took him to Egypt" (Gen. 37:26-28).

Joseph's brothers had stripped him of the ornamented robe which his father had given him, but now they had to return to Jacob and explain Joseph's disappearance.

> ³¹*"Then they got Joseph's robe, slaughtered a goat and dipped the robe in the blood. ³²They took the ornamented robe back to their father and said, 'We found this. Examine it to see whether it is your son's robe.'*
>
> ³³*He recognized it and said, 'It is my son's robe! Some ferocious animal has devoured him. Joseph has surely been torn to pieces.'*
>
> ³⁴*Then Jacob tore his clothes, put on sackcloth and mourned for his son many days. ³⁵All his sons and daughters came to comfort him, but he refused to be comforted. 'No,' he said, 'in mourning will I go down to the grave to my son.' So his father wept for him.*
>
> ³⁶*Meanwhile, the Midianites sold Joseph in Egypt to Potiphar, one of Pharaoh's officials, the captain of the guard"* (Gen. 37:31-36).

Joseph served the Lord. Even though he had been hated by his brothers, and was treated shamefully by them, he did not allow this traumatic experience to get the best of him. The life he lived in Egypt testified to his faith in God, and God blessed him in that land.

> ¹*"Now Joseph had been taken down to Egypt. Potiphar, an Egyptian who was one of Pharaoh's officials, the captain of the guard, bought him from the Ishmaelites who had taken him there.*
>
> ²*The LORD was with Joseph and he prospered, and he lived in the house of his Egyptian master. ³When his master*

---

⁹ [] Bracketed insertion added

saw that the LORD was with him and that the LORD gave him success in everything he did, 4Joseph found favor in his eyes and became his attendant. Potiphar put him in charge of his household, and he entrusted to his care everything he owned. 5From the time he put him in charge of his household and of all that he owned, the LORD blessed the household of the Egyptian because of Joseph. The blessing of the LORD was on everthing Potiphar had both in the house and in the field. 6So he left in Joseph's care everything he had; with Joseph in charge, he did not concern himself with anything except the food he ate" (Gen. 39:1-6).

But trouble was brewing for Joseph.

"Now Joseph was well-built and handsome, 7and after a while his master's wife took notice of Joseph and said, 'Come to bed with me!'

8But he refused. 'With me in charge,' he told her, 'my master does not concern himself with anything in the house; everything he owns he has entrusted to my care. 9No one is greater in this house than I am. My master has withheld nothing from me except you, because you are his wife. How then could I do such a wicked thing and sin against God?' 10And though she spoke to Joseph day after day, he refused to go to bed with her or even be with her.

11One day he went into the house to attend to his duties, and none of the household servants was inside. 12She caught him by his cloak and said, 'Come to bed with me!' But he left his cloak in her hand and ran out of the house.

13When she saw that he had left his cloak in her hand and had run out of the house, 14she called her household servants. 'Look,' she said to them, 'this Hebrew has been brought to us to make sport of us! He came in here to sleep with me, but I screamed. 15When he heard me scream for help, he left his cloak beside me and ran out of the house.'

16She kept his cloak beside her until his master came home. 17Then she told him this story: 'That Hebrew slave you brought us came to me to make sport of me. 18But as soon as I screamed for help, he left his cloak beside me and ran out of the house.'

[19]When his master heard the story his wife told him, saying, 'This is how your slave treated me,' he burned with anger. [20]Joseph's master took him and put him in prison, the place where the king's prisoners were confined...' (Gen. 39:6-20).

So, Joseph was cast into prison, but we see that even in prison, Joseph was found to be most excellent in all that he did.

[20]"... But while Joseph was there in the prison, [21]the LORD was with him; he showed him kindness and granted him favor in the eyes of the prison warden. [22]So the warden put Joseph in charge of all those held in the prison, and he was made responsible for all that was done there. [23]The warden paid no attention to anything under Joseph's care, because the LORD was with Joseph and gave him success in whatever he did" (Gen. 39:20b-23).

It was while he was in prison that two men who had formerly served Pharaoh were also thrown into prison for offending their master. One had been Pharaoh's baker, and the other had been his cupbearer. Each of these men had a dream the same night, and each dream had a meaning of its own.

[6]"When Joseph came to them the next morning, he saw that they were dejected. [7]So he asked Pharaoh's officials who were in custody with him in his master's house, 'Why are your faces so sad today?'

[8]'We both had dreams,' they answered, 'but there is no one to interpret them.'

Then Joseph said to them, 'Do not interpretations belong to God? Tell me your dreams'" (Gen. 40:6-8).

Both men told Joseph their dreams and Joseph, by the help of God, was able to interpret the dreams for them. The dreams indicated that in three days one of the men would be restored by Pharaoh to his former position as cupbearer, whereas the one who had formerly been Pharaoh's baker would be put to death.

When Joseph had finished interpreting the dream for the cupbearer, he said to him:

> [14]*"But when all goes well with you, remember me and show me kindness; mention me to Pharaoh and get me out of this prison.* [15]*For I was forcibly carried off from the land of the Hebrews, and even here I have done nothing to deserve being put in a dungeon"* (Gen. 40:14-15).

The interpretation of the dreams came to pass just as Joseph had said. The baker was put to death, and the cupbearer was restored to his former position with Pharaoh. However, when the chief cupbearer was once again at Pharaoh's side, he did not remember Joseph, but forgot all about him.

Two full years passed with no change in Joseph's status, but then, Pharaoh had two troubling dreams. He sent for all the magicians and wise men of Egypt and told them his dreams hoping that someone would be able to tell him the meaning of them, but no one could.

It was at this time that Pharaoh's chief cupbearer remembered Joseph.

> [9]*"Then the chief cupbearer said to Pharaoh, 'Today I am reminded of my shortcomings.* [10]*Pharaoh was once angry with his servants, and he imprisoned me and the chief baker in the house of the captain of the guard.* [11]*Each of us had a dream the same night, and each dream had a meaning of its own.* [12]*Now a young Hebrew was there with us, a servant of the captain of the guard. We told him our dreams, and he interpreted them for us, giving each man the interpretation of his dream.* [13]*And things turned out exactly as he interpreted them to us: I was restored to my position, and the other man was hanged.'*

[14]*So Pharaoh sent for Joseph, and he was quickly brought from the dungeon. When he had shaved and changed his clothes, he came before Pharaoh.*

[15]*Pharaoh said to Joseph, 'I had a dream, and no one can interpret it. But I have heard it said of you that when you hear a dream you can interpret it.'*

[16]*'I cannot do it,' Joseph replied to Pharaoh, 'but God will give Pharaoh the answer he desires...'"* (Gen. 41:9-16).

Pharaoh then told Joseph his dreams, and Joseph was able to interpret them. The dreams provided a warning of a famine which was soon to come. Joseph told Pharaoh...

[28]*"...God has shown Pharaoh what he is about to do.* [29]*Seven years of great abundance are coming throughout the land of Egypt,* [30]*but seven years of famine will follow them. Then all the abundance in Egypt will be forgotten, and the famine will ravage the land.* [31]*The abundance in the land will not be remembered, because the famine that follows it will be so severe.* [32]*The reason the dream was given to Pharaoh in two forms is that the matter has been firmly decided by God, and God will do it soon.*

[33]*And now let Pharaoh look for a discerning and wise man and put him in charge of the land of Egypt.* [34]*Let Pharaoh appoint commissioners over the land to take a fifth of the harvest of Egypt during the seven years of abundance.* [35]*They should collect all the food of these good years that are coming and store up the grain under the authority of Pharaoh, to be kept in the cities for food.* [36]*This food should be held in reserve for the country, to be used during the seven years of famine that will come upon Egypt, so that the country may not be ruined by the famine'"* (Gen.41:28b-36).

Pharaoh was impressed by Joseph and all that he had revealed.

[37]"The plan seemed good to Pharaoh and to all his officials. [38]So Pharaoh asked them, 'Can we find anyone like this man, one in whom is the spirit of God?'

[39]Then Pharaoh said to Joseph, 'Since God has made all this known to you, there is no one so discerning and wise as you. [40]You shall be in charge of my palace, and all my people are to submit to your orders. Only with respect to the throne will I be greater than you.'

[41]So Pharaoh said to Joseph, 'I hereby put you in charge of the whole land of Egypt.' [42]Then Pharaoh took his signet ring from his finger and put it on Joseph's finger. He dressed him in robes of fine linen and put a gold chain around his neck. [43]He had him ride in a chariot as his second-in-command, and men shouted before him, 'Make way!' Thus he put him in charge of the whole land of Egypt.

[44]Then Pharaoh said to Joseph, 'I am Pharaoh, but without your word no one will lift hand or foot in all Egypt.' [45]Pharaoh gave Joseph the name Zaphenath-Paneah and gave him Asenath daughter of Potiphera, priest of On, to be his wife. And Joseph went throughout the land of Egypt.

[46]Joseph was thirty years old when he entered the service of Pharaoh king of Egypt. And Joseph went out from Pharaoh's presence and traveled throughout Egypt. [47]During the seven years of abundance the land produced plentifully. [48]Joseph collected all the food produced in those seven years of abundance in Egypt and stored it in the cities. In each city he put the food grown in the fields surrounding it. [49]Joseph stored up huge quantities of grain, like the sand of the sea; it was so much that he stopped keeping records because it was beyond measure.

[50]Before the years of famine came, two sons were born to Joseph by Asenath daughter of potiphera, priest of On. [51]Joseph named his firstborn Manasseh and said, 'It is because God has made me forget all my trouble and all my father's household.' [52]The second son he named Ephraim and said, 'It is because God has made me fruitful in the land of my suffering.'

[53]The seven years of abundance in Egypt came to an end, [54]and the seven years of famine began, just as Joseph

had said. There was famine in all the other lands, but in the whole land of Egypt there was food. ⁵⁵When all Egypt began to feel the famine, the people cried to Pharaoh for food. Then Pharaoh told all the Egyptians, 'Go to Joseph and do what he tells you.'

⁵⁶When the famine had spread over the whole country, Joseph opened the storehouses and sold grain to the Egyptians, for the famine was severe throughout Egypt. ⁵⁷And all the countries came to Egypt to buy grain from Joseph, because the famine was severe in all the world'" (Gen. 41:37-56).

This famine had its effect on the land where Jacob/Israel and Joseph's brothers and sister lived, and they were in need of food.

¹"When Jacob learned that there was grain in Egypt, he said to his sons, 'Why do you just keep looking at each other?' ²He continued, 'I have heard that there is grain in Egypt. Go down there and buy some for us, so that we may live and not die.'

³Then ten of Joseph's brothers went down to buy grain from Egypt. ⁴But Jacob did not send Benjamin, Joseph's brother, with the others, because he was afraid that harm might come to him. ⁵So Israel's sons were among those who went to buy grain, for the famine was in the land of Canaan also" (Gen. 42:1-5).

So it was necessary for the brothers to go down to Egypt, and this brought them face to face with their brother Joseph.

⁶"Now Joseph was the governor of the land, the one who sold grain to all its people. So when Joseph's brothers arrived, they bowed down to him with their faces to the ground. ⁷As soon as Joseph saw his brothers, he recognized them, but he pretended to be a stranger and spoke harshly to them. 'Where do you come from?' he asked.

'From the land of Canaan,' they replied, 'to buy food.'
8Although Joseph recognized his brothers, they did not recognize him" (Gen. 42:6-8).

Joseph did not reveal himself to his brothers for some time. He accused them of possibly being spies, come to see where the land was unprotected. Therefore, he said he would have to test them to see if they were honest men.

18"On the third day, Joseph said to them, 'Do this and you will live, for I fear God: 19If you are honest men, let one of your brothers stay here in prison, while the rest of you go and take grain back for your starving households. 20But you must bring your youngest brother to me, so that your words may be verified and that you may not die.' This they proceeded to do" (Gen. 42:18-20).

Joseph had Simeon taken from them and bound before their eyes. He gave orders to fill their bags with grain, to put each man's silver back in his sack, and to give them provisions for their journey. After this was done for them, they loaded their grain on their donkeys and left.

They arrived home and told their father all that had occurred. He was not willing that Benjamin should go to Egypt. He considered that Joseph was dead and feared greatly the loss of his youngest offspring and the only remaining child of Rachel. He said that if harm were to come to Benjamin, it would bring his gray head down to the grave in sorrow.

When all the grain they had brought back from Egypt was used up, they could no longer delay to return to Egypt for more food, but the only way that they could return was if they had Benjamin with them. In consideration of their father's concerns, Reuben offered his two sons as security for Benjamin.

"...Reuben said to his father, 'You may put both of my sons to death if I do not bring him back to you. Entrust him to my care, and I will bring him back'" (Gen. 42:37).

Judah also offered himself as security that he would bring Benjamin back.

[8]"Then Judah said to Israel his father, 'Send the boy along with me and we will go at once, so that we and you and our children may live and not die. [9]I myself will guarantee his safety; you can hold me personally responsible for him. If I do not bring him back to you and set him here before you, I will bear the blame before you all my life. [10]As it is, if we had not delayed, we could have gone and returned twice'" (Gen. 43:8-10).

So Jacob reluctantly agreed and the sons returned to Egypt.

When they arrived, Joseph received them into his own home, but still did not identify himself to them. Simeon was brought out to them, and they were served food in Joseph's home. Joseph was deeply moved at seeing his brother Benjamin, and so as not to reveal who he was, he had to hurry out to look for a place to weep.

Joseph told the steward of his house to fill the men's sacks with as much food as they could carry. He also instructed the steward to put Joseph's personal cup, a silver one, in the mouth of Benjamin's sack before he closed it up.

When morning came, the men were sent on their way with the donkeys. After they had gone, Joseph instructed his steward to go after the men at once and when he had caught up with them to confront them about the missing silver cup.

When the steward caught up with the men, he charged them with stealing from Joseph. At hearing this, the brothers were dumbfounded. They each opened their sack. Sure enough, the missing cup was found in Benjamin's. At this, they tore their clothes in dismay. When they had all re-loaded their donkeys, they returned to the city.

Upon their arrival, Joseph showed great displeasure at the apparent theft of his cup.

> [16]*"What can we say to my lord?" Judah replied. "What can we say? How can we prove our innocence? God has uncovered your servants' guilt. We are now my lord's slaves—we ourselves and the one who was found to have the cup."*
>
> [17]*But Joseph said, 'Far be it from me to do such a thing! Only the man who was found to have the cup will become my slave. The rest of you, go back to your father in peace'"* (Gen. 44:16-17).

Judah then asked Joseph to allow him to speak. As he did so, he pleaded with Joseph that if he did not bring Benjamin back with him, then surely his father would die.

> [27]*"Your servant my father said to us, 'You know that my wife bore me two sons.* [28]*One of them went away from me, and I said, 'He has surely been torn to pieces. And I have not seen him since.* [29]*If you take this one from me too and harm comes to him, you will bring my gray head down to the grave in misery.'*
>
> [30]*So now, if the boy is not with us when I go back to your servant my father and if my father, whose life is closely bound up with the boy's life,* [31]*sees that the boy isn't there, he will die. Your servants will bring the gray head of our father down to the grave in sorrow.* [32]*Your servant guaranteed the boy's safety to my father. I said, 'If I do not bring him back to you, I will bear the blame before you, my father, all my life!'*
>
> [33]*'Now then, please let your servant remain here as my lord's slave in place of the boy, and let the boy return with his brothers.* [34]*How can I go back to my father if the boy is not with me? No! Do not let me see the misery that would come upon my father'"* (Gen. 44:27-34).

Joseph was a godly man. Even though his brothers had treated him terribly, he could not continue to bring such distress upon his father and his brothers. He also recognized that God was working good out of the evil that had come his way.

¹*"Then Joseph could no longer control himself before all his attendants, and he cried out, "Have everyone leave my presence!" So there was no one with Joseph when he made himself known to his brothers. ²And he wept so loudly that the Egyptians heard him, and Pharaoh's household heard about it.*

³*Joseph said to his brothers, "I am Joseph! Is my father still living?" But his brothers were not able to answer him, because they were terrified at his presence.*

⁴*Then Joseph said to his brothers, 'Come close to me.' When they had done so, he said, 'I am your brother Joseph, the one you sold into Egypt! ⁵And now, do not be distressed and do not be angry with yourselves for selling me here, because it was to save lives that God sent me ahead of you. ⁶For two years now there has been famine in the land, and for the next five years there will not be plowing and reaping. ⁷But God sent me ahead of you to preserve for you a remnant on earth and to save your lives by a great deliverance.'*

⁸*"So then, it was not you who sent me here, but God. He made me father to Pharaoh, lord of his entire household and ruler of all Egypt. ⁹Now hurry back to my father and say to him, 'This is what your son Joseph says: God has made me lord of all Egypt. Come down to me; don't delay. ¹⁰You shall live in the region of Goshen and be near me— you, your children and grandchildren, your flocks and herds, and all you have. ¹¹I will provide for you there, because five years of famine are still to come. Otherwise you and your household and all who belong to you will become destitute.'*

¹²*'You can see for yourselves, and so can my brother Benjamin, that it is really I who am speaking to you. ¹³Tell my father about all the honor accorded me in Egypt and about everything you have seen. And bring my father down here quickly.'*

¹⁴Then he threw his arms around his brother Benjamin and wept, and Benjamin embraced him, weeping. ¹⁵And he kissed all his brothers and wept over them. Afterward his brothers talked with him" (Gen. 45:1-15).

What a tremendous picture Joseph presents in his for-giveness, love, and above all, submission to the will of God. A true picture of Christ, who, in submission to the will of the Father was the object of such great evil at the hands of men, to the point of crucifixion. The words we hear Joseph say to his brothers, are the ones Jesus speaks to the Jews, "And now, do not be distressed and do not be angry with your-selves for selling me here, because it was to save lives that God sent me ahead of you...God sent me ahead of you to preserve for you a remnant on earth and to save your lives by a great deliverance." The great evil perpetrated against Jesus Christ resulting in His crucifixion, has been worked for our good by God, bringing a way of salvation to all who will receive it.

Joseph told his brothers to bring his father down to Egypt quickly, and when Pharaoh heard that Joseph's brothers had come, he and all his officials were pleased.

¹⁷"Pharaoh said to Joseph, 'Tell your brothers, Do this: Load your animals and return to the land of Canaan, ¹⁸and bring your father and your families back to me. I will give you the best of the land of Egypt and you can enjoy the fat of the land'" (Gen. 45:17-18).

So Jacob's sons returned to him in the land of Canaan.

²⁶"They told him, 'Joseph is still alive! In fact, he is ruler of all Egypt.' Jacob was stunned; he did not believe them. ²⁷But when they told him everything Joseph had said to them, and when he saw the carts Joseph had sent to carry him back, the spirit of their father Jacob revived. ²⁸And Israel said, 'I'm convinced! My son Joseph is still alive. I will go and see him before I die'" (Gen. 45:26-28).

As far as Israel was concerned, Joseph had come back from the dead. He who was dead is alive. Again, a beautiful picture of Christ who was killed at the hands of His earthly brothers, the Jews, raised from the dead to the position of authority at the right hand of the Father, and who one day will reveal himself to the Jews as the true Messiah. One who suffered much at their hands, yet who suffered that they might be saved. He is not dead, He is alive!

[1]"So Israel set out with all that was his, and when he reached Beersheba, he offered sacrifices to the God of his father Isaac.

[2]And God spoke to Israel in a vision at night and said, 'Jacob! Jacob!'

'Here I am,' he replied.

[3]'I am God, the God of your father,' he said. 'Do not be afraid to go down to Egypt, for I will make you into a great nation there. [4]I will go down to Egypt with you, and I will surely bring you back again. And Joseph's own hand will close your eyes.'

[5]Then Jacob left Beersheba, and Israel's sons took their father Jacob and their children and their wives in the carts that Pharaoh had sent to transport him. [6]They also took with them their livestock and the possessions they had acquired in Canaan, and Jacob and all his offspring went to Egypt. [7]He took with him to Egypt his sons and grandsons and his daughters and granddaughters—all his offspring" (Gen. 46:1-7).

[26]"All those who went to Egypt with Jacob—those who were his direct descendants, not counting his sons' wives— numbered sixty-six persons. [27]With the two sons who had been born to Joseph in Egypt, the members of Jacob's family, which went to Egypt, were seventy in all" (Gen. 46:26-27).

[27]"Now the Israelites settled in Egypt in the region of Goshen. They acquired property there and were fruitful and increased greatly in number" (Gen. 47:27).

When Jacob was getting along in years, he became ill, and Joseph went to see him, bringing his two sons, Manasseh and Ephraim, with him.

> *³"Jacob said to Joseph, 'God Almighty appeared to me at Luz in the land of Canaan, and there he blessed me ⁴and said to me, 'I am going to make you fruitful and will increase your numbers. I will make you a community of peoples, and I will give this land as an everlasting possession to your descendants after you.'*
>
> *⁵Now then, your two sons born to you in Egypt before I came to you here will be reckoned as mine; Ephraim and Manasseh will be mine. ⁶Any children born to you after them will be yours; in the territory they inherit they will be reckoned under the names of their brothers'"* (Gen. 48:3-6).

As has been said earlier, Jacob had twelve sons. These sons, in order by their age were: Reuben, Simeon, Levi, Judah, Dan, Naphtali, Gad, Asher, Issachar, Zebulun, Joseph and Benjamin. Now we see Jacob in essence adopting the two sons of Joseph as his own. They would be reckoned as though they were his.

In Genesis 48:10-20, we see Israel giving his blessing to Ephraim and Manasseh. In Genesis 49, Israel prophesies over his sons. At the conclusion of this passage in Gen 49, it says:

> *²⁸All these are <u>the twelve tribes of Israel,</u> and this is what their father said to them when he blessed them, giving each the blessing appropriate to him. (Gen. 49:28)*

The nation of Israel was established with twelve tribes. When you consider that Israel had twelve sons and adopted two more, Ephraim and Manasseh, then this would be the basis for fourteen tribes. However, no tribe of Joseph was established. Instead, he was the father of two tribes established through his sons, Ephraim and Manasseh. Also, Levi was not among the tribes given land allotments after the conquest of Canaan. Instead, the Levites were set apart as belonging to the Lord to serve as priests to the nation of Israel. The priests were given 48 towns located throughout Israel as their dwelling places.

As we have previously seen, Jacob's name was changed to Israel when he wrestled with God at Peniel. As patriarch of the 12 tribes, he bequeathed his new name to the nation.

In Genesis 17 we previously read God's promises to Abraham...

> [8]*The whole land of Canaan, where you are now an alien, I will give as an **everlasting possession**[y] to you and your descendants after you; and I will be their God.*

Today Israel's right to the land is hotly contested by the Arabs. It is significant to note that the Arabs are descended from Ishmael, Abraham's son born to Hagar, Sarah's handmaiden. The land of Israel was not promised to the Arabs, Ishmael's descendants, but was given by God as an everlasting possession to the nation of Israel.

In this chapter we have seen the beginnings of the nation of Israel and the promises given by God concerning them. We have also seen how it was that they had to leave the land promised to them, the land of Canaan, to come and live as strangers in the land of Egypt.

Based on the Genesis account, the descendancy from Abraham to the twelve tribes of the nation of Israel is depicted on the chart which follows on page 356.

When Jacob/Israel died, Joseph's brothers became very concerned.

---

[y] Emphasis added

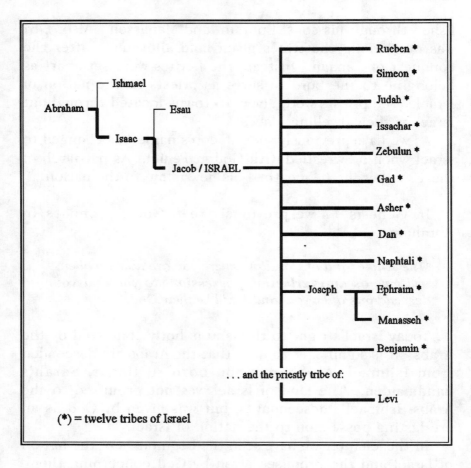

Abraham
— Ishmael
— Isaac
— Esau
— Jacob / ISRAEL
Rueben *
Simeon *
Judah *
Issachar *
Zebulun *
Gad *
Asher *
Dan *
Naphtali *
Joseph
Ephraim *
Manasseh *
Benjamin *

. . . and the priestly tribe of:
Levi

(*) = twelve tribes of Israel

¹⁵When Joseph's brothers saw that their father was dead, they said, "What if Joseph holds a grudge against us and pays us back for all the wrongs we did to him?" ¹⁶So they sent word to Joseph, saying, "Your father left these instructions before he died: ¹⁷'This is what you are to say to Joseph: I ask you to forgive your brothers the sins and the wrongs they committed in treating you so badly.' Now please forgive the sins of the servants of the God of your father." When their message came to him, Joseph wept.

¹⁸His brothers then came and threw themselves down before him. "We are your slaves," they said.

¹⁹But Joseph said to them, "Don't be afraid. Am I in the place of God? ²⁰You intended to harm me, but God intended it for good to accomplish what is now being done, the saving of many lives. ²¹So then, don't be afraid. I will provide for you and your children." And he reassured them and spoke kindly to them (Gen. 50:15-21).

Can you not see Jesus Christ in these verses?

In Zech. 12:10-14 and 13:1 it says (speaking of a future time which I believe is yet to come):

¹⁰"And I will pour out on the house of David and the inhabitants of Jerusalem a spirit of grace and supplication. They will look on me, the one they have pierced, and they will mourn for him as one mourns for an only child, and grieve bitterly for him as one grieves for a firstborn son. ¹¹On that day the weeping of Jerusalem will be great, like the weeping of Hadad Rimmon in the plain of Megiddo. ¹²The land will mourn, each clan by itself, with their wives by themselves: the clan of the house of David and their wives, the clan of the house of Nathan and their wives, the clan of the house of Levi and their wives, the clan of Shimei and their wives, and all the rest of the clans and their wives.

¹"On that day a fountain will be opened to the house of David and the inhabitants of Jerusalem, to cleanse them from sin and impurity."

When the time comes spoken of in these verses, the Jews will see the One whom they crucified. It will be a time for great mourning. A fountain of forgiveness will be opened to cleanse them from sin and impurity. While they might have every reason in the natural to fear the Almighty King of Kings and Lord of Lords, that one whom they crucified, I can hear Jesus say, "Don't be afraid. You intended to harm me, but God intended it for good to accomplish what is now being done, the eternal salvation of many souls. So then, don't be afraid. I will provide for you and your children." The Lord will reassure them and speak kindly to them.

The offspring of Abraham, Isaac and Jacob who came into Egypt were treated well by Pharaoh and the Egyptians. This can be seen clearly in the events recorded in Genesis 45:16 through chapter 50. But as we now begin to read in the book of Exodus, we see that this gracious hospitality was not to last.

> [6]*Now Joseph and all his brothers and all that generation died,* [7]*but the Israelites were fruitful and multiplied greatly and became exceedingly numerous, so that the land was filled with them.*
>
> [8]*Then a new king, who did not know about Joseph, came to power in Egypt.* [9]*"Look," he said to his people, "the Israelites have become much too numerous for us.* [10]*Come, we must deal shrewdly with them or they will become even more numerous and, if war breaks out, will join our enemies, fight against us and leave the country."*
>
> [11]*So they put slave masters over them to oppress them with forced labor, and they built Pithom and Rameses as store cities for Pharaoh.* [12]*But the more they were oppressed, the more they multiplied and spread; so the Egyptians came to dread the Israelites* [13]*and worked them ruthlessly.* [14]*They made their lives bitter with hard labor in brick and mortar and with all kinds of work in the fields; in all their hard labor the Egyptians used them ruthlessly.*
>
> [15]*The king of Egypt said to the Hebrew midwives, whose names were Shiphrah and Puah,* [16]*"When you help the Hebrew women in childbirth and observe them on the delivery stool, if it is a boy, kill him; but if it is a girl, let her live."* [17]*The midwives, however, feared God and did not do what the king of Egypt had told them to do; they let the boys live.* [18]*Then the king of Egypt summoned the midwives and asked them, "Why have you done this? Why have you let the boys live?"*
>
> [19]*The midwives answered Pharaoh, "Hebrew women are not like Egyptian women; they are vigorous and give birth before the midwives arrive."*

²⁰So God was kind to the midwives and the people increased and became even more numerous. ²¹And because the midwives feared God, he gave them families of their own.

²²Then Pharaoh gave this order to all his people: "Every boy that is born you must throw into the Nile, but let every girl live." (Exod. 1:6-22)

MOSES

This is the environment into which a particular Hebrew boy was born. His name was Moses. Based on Pharaoh's command, he was marked for death. His mother hid him for three months to keep him from being killed.

³But when she could hide him no longer, she got a papyrus basket for him and coated it with tar and pitch. Then she placed the child on it and put it among the reeds along the bank of the Nile. ⁴His sister stood at a distance to see what would happen to him.

⁵Then Pharaoh's daughter went down to the Nile to bathe, and her attendants were walking along the river bank. She saw the basket among the reeds and sent her slave girl to get it. ⁶She opened it and saw the baby. He was crying, and she felt sorry for him. "This is one of the Hebrew babies," she said. (Exod. 2:3-6)

⁷Then his sister asked Pharaoh's daughter, "Shall I go and get one of the Hebrew women to nurse the baby for you?"

⁸"Yes, go," she answered. And the girl went and got the baby's mother. ⁹Pharaoh's daughter said to her, "Take this baby and nurse him for me, and I will pay you." So the woman took the baby and nursed him. ¹⁰When the child grew older, she took him to Pharaoh's daughter and he became her son. She named him Moses, saying, "I drew him out of the water." (Exod. 2:3-10)

Moses grew up in Pharaoh's house. Pharaoh's daughter knew that the baby was an Israelite child, and perhaps she even came to know that the woman who nursed the child was his mother. It is very probable that he continued to see his real mother as he was growing up. While Moses was schooled in all the ways of the Egyptians, it is clear that he also knew about his Hebrew heritage. He undoubtedly learned the history of his forefathers, Abraham, Isaac and Jacob, and had come to know the God they served.

I believe God may have shown Moses that he would be used in some way to bring deliverance to his people from Egypt's cruel domination. Many of the Bible's leading characters received such insights from God years in advance of the actual total fulfillment of their call. Abraham was told that he would have a unique son who would be the beginning of a great nation. This was revealed to him years before its actual fulfillment. Joseph had his dreams which gave a hazy view that someday he would be exalted to a position of authority. We have seen though that Joseph had to undergo years of difficulty before the early dream he received was finally fulfilled. David was shown that he would be king of Israel years before it came to pass. This occurred with others as well. Standing between the time of their initial call and the fulfillment of that call stood a time of testing and growth in God. A time where their obedience and faith had to be proven and strengthened. It seems that the greater the calling and task to be performed, the longer the period of testing.

As we have seen, Abraham and Sarah grew impatient waiting for God to fulfill his promise and took matters into their own hands. As a result, Ishmael was born. In the same way it appears that Moses also tried to accomplish God's call in his own way and strength. In the New Testament we read a summary account given by Stephen of Moses early life and the deliverance he tried to bring about in his own strength.

> [20]*"At that time Moses was born, and he was no ordinary child. For three months he was cared for in his father's house. [21]When he was placed outside, Pharaoh's daughter took him and brought him up as her own son. [22]Moses was educated in all the wisdom of the Egyptians and was powerful in speech and action.*
>
> [23]*"When Moses was forty years old, he decided to visit his fellow Israelites. [24]He saw one of them being mistreated by an Egyptian, so he went to his defense and avenged him by killing the Egyptian. [25]Moses thought that his own people would realize that God was using him to rescue them, but they did not. [26]The next day Moses came upon two Israelites who were fighting. He tried to reconcile them by saying, 'Men, you are brothers; why do you want to hurt each other?'*
>
> [27]*"But the man who was mistreating the other pushed Moses aside and said, 'Who made you ruler and judge over us? [28]Do you want to kill me as you killed the Egyptian yesterday?' [29]When Moses heard this, he fled to Midian, where he settled as a foreigner and had two sons.'* (Acts 7:20-29)

Moses was forty when he fled from Egypt. He went to a land that by contrast to Egypt was very barren. Midian was located in the southeastern portion of the Sinai peninsula. In that rather barren place, Moses' life was vastly different from his life in the royal dwelling of the Pharaoh. It appears that in Midian he became a sheep herder (Exod. 3:1).

Moses remained in Midian for forty years.

> [23]*During that long period, the king of Egypt died. The Israelites groaned in their slavery and cried out, and their cry for help because of their slavery went up to God. [24]God heard their groaning and he remembered his covenant with Abraham, with Isaac and with Jacob. [25]So God looked on the Israelites and was concerned about them.* (Exod. 2:23-25)

We conclude with Stephen's account in the book of Acts...

30"After forty years had passed, an angel appeared to Moses in the flames of a burning bush in the desert near Mount Sinai. 31When he saw this, he was amazed at the sight. As he went over to look more closely, he heard the Lord's voice: 32'I am the God of your fathers, the God of Abraham, Isaac and Jacob.' Moses trembled with fear and did not dare to look.

33"Then the Lord said to him, 'Take off your sandals; the place where you are standing is holy ground. 34I have indeed seen the oppression of my people in Egypt. I have heard their groaning and have come down to set them free. Now come, I will send you back to Egypt.'

35"This is the same Moses whom they had rejected with the words, 'Who made you ruler and judge?' was sent to be their ruler and deliverer by God himself, through the angel who appeared to him in the bush (Acts 7:30-35).

To order additional copies of

Stand By Faith ... Or Not At All

please call 1-800-917-BOOK.